Iraq: from war to a new authoritarianism

Toby Dodge

Iraq: from war to a new authoritarianism

Toby Dodge

IISS The International Institute for Strategic Studies

The International Institute for Strategic Studies
Arundel House | 13–15 Arundel Street | Temple Place | London | WC2R 3DX | UK

First published December 2012 by **Routledge**
4 Park Square, Milton Park, Abingdon, Oxon, OX14 4RN

for **The International Institute for Strategic Studies**
Arundel House, 13–15 Arundel Street, Temple Place, London, WC2R 3DX, UK
www.iiss.org

Simultaneously published in the USA and Canada by **Routledge**
270 Madison Ave., New York, NY 10016

Routledge is an imprint of Taylor & Francis, an Informa Business

DIRECTOR-GENERAL AND CHIEF EXECUTIVE Dr John Chipman
EDITOR Dr Nicholas Redman
ASSISTANT EDITOR Alexa van Sickle
COPY EDITOR Matthew Foley
EDITORIAL Sarah Johnstone, Mona Moussavi
COVER/PRODUCTION John Buck, Kelly Verity
COVER ILLUSTRATION Steve Dell

The International Institute for Strategic Studies is an independent centre for research, information and debate on the problems of conflict, however caused, that have, or potentially have, an important military content. The Council and Staff of the Institute are international and its membership is drawn from almost 100 countries. The Institute is independent and it alone decides what activities to conduct. It owes no allegiance to any government, any group of governments or any political or other organisation. The IISS stresses rigorous research with a forward-looking policy orientation and places particular emphasis on bringing new perspectives to the strategic debate.

The Institute's publications are designed to meet the needs of a wider audience than its own membership and are available on subscription, by mail order and in good bookshops. Further details at www.iiss.org.

Printed and bound in Great Britain by Bell & Bain Ltd, Thornliebank, Glasgow

British Library Cataloguing in Publication Data
A catalogue record for this book is available from the British Library

Library of Congress Cataloging in Publication Data

ADELPHI series
ISSN 1944-5571

ADELPHI 434–435
ISBN 978-0-415-83485-8

Contents

ACKNOWLEDGEMENTS

The subject of this book, the arguments made in it and the conclusions drawn mean that it is not possible to specifically thank a number of Iraqis who gave very generously of their time and knowledge in order to help me better understand the politics of their country. I would like to thank them all.

The idea for the book originated in a discussion between John Chipman and Alex Nicoll at the International Institute for Strategic Studies. I would like to thank them for encouraging me to write it. I would also like to thank Adam Ward and especially Nick Redman for overseeing the book's research, writing and publication with great insight and diplomacy. I have had many long, passionate and informative discussions about Iraqi politics at the institute with Dana Allin, Ben Barry, Mamoun Fandy, James Hackett, Emile Hokayem, Andrew Parasiliti and especially the late Hilary Synnott. I would like to thank them all for taking the time. At IISS headquarters in London I would like to thank John Buck for all the design work and Alexa van Sickle for the copy-editing. At IISS–Middle East I would like to thank Wafa Alsayed for the excellent research she put into the election tables and Mark Allworthy for his support. At IISS–US I would like to thank Nathaniel Markowitz who, while working as an intern, helped with the translations, and Becca Wasser for her support.

This book was started while I was teaching in the Department of Politics and International Relations at Queen Mary, University of London and was finished at the Department of International Relations at the London School of Economics and Political Science. Within both institutions I would like to thank Jeremy Jennings, Lee Jones, Ray Keily, George Lawson, Bryan Mabee and Brendan O'Duffy and David Williams for their insights. I would also like to thank Mick Cox and Arne Westad for providing me with an inspiring intellectual home at LSE Ideas.

Within the wider community of Iraq watchers a number of people have been very generous with their time and insights. These include George Adair, Raad Alkadiri, Jane Arraf, Stuart Bowen, Jason Burke, Patrick Cockburn, Juan Cole, Larry Diamond, Alice Fordham, Michael Gfoeller, Michael Gordon, Fanar Haddad, Peter Harling, Derek Harvey, Khair el-Din Haseeb, Joost Hiltermann, Faleh Jabar, Isam al-Khafaji, Laleh Khalili, Rubina Khan, Ali Khedery, Yousif al-Khoei, David Kilcullen, Michael Knights, David Malone, Ramzy Mardini, Phebe Marr, Regis Matlak, H. R. McMaster, Roel Meijer, John Moore, Denise Natali, Ned Parker, Sam Parker, Nick Pelham, David Petraeus, Molly Phee, Andrew Rathmell, Joel Rayburn, Tom Ricks, Nir Rosen, Yahia Said, Joseph Sassoon, Oubai Shahbandar, Jonathan Shaw, Emma Sky, John Sloboda, Peter Sluglett, Charles Tripp, Reidar Visser and Sami Zubaida.

A very early version of the arguments at the centre of this book was presented at the Watson Institute for International Studies at Brown University. I thank Shia Balaghi and Michael Kennedy for the invitation. Clare has read every word of this book and everything else I have ever written. I thank her for her support, tolerance and perseverance.

This book is respectfully dedicated to the memory of one of my oldest and dearest Iraqi friends, Zuhair al-Kadiri. He looked after me in Baghdad, and took a great deal of time to explain to me the many intricacies of Iraqi politics and history, but sadly did not live to see the influence of his wise words on this publication.

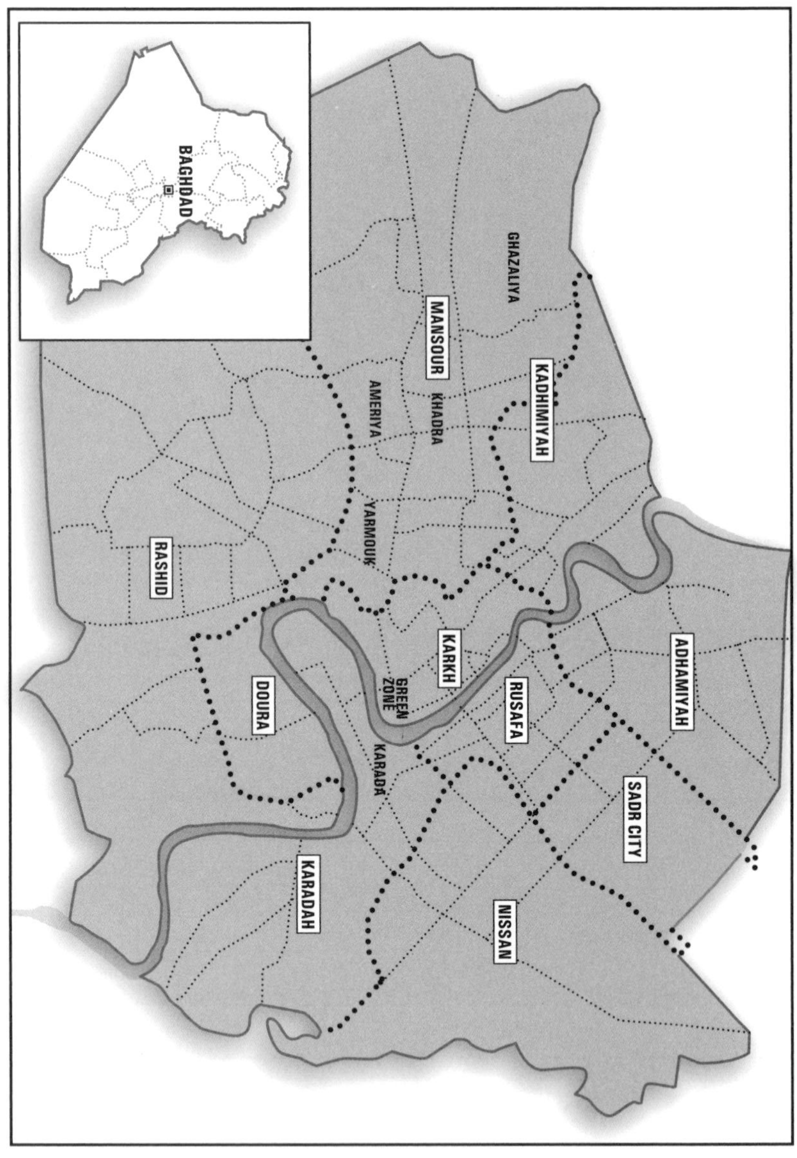
BAGHDAD
GHAZALIYA
MANSOUR
KADHIMIYAH
AMERIYA
KHADRA
YARMOUK
RASHID
KARKH
GREEN ZONE
RUSAFA
ADHAMIYAH
DOURA
KARADA
SADR CITY
KARADAH
NISSAN

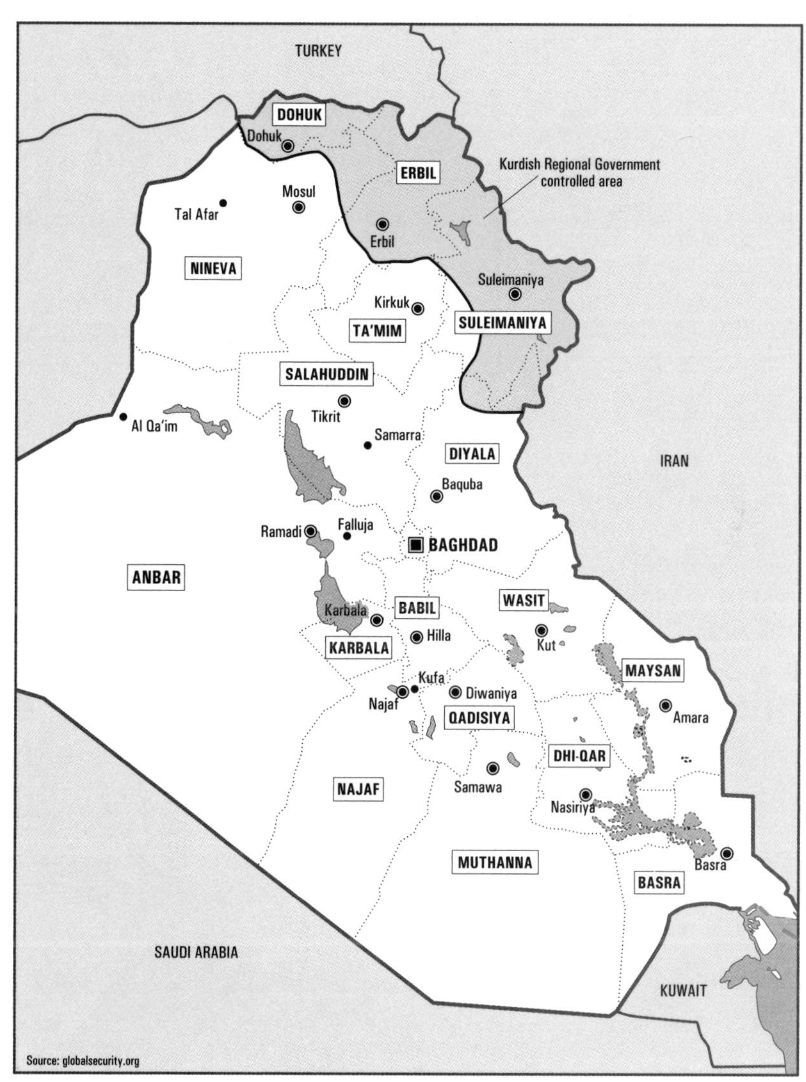
TURKEY
DOHUK
Dohuk
ERBIL
Kurdish Regional Government controlled area
Mosul
Tal Afar
Erbil
NINEVA
Suleimaniya
Kirkuk
TA'MIM
SULEIMANIYA
SALAHUDDIN
Tikrit
Al Qa'im
Samarra
DIYALA
IRAN
Baquba
Ramadi
Falluja
BAGHDAD
ANBAR
WASIT
BABIL
Karbala
Hilla
Kut
KARBALA
MAYSAN
Kufa
Diwaniya
Najaf
QADISIYA
Amara
DHI-QAR
NAJAF
Samawa
Nasiriya
MUTHANNA
Basra
BASRA
SAUDI ARABIA
KUWAIT
Source: globalsecurity.org

In memory of Zuhair al-Kadiri

INTRODUCTION

Assessing the future of Iraq

A sovereign Iraq

On 15 December 2011, in a fortified compound at Baghdad International Airport, United States Secretary of Defense Leon Panetta oversaw the formal end of the American military presence in Iraq. The event marked the final departure of US troops, eight years and nine months after the invasion. Panetta's farewell speech was sober and downbeat. He placed emphasis on the joint sacrifices that Iraqis and Americans had made during the years of occupation.[1]

The restraint in Panetta's speech is understandable for two reasons. The first is that the US military was ultimately forced out of the country by Iraqi political opinion. The Status of Forces Agreement (SOFA) negotiated by the George W. Bush administration in 2008 set the end of 2011 as the non-negotiable deadline for the departure of all US forces. Under the agreement, US combat troops were removed from Iraq's towns and cities in June 2009. To meet his election promises, President Barack Obama then accelerated the removal of all American combat forces from Iraq by August 2010. However, by April 2011 it was clear that the US government wished to renegotiate the SOFA in order to keep 10,000 to 20,000 American troops in Iraq past the original deadline. The Secretary of Defense Robert Gates and the chairman of the Joint Chiefs of Staff, Admiral Mike Mullen, both visited Baghdad in an attempt to gain permission from the Iraqi government for a number of American troops to stay. They also wanted to secure them legal protection from Iraqi law and win approval for this from the Iraqi parliament. In late May, Gates indicated that the United States wanted to keep a minimum of 8,000 soldiers in the country after December 2011, to meet its ongoing commitments to train Iraqi forces.[2] However, Iraq's ruling elite would not tolerate this. As early as December 2010, Prime Minister Nuri al-Maliki made this clear: 'The withdrawal of forces agreement expires on December 31, 2011. The last American soldier will leave Iraq (by then).'[3] By October 2011, it was apparent that senior members of Iraq's ruling coalition, constrained by strong popular opinion, could not give the US military even the minimum terms they needed to remain in the country.[4] In effect, American troops would be forced out of Iraq.

The second, more important reason for the reticence of Panetta's farewell speech concerns profound doubts about the stability and sustainability of the Iraqi state that the US had attempted to rebuild after regime change. In the aftermath of the invasion in March 2003, the US administration explicitly set out to transform Iraq into a democratic state with a free-market economy. To that end it disbanded the Iraqi Army and drove the previous ruling elite from power. When faced with the resultant insurgency and later civil war, American policy aims were dramatically reduced. In place of transformation, the United States tried to establish civil and military institutions that would be robust enough to allow it to disengage.[5] Although it has succeeded in this more limited ambition, there remain profound doubts about the future political trajectory of the country the United States left in December 2011.

It was Iraq's propensity to destabilise the Middle East that drove the US, at the head of a multinational coalition, to invade in March 2003. The fact that Iraq has the third-largest oil reserves in the world, combined with a population of 33 million people, ensures its position as one of the most strategically important countries in the region. The history of Iraq's foreign relations over the last 30 years has also made it a major source of instability in the Gulf. Iraq's geostrategic significance combined with the role it has played in destabilising Middle Eastern politics places it at the centre of the Gulf region.

This book seeks to judge what Iraq's future holds, now that it has regained full independence. It does this by seeking to address three questions. Firstly, can Iraq avoid sliding back into civil war and can it reduce the still appreciable levels of lethal violence seen since 2010? Secondly, will Iraq evolve into a law-governed, pluralistic polity that in some way resembles the interventionists' dream of an Arab democracy? Finally, will Iraq once again pose a security threat to its neighbours? Customarily this threat has emanated from the state's autonomy, strength and ambition, yet the 2003–12 period showed that an enfeebled Iraqi state can pose security problems in its region in other ways. The factual basis from which these judgements will be derived will be provided by an analysis of the country's political and security situation since the 2003 invasion. Particular attention will be given to the three different but interlinked dynamics that drove the country into civil war: socio-cultural factors; the weakness of the state's administrative and coercive institutions; and the nature of the constitutional settlement that structures its post-invasion politics.

Measuring stability after the invasion

One of the most common but statistically disputed approaches to judging the stability of Iraq is to assess the rate of civilian deaths. Given the ferocity of the conflict, the data on casualties are understandably variable and open to dispute. One of the most widely accepted medical surveys of Iraqi casualties was published in *The New England Journal of Medicine* in January 2008. It estimated that, between January 2002 and June 2006, 151,000 people had died violent deaths.[6] The non-governmental organisation Iraq Body Count has collected documentary evidence from the media and leaked US government documents which suggests that between 109,720 and 119,879 civilians were murdered between the invasion and November 2012.[7] The Brookings Institution's *Iraq Index* also publishes estimates of civilian deaths in Iraq drawn from an amalgamation of the ongoing Iraq Body Count data and statistics released by the Iraqi Interior Ministry and the US military. It has estimated that 116,409 civilians were killed from the the start of the invasion to June 2012.[8]

Beyond the controversy surrounding the headline numbers, a clear trend in civilian casualty figures is detectable (see Figure 1), and gives an indication of the country's changing levels of stability. Leaving aside several specific spikes, the number of violent civilian deaths steadily increased from May 2003 until February 2006. Iraq Body Count estimates that the number of civilians killed daily rose steadily, peaking at 73 a day between March 2006 and March 2007.[9] *Iraq Index* tracked the yearly civilian death rates starting at 7,300 in 2003 and peaking at 34,500 in 2006.

By the time Iraq's first post-invasion national elections were held in 2005, the conflict undoubtedly met the widely accepted scholarly definition of a civil war, which places the casualty threshold at 1,000 battlefield deaths per year in a 'primarily internal' conflict, 'pitting central government forces against an insurgent force capable of effective resistance'.[10] The rate of violent civilian deaths continued to steeply increase after 22 February 2006, when the al-Askariyya Mosque in the northern Iraqi city of Samara, a site revered in Shia Islam, was destroyed in an incident calculated to accelerate the sectarian murder rate. In the aftermath of the al-Askariyya bombing, the United Nations in Baghdad estimated that 34,452 civilians were killed in 2006.[11] If there were any doubts that these figures amounted to a civil war, the nature of the violence and the associated population transfers should have put paid to them. After the al-Askariyya bombing, estimates based on anecdotal evidence placed the number of Sunnis murdered in extra judicial killings in Baghdad at 1,000 per month, with 365,000 Iraqis forced from their homes.[12] According to Nicholas Sambanis, an expert on the causes of civil war: 'The level of violence is so extreme that it far surpasses most civil wars since 1945.'[13]

The violence associated with the civil war reached its peak in October 2006, when *Iraq Index* estimated that 3,709 civilians had been killed in just one month. In a televised speech to the American people on 10 January 2007, President Bush announced a dramatic shift in US policy towards Iraq: the 'surge'. This involved sending a total of 39,000 extra US troops to the country and deploying them in the midst of Iraqi society. From February 2007 onwards, civilian casualties in Iraq steadily declined. By mid-2008, fewer than 500 people were being killed every month. From then on the figure fell to about 300 a month. Statistically, this means that Iraq at the time of writing is still caught in a civil war. However, compared with the peak of the violence in 2006, the conflict has declined markedly in ferocity and scope.

The US government has used a series of different benchmarks to assess Iraq's progress towards stability in the

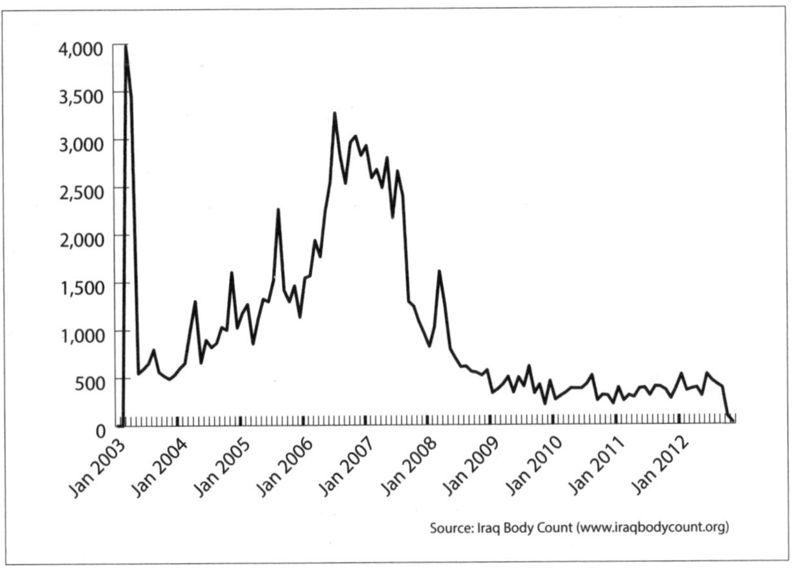

Figure 1: **Documented civilian deaths from violence in Iraq, by month, March 2003–November 2012**

aftermath of regime change. Until 2007, Washington tended to celebrate what were labelled at the time as major 'turning-points' in Iraq's post-invasion history. The first such event was the capture of President Saddam Hussein by US forces in mid-December 2003. This was followed by the handing over of sovereignty from the Coalition Provisional Authority (CPA), run by former American diplomat Paul Bremer, to an interim Iraqi government headed by the former long-term exile Ayad Allawi in June 2004. However, neither of these two events stopped the rising tide of politically motivated violence.

The next event to be seized upon by the Bush administration as definitive proof of progress was the national election held at the end of January 2005. This brought to power an interim government headed by Ibrahim al-Jaafari. A new constitution was then written by members of the recently elected national assembly and was successfully put to a national referendum in October 2005. Finally, Iraq went back to the polls to elect its first, full-term government in December 2005. Although it took 156 days after that election for Iraq's ruling elite to pick a new prime minister, Nuri al-Maliki, both the elections themselves and the rather belated selection of a new leader for the country were celebrated in Washington as evidence that Iraq was turning yet another corner and heading towards peace and sustainable stability.

Despite these undoubtedly historic events, 2005 was also the year when Iraq descended into an internecine conflict that met the all conventional definitions of a civil war.[14] If the handover of sovereignty to Iraqis and then the election of two Iraqi governments did not hasten Iraq's descent into civil war, then they certainly did nothing to slow the process down or herald a new dawn for the long-suffering population. With a rising tide of violence in Iraq and increasing public opposition to the war in America, the Bush administration was forced to move to a more rigorous set of metrics to judge Iraq's progress towards political and military stability, and to sell that assessment to its own increasingly hostile electorate. Over 2006 and 2007, a series of metrics or 'benchmarks' were devised in an attempt to force the Iraqi government to deliver policies that Washington judged would stabilise the country.

In October 2006, the then-head of the Multi-National Force–Iraq, General George Casey, and the American Ambassador to Baghdad, Zalmay Khalilzad, drafted what they called a 'blueprint' or 'schedule of specific milestones' against which Prime Minister Maliki's performance and the country's move towards stability would be judged. These included disarming the sectarian militias that were driving Iraq deeper into civil war, as well as a broader set of economic and military commitments to stabilise the country.[15] To the astonishment of American diplomats in Baghdad, this triggered howls of outrage from Maliki, who, citing his democratic mandate, dismissed Casey and Khalilzad's right to set a timetable for his government to meet any specific policy goals.[16]

By the end of 2006, the Bush administration was forced to face the fact that American policy was failing and had to be radically changed if the disintegration of Iraq and US defeat were to be avoided. With this in mind, US Iraq policy once again deployed a set of overt benchmarks at the centre of its new 'surge' strategy. In a January 2007 nationwide television broadcast announcing the new strategy, Bush said that he would hold the Iraqi government responsible for delivering six new benchmark commitments, namely: responsibility for security in all of Iraq's provinces; passing legislation to share oil revenues; spending $10 billion of its own money on reconstruction and infrastructure projects; holding provincial elections; reforming de-Ba'athification laws; and 'establishing a fair process for considering amendments to Iraq's constitution'.[17]

The eventual commitment to deploy a further 39,000 US troops to Iraq as part of the surge caused consternation among the Democratic members of the US Congress, newly empowered by their November 2006 mid-term election victories. In order to assert some form of control over US Iraq policy, Congress tied agreement to US$95bn of additional funding to an extended set of 18 benchmarks. These would be used to judge the success of US policy, allowing Congress to demand change, should the policy be found wanting.[18] A number of the congressional benchmarks, passed into law in May 2007, simply replicated those outlined in January by Bush. The rest focused on disarming the militias, guaranteeing the independence of both the Iraqi judiciary and the armed forces, and compelling the Iraqi government to expand and strengthen its security services.[19]

In 2007, once the administration and Congress accepted that Iraq was in the midst of a bloody civil war that risked delivering America a major strategic defeat, attempts at rectifying the situation implicitly recognised that the drivers of conflict were multi-faceted. Economically, both Bush and Congress stressed that oil revenues should be equally distributed across the whole of Iraq's population, and that the state should play a greater role in reconstruction. Bush, in the benchmarks he demanded the Iraqi government meet, tended to stress political initiatives and legislation designed to bring about reconciliation, attempting to reduce the alienation of the Sunni population. These included diluting the punitive nature of de-Ba'athification, holding provincial elections and reforming the constitution. Congress, on the other hand, identified the weakness of Iraq's security services and the power of sectarian militias as the key problems that needed attention before Iraq could be stabilised. Both Bush and Congress were right to see the post-war political settlement and state weakness as major contributing factors to driving the Iraqi civil war forward.

Assessing the causes of instability and violence

Following the start of the Bush administration's new Iraq policy, civilian murders certainly declined, from a peak of 3,079 people killed in October 2006 to rates of between 200 and 500 civilian deaths per month in late 2012.[20] It is, however, more difficult to assess the cause of this dramatic reduction in lethal violence and, more importantly, to judge whether it represents a move towards a stable and sustainable future for the country as a whole. The relationship between the decline in violence and the benchmarks set by the US government is rather obscure. The Iraqi government's record on meeting the 18 congressional benchmarks was mixed. Eleven had been partially or wholly met by October 2010, including military support for US troops during the surge, the expansion of the security services and the reduction of militia influence in the police force. However, even today there has been limited or no progress made on passing new legislation such as an oil law, de-Ba'athification and redrafting the constitution. Finally, and most importantly, although progress has certainly been made in challenging the sectarian militias' control of Baghdad and Basra, they have not been disarmed by the government and they still operate, albeit at a greatly reduced level, across the country.[21]

Against this background, a reliable analysis of Iraq's contemporary development and its future stability needs to move beyond the specificities of the 'shopping list' approach laid out above. This analysis should systematically assess a broader range of the potential causes of violence in Iraq. This would certainly include those issues identified as meriting inclusion in the US government's benchmarks. It would however seek to deploy an assessment of Iraq's initial descent into civil war, identifying what caused such profound destabilisation over the four years from the invasion to 2007. It would then analyse the extent to which these motors of instability were tackled between 2007 and 2012. How far did the US-led surge and Iraqi government policy in its aftermath reduce or completely remove the factors that caused the civil war?

Comparative examination of the causes of civil wars and the end of such conflicts focuses on three major themes: the socio-cultural factors that give rise to violent conflict; the institutional weakness of the state, both administrative and coercive, that created the space for violence to flourish; and the nature of the constitutional settlement that shapes how politics function, who can have access to power and how that power is shared.[22] These three broad factors have a key role in the analysis of the rising tide of violence in Iraq. The future stability of the country is partly dependent on the extent to which the US surge and subsequent Iraqi government policy have dealt with these major drivers of conflict. However, beyond the possibility of a return to civil war, there is the danger that the state has become too dominant, that its military power gives those in charge the ability not only to guarantee order, but also to suppress society. The political evolution of Iraq and its role in the wider region will be driven by these two dangers, civil war and a new authoritarianism.

The regional and global significance of Iraq

The regional importance of these questions is hard to overestimate. Iraq's influence on the wider Middle East partly originates from its geography. Iraq lies across two of the major population faultlines in the region. Demographically, the country, with its population of over 32m, sits between its much smaller oil-rich Gulf neighbours (including Saudi Arabia and Kuwait) and the considerably larger population of Iran, with nearly 72m people.[23] Economically, Iraq has the third-largest oil reserves in the world and has the potential to produce 8m barrels per day, making it the world's second-largest oil exporter. According to a 2012 report from the International Energy Agency, Iraq is key to meeting global oil demand over the next few decades.[24] It is this comparatively large population, combined with its oil-sector potential, that has historically given Iraq a dominant role in the Gulf and in wider Middle Eastern politics. Religiously, Iraq, with its majority Shia population, also sits between the Arab-majority Sunni regions of the Middle East and Iran's overwhelmingly Shia majority.

Even a cursory glance at the contemporary history of the Middle East indicates how these demographic, economic and religious dynamics have combined to give Iraq a major role in destabilising the region over the last 40 years. It is undoubtedly Iraq's combination of oil reserves and population size that has given its ruling elites the comparative autonomy they enjoy, both from their own society and from the international system; and which has been wielded to foment regional instability. Iraq's destabilising role began in earnest after the UK announced its withdrawal from the Gulf in 1968.[25] The removal of an external hegemon coincided with the seizure of power in Baghdad by the Ba'athist regime, first led by Hasan al-Bakr from July 1968 and then by Saddam from July 1979. The Ba'athist leadership's autonomy, both domestically and internationally, rose in tandem with the nationalisation of the Iraq Petroleum Company in 1972. This allowed the Iraqi government to sharply increase oil production to suit its own development needs. After the oil price shocks of 1973–74, the money flowing into Baghdad's coffers was drastically augmented with an 18-fold increase in the revenue the Iraqi government received from oil exports.[26] The overall result was a 40-fold increase in Iraq's oil revenues in a decade.[27]

Iraq's rulers used their newfound domestic and regional autonomy to secure dominance over the own population and then to project the state's power into the Gulf area. Thus, Baghdad became a major cause of instability in the Middle East. It started two of the most costly and prolonged conflicts in the region, the 1980–88 Iran–Iraq War and the 1990 invasion of Kuwait, which led in turn to the imposition of no-fly zones and international sanctions. Iraq invaded Iran in September 1980 for two reasons. One was to gain a more favourable border settlement along the disputed Shatt al-Arab waterway. More importantly, the invasion was launched in an attempt to neutralise the revolutionary threat posed by the leadership of Ayatollah Khomeini in Tehran. Khomeini called for Iraq's Shia population to rise up and overthrow the secular nationalist leadership of Saddam and the Ba'ath Party. The resulting eight-year conflict failed to achieve either of these aims. It cost over half a million lives and the loss of US$100bn to US$200bn in oil-export revenue, and forced Iraq to become heavily indebted to both the Arab Gulf states and Europe.[28]

The failure of Iraq's invasion of Iran, and the indebtedness that followed, triggered the August 1990 invasion of Kuwait. Iraq's violent attempt to annex Kuwait transgressed one of the cardinal rules of international law. In a world emerging from the bipolarity of the Cold War, condemnation by the permanent members of the UN Security Council was quick and unambiguous. With something approaching an international consensus, sanctions were rapidly imposed by the UN and Iraqi troops were expelled from Kuwait by an American-led coalition in an air bombardment and land offensive that lasted a little over six weeks. In the aftermath of this apparently triumphant military victory, the Security Council passed Resolutions 687 and 688. The sanctions imposed on Iraq by these resolutions not only 'achieved the greatest degree of international cooperation in modern history' but were to become, over the 13 years of their application, the 'most comprehensive and severe ever imposed against one nation'.[29] However, because of the international and domestic autonomy it had successfully established since 1968, the Ba'athist regime in Baghdad survived over a decade of this coercive diplomacy.[30]

The US invaded Iraq in March 2003 to remove the Ba'athist government. In doing so it also wanted to break the domestic and regional autonomy of the Iraqi state, and hence remove one of the central drivers of instability in the region. In fact, this ambitious attempt to use American military power to reform a major Arab state gave rise to another unintended source of regional instability as the Iraqi state collapsed into violence and civil war that threatened to spill across its borders. There is a profound irony that, after 2003, Iraq's position as a failed state might have been more destabilising for the region than the rogue state run by Saddam.

Iraq at the crossroads

Two periods of Iraq's contemporary history, 1968 to 2003 and 2003 to 2011, reflect the opposing dynamics that played a central role in Iraq's domestic and regional instability. Under Ba'athist rule from 1968 onwards, the state's military and economic power was such that it could forcibly break any domestic opposition it faced and then project its own coercive strength across the region as a whole. In the aftermath of regime change in 2003, the reverse happened. The UN sanctions imposed on the country in 1990, combined with the three wars it had fought since 1980, brought the Iraqi state to the edge of collapse. The US-led invasion and the policy pursued by the occupation authorities in its aftermath reduced the power of the Iraqi state to such an extent that it could no longer impose order on its own population or guarantee the security of its borders. Domestically, the collapse of state capacity, the rise of militias legitimised in the name of sectarian politics and the structure of the political settlement imposed on the country in the aftermath of regime change drove it into civil war. Regionally, the occupation of Iraq by US forces, the profound weakness of the state and the sectarian warfare that dominated the country made Iraq a cockpit for the foreign policy disputes of its neighbours.

After 2012, when Iraq has regained its full sovereignty, the country's immediate future will be shaped by the dynamics unleashed in the aftermath of the invasion. Can the Iraqi state, led by Maliki, escape the social and political pressures that drove it into civil war? Do the institutions of the state have the autonomous capacity to constrain and then disarm the militias that played such a central role in the civil war? Beyond the threat of societal actors driving the country back into civil war, there remains a larger question mark over the role of the state itself. In particular, Maliki has shown a trenchant ability to impose his own personal rule on the institutions of the state. It is this pervasive fear amongst Iraq's ruling elite that Maliki is returning the country to dictatorship that caused the nine-month delay in forming a government after the elections in March 2010.

Iraq's near future is haunted by two different spectres. The first is the fear that the forces that overwhelmed the state and drove it into civil war will return. Iraq's population could then, once again, face a war of all against all where life would be nasty, brutish and short. The second older spectre is the one feared by politically active Iraqis: that another dictator could emerge, this time in the form of Maliki, and use the coercive power of the state to dominate society and stifle any chance of political opposition to his rule. With both these spectres hanging over it, Iraq has the potential to once again menace its neighbours and destabilise the Gulf region.

Notes

1 Secretary of Defense Leon E. Panetta, 'US Forces-Iraq End of Mission Ceremony', 15 December 2011, http://www.defense.gov/speeches/speech.aspx?speechid=1641.

2 John D. Banusiewicz, 'Gates Shares Views on Iraq, Afghanistan, Pakistan', *American Forces Press Service*, 19 May 2011, http://www.defense.gov//News/NewsArticle.aspx?ID=64011.

3 Sam Dagher, 'Transcript: Maliki on Iraq's Future', *Wall Street Journal*, 28 December 2010, http://online.wsj.com/article/SB10001424052970203430404577092512821791908.html.

4 Tim Arango and Michael S. Schmidt, 'Iraq Denies Legal Immunity to US Troops After 2011', *New York Times*, 4 October 2011, http://www.nytimes.com/2011/10/05/world/middleeast/iraqis-say-no-to-immunity-for-remaining-american-troops.html?_r=1&ref=middleeast.

5 On the changing parameters of the United States' Iraq policy see Toby Dodge, 'The Ideological Roots of Failure: The Application of Kinetic Neo-Liberalism to Iraq', *International Affairs*, vol. 86, no. 6, November 2010, pp. 1,269–86.

6 Iraq Family Health Survey Study Group, 'Violence-Related Mortality in Iraq from 2002 to 2006', *New England Journal of Medicine*, vol. 358, no. 5, 31 January 2008, pp. 484–93, http://content.nejm.org/cgi/content/full/NEJMsa0707782.

7 http://www.iraqbodycount.org. I thank John Sloboda of Iraq Body Count for his advice on casualty figures.

8 Michael E. O'Hanlon and Ian Livingston, *Iraq Index: Tracking Variables of Reconstruction and Security in Post-Saddam Iraq*, July 2012, http://www.brookings.edu/~/media/Centers/saban/iraq%20index/index201207.pdf, p. 3. For their methodology see *Iraq Index*, fn. 1, p. 11.

9 Iraq Body Count, 'Year Four: Simply the Worst', 18 March 2007, http://www.iraqbodycount.org/analysis/numbers/year-four.

10 Errol A. Henderson and J. David Singer, 'Civil War in the Post-Colonial World, 1946–92', *Journal of Peace Research*, vol. 37, no. 3, May 2000, p. 284.

11 Damien Cave and John O'Neil, 'UN Puts '06 Iraq Toll of Civilians at 34,000', *International Herald Tribune*, 17 January 2007; and Associated Press, 'Iraq Sets Toll of Civilians at 12,000 for 2006', *New York Times*, 3 January 2007.

12 Based on interviews by the author and commentator Fareed Zakaria, 'Rethinking the Way Forward', *Newsweek*, 6 November 2006, p. 26.

13 Quoted in Edward Wong, 'A Matter of Definition: What Makes a Civil War, and Who Declares It So?', *New York Times*, 26 November 2006, http://www.nytimes.com/2006/11/26/world/middleeast/26war.html?_r=1&scp=1&sq=Iraq%20civil%20war%20Edward%20Wong&st=cse.

14 Beyond the number of battlefield casualties, if the issue of defining the Iraq conflict as a civil war also rests on the indigenous nature of the forces fighting then it was not until May 2005 that Iraqi government forces outnumbered US and allied troops. From then on, Iraqi force numbers continued to grow and the weight of responsibility for fighting the insurgency is reflected in the increasing loss of life suffered. In the 18 months from June 2003 to January 2005, 1,300 members of the Iraqi security services were killed, with more than 2,000 killed in 2005 and 2006. See O'Hanlon and Livingston, *Iraq Index*, pp. 5, 19, 23. On the balance of exogenous and indigenous forces in defining a civil war, see Henderson and Singer, 'Civil War in the Post-Colonial World', p. 276; James D. Fearon and David D. Laitin, 'Ethnicity, Insurgency and Civil War', *American Political Science Review*, vol. 97, no. 1, February 2003, p. 76; and Nicholas Sambanis, 'What Is Civil War? Conceptual and Empirical Complexities of an Operational Definition', *Journal of Conflict Resolution*, vol. 48, no. 6, December 2004, p. 829.

15 David S. Cloud, 'US To Hand Iraq a New Timetable on Security Role', *New York Times*, 22 October 2006, http://www.nytimes.com/2006/10/22/world/middleeast/22policy.html?scp=67&sq=Iraq+benchmarks&st=nyt.

16 John F. Burns, 'Fighting Split, US and Iraq Renew Vow To Work for Peace', *New York Times*, 28 October, 2006, http://www.nytimes.com/2006/10/28/world/middleeast/28iraq.html?scp=71&sq=Iraq+benchmarks&st=ny.

17 George W. Bush, 'President's Address to the Nation', 10 January 2007, http://georgewbush-whitehouse.archives.gov/news/releases/2007/01/20070110-7.html.

18 'US Troop Readiness, Veterans' Care, Katrina Recovery, and Iraq Accountability Appropriations Act, 2007', Bill 1314, available at http://frwebgate.access.gpo.gov/cgi-bin/getdoc.cgi?dbname=110_cong_bills&docid=f:h2206enr.txt.pdf.

19 The 18 congressional benchmarks: (1) Forming a Constitutional Review

Committee and then completing the constitutional review; (2) Enacting and implementing legislation on de-Ba'athification; (3) Enacting and implementing legislation to ensure the equitable distribution of hydrocarbon resources; (4) Enacting and implementing legislation on procedures to form semi-autonomous regions; (5) Enacting and implementing legislation establishing an Independent High Electoral Commission, provincial elections law, provincial council authorities and a date for provincial elections; (6) Enacting and implementing legislation addressing amnesty; (7) Enacting and implementing legislation establishing a strong militia disarmament programme to ensure that such security forces are accountable only to the central government and loyal to the Constitution of Iraq; (8) Establishing supporting political, media, economic and services committees in support of the Baghdad Security Plan; (9) Providing three trained and ready Iraqi brigades to support Baghdad operations; (10) Providing Iraqi commanders with all authorities to execute this plan and to make tactical and operational decisions, in consultation with US commanders, without political intervention, to include the authority to pursue all extremists, including Sunni insurgents and Shiite militias; (11) Ensuring that the Iraqi Security Forces are providing even handed enforcement of the law; (12) Ensuring that, according to President Bush, Prime Minister Maliki said 'the Baghdad security plan will not provide a safe haven for any outlaws, regardless of [their] sectarian or political affiliation'; (13) Reducing the level of sectarian violence in Iraq and eliminating militia control of local security; (14) Establishing all of the planned joint security stations in neighborhoods across Baghdad; (15) Increasing the number of Iraqi security force units capable of operating independently; (16) Ensuring that the rights of minority political parties in the Iraqi legislature are protected; (17) Allocating and spending $10 billion in Iraqi revenues for reconstruction projects, including delivery of essential services, on an equitable basis; (18) Ensuring that Iraq's political authorities are not undermining or making false accusations against members of the Iraqi security forces.

20 See *Iraq Index* and http://www.iraqbodycount.org/database/.

21 Kenneth Katzman, *Iraq: Politics, Elections, and Benchmarks*, Congressional Research Service, 4 October 2010, pp. 23–4.

22 See Astri Suhrke, 'Introduction', in Mats Berdal and Astri Suhrke (eds), *The Peace In Between: Violence in Post-war States* (Abingdon: Routledge, 2012).

23 See http://data.worldbank.org/indicator/SP.POP.TOTL?cid=GPD_1.

24 International Energy Agency, 'Iraq poised to become game-changer for world markets, landmark IEA report says,' 9 October 2012, accessed at http://www.iea.org/newsroomandevents/pressreleases/2012/october/name,32060,en.html.

25 Tim Niblock, 'Iraqi Policies Towards the Arab States of the Gulf, 1958–1981', in Tim Niblock (ed.), *Iraq: The Contemporary State* (London: Croom Helm, 1982), p. 126.

26 Charles Tripp, *A History of Iraq* (Cambridge: Cambridge University Press, 2000), p. 214.

27 Fanar Haddad, *Sectarianism in Iraq; Antagonistic Visions of Unity* (London: Hurst & Co., 2011), p. 89.

28 Phebe Marr, 'Iraq: Balancing Foreign and Domestic Realities', in L. Carl Brown (ed.), *Diplomacy in the Middle East: The International Relations of Regional and Outside Powers* (London: I.B. Tauris, 2006), p. 89.

29 Daniel W. Drezner, *The Sanctions Paradox: Economic Statecraft and International Relations* (Cambridge: Cambridge University Press, 1999), p. 1; and Jeffrey A. Meyer and Mark G. Califano, *Good Intentions Corrupted: The Oil-for-Food Scandal and the Threat to the UN* (New York: Public Affairs, 2006), p. 2.

30 See Toby Dodge, 'The Failure of Sanctions and the Evolution of International Policy Towards Iraq 1990–2003', *Contemporary Arab Affairs*, vol. 3, no. 1, January 2010, pp. 82–90.

CHAPTER ONE

Understanding the drivers of violence in Iraq

In order to assess what Iraq's future will be, the causes of the violent instability that plagued the country from 2003 onwards need to be analysed. Firstly, what were the factors that drove Iraq into civil war, and have events since 2007 reduced or removed them from the political arena? A close examination of civil wars across the world from 1945 onwards reveals three different but interlinked drivers of violent conflict that are relevant to what has happened in Iraq since 2003. These can be labelled socio-cultural factors, broadly meaning, the ideological trends within a society that encourage the non-state use of violence; the weakness of the state's administrative and coercive institutions; and the nature of the constitutional settlement that structures politics.[1]

Socio-cultural factors in Iraq's descent into civil war

Two intertwined dynamics tend to be highlighted when the role of socio-cultural factors in causing violence is examined: the 'general legitimation of violence stemming from wartime reversal of customary prohibitions on killings' and 'the rise in prominence of people with a propensity for violence'.[2]

The Ba'athist dictatorship that ran the country for 35 years deployed high levels of state-sanctioned violence while seeking to realise its totalitarian aspirations. However, it also worked hard from 1968 onwards to ensure that the Iraqi state had a secure grip on the collective deployment of violence within society, and severely punished those who used violence without its permission. The regime also used inter-state warfare, first invading Iran and then Kuwait, as a tool for controlling its own society.[3]

It was the aftermath of the 1990–91 Gulf War that may have had the greatest impact on customary prohibitions on killing. By the mid-1990s, under the pressure of UN sanctions, the Iraqi state began to lose control of its monopoly on violence. This allowed criminality to flourish and privatised coercion to serve the pursuit of personal interest as well as state-driven repression.[4] This was when state and societal prohibitions on killing lost their purchase. There is a direct link between the suffering imposed on the Iraqi people under the sanctions regime and the explosion of violence after 2003.[5] Iraqi author Zuhair al-Jezairy graphically describes the violence at the heart of Iraqi society when he returned in 2003:

> In the trenches, in the training camps, in the atmosphere of total militarization, three generations had grown up inculcated with the idea of violence as a form of self-expression and protest. They were unbound by any law, or even any social norms … unless it was under force of compulsion. The sanctions imposed on Iraq in the 90s reinforced this culture of violence by diminishing the position of the educated middle class, who had been the leaders of modernism and progress in the country.[6]

War and sanctions left Iraq a highly militarised society that had been involved in three conflicts in 20 years. At the peak of its militarisation in 1989, Iraq had a standing army of one million men, with a weapons stockpile estimated to contain 4.2m firearms.[7] This militarisation led to high civilian gun ownership, with 3.2m firearms in the hands of ordinary Iraqis. The combination of a large standing army, conscription and government-formed militias gave rise to a steady proliferation of small arms across society.[8] By 2003, this proliferation had turned into a flood. The rapid collapse of the Iraqi armed forces in the face of the US invasion led to the looting of its weapons stockpile. The 4.2m guns once controlled by the Iraqi security services spread across the whole of Iraqi society. Thus, societal trauma, extreme violence as a common currency in both politics and crime, and high levels of private gun ownership (both legal and illicit), combined to make the rise of collective violence in Iraq after 2003 comparatively easy to organise.

The socio-cultural factors more commonly deployed to explain the violence in Iraq focus on the ethnic and religious divisions within Iraqi society. At first glance, this does not appear to be a fruitful area for uncovering explanations for the Iraqi civil war. Cross-regional examinations of other civil wars have a tendency to downplay the ethnically or religiously divided nature of societies in explaining their descent into strife.[9] As Fanar Haddad has cogently argued, before 2003, 'traditional Iraq discourse, whether from above or below, has struggled to openly address "sectarianism"'.[10] Yet as the violence in Iraq mutated from an insurgency into a civil war, the rhetoric used to justify the increasing killings of civilians, the population transfers and mass-casualty attacks was infused with sectarian language. As journalist and author Nir Rosen notes:

> Sunnis and Shi'as began using new terms to refer to each other. To Shi'as, Sunnis were Wahhabis, Saddamists, and nawasib. To Sunnis, Shi'as were al rafidha or al turs. Rafidha, meaning 'rejectionists', refers to those who do not recognize the Islamic caliphs and want instead a caliphate from the descendent of Imam Ali.[11]

Clearly, by 2006, the conflict was being justified in aggressively divisive sectarian language. Such forms of political mobilisation based on religious and ethnic identity do not operate wholly on a rational, instrumental or even fully conscious basis, as 'the political genius of ethnicity in the contemporary developed world lies precisely in its ability to combine emotional sustenance with calculated strategy'.[12]

Haddad makes the distinction between three states of ethnic and religious identity: aggressive, passive and banal.[13] In times of profound insecurity, competition for scarce resources and the aggressive assertion of competing identity claims are likely to move a group's collective sense of itself from banal or passive to the violently assertive, as the group struggles for survival. For these communalistic identities to triumph as an organising principle in this fluid and unpredictable situation it also requires the existence of a certain type of sub-national political elite. These 'ethnic entrepreneurs' have to supply what the wider community desperately needs, namely a degree of stability and certainty. They can then legitimise their role in terms of a communalistic identity that aids them in the competition for scarce resources.[14] In these circumstances, people will look to whatever grouping, militia or identity offers them the best chance of survival.[15] This unstable and violent process will be shaped by path dependencies built up before the collapse of the state and the actions of political entrepreneurs in its wake.

Local, sub-state and ethnic identities will emerge from the wreckage of state collapse to provide channels for mobilisation and the immediate basis for political organisation.[16]

Once this process has been set in motion, when ethnic entrepreneurs have mobilised a significant section of the population on the basis of communalistic identity, this dynamic can quickly solidify.[17] Previously 'fuzzy' or passive identity traits can become politicised and 'enumerated'.[18] Survival, or a degree of predictability for individuals and their families, becomes primarily obtainable through the increasingly militant deployment of ethnic or sectarian identity. There is nothing inevitable about the unfolding of this process; the primary cause is the collapse of the state and the subsequent security vacuum, not the communalist conflict that emerges in its wake.

In pre-2003 Iraq, the state promoted an Iraqi nationalism that at first glance appeared to be without religious bias. Although, from the mid-1990s onwards, Saddam had injected Islamism into his party's ruling ideology, examples of the state using blatantly sectarian rhetoric were comparatively rare. However, on closer inspection, the ruling ideology, based as it was on Arab nationalism, relied on a passive but nonetheless important affinity with Sunni Islam. As Haddad argues, although Ba'athist ideology in Iraq attempted to integrate both Sunni and Shia imagery, it was clearly more inclusive of Sunni symbolism than Shia.[19] In addition, it was Sunni Islam that was taught in state schools, and various aspects of Shia religious practice were banned under the Ba'athist regime.[20]

This favouring of Sunni symbolism and the suppression of Shia Islam came to a shuddering halt when the Ba'athist regime fell in April 2003, freeing the majority Shia population to actively promote their religious identity. Only a few weeks after the fall of the Ba'ath Party, up to three million Shia pilgrims descended on the holy city of Karbala to take part in the previously banned *arba'in* ceremony.[21] In a country with little government and no order, the Shia religious hierarchy, the *hawza*, became the focus of loyalty and hope.[22] Once governing institutions were tentatively set up, their senior ranks quickly filled with formerly exiled politicians and parties that actively asserted the centrality of their Shia religious beliefs to the country's new politics, and the desire to remould Iraqi nationalism, placing Shi'ism at its heart. This assertive promotion of religious identity produced a backlash across the Sunni section of Iraqi society. In an increasingly lawless country politically dominated by overtly Shia parties and the *hawza*, those Sunnis who had previously found comfort and certainty in Iraqi nationalism began to look elsewhere. An increasingly militant assertion of a rival Sunni Islamism was forged that was both radicalised and, at its fringes, increasingly violent.[23]

The weakness of the Iraqi state after 2003

Socio-cultural explanations for rising violence are directly linked to the power of the state's institutions, both its army and police force, and its ability to deliver services to the population. The decline in 'customary prohibitions on killings' and the rise in the aggressive assertion of sub-state identities are driven by a dramatic reduction in state power. The withdrawal of institutional power from society creates the space for both ethnic entrepreneurs to mobilise society and the purveyors of violence to exploit lawlessness. Against this background, an analytical explanation of violence in Iraq after regime change would have to factor in the drastic reduction in state capacity from April 2003 onwards. This would be in line with Fearon and Laitin's argument that 'financially, organizationally and politically weak central governments render insurgency more feasible and attractive due to weak local policing or inept and corrupt counterinsurgency practices'.[24]

A coherent state relies on its ability to impose order on the population and to monopolise the deployment of collective violence across the whole of its territory.[25] Once a state has obtained the ability to impose and guarantee order, the basis of its sustainability and legitimacy moves to infrastructural power, the ability to deliver services the population benefits from whilst also operating across society unopposed.[26] The degree to which a state has reached this ideal type can be judged by the ability of its institutions firstly to impose and guarantee the rule of law, then to penetrate society and mobilise the population, and finally to regularly extract resources in the form of taxation.[27] Ultimately, the stability of the state depends on the extent to which its actions are judged to be legitimate in the eyes of the majority of its citizens, and the ability of its ruling elite to foster consent.[28]

The initial causes of the security vacuum in Iraq lies in the lack of troops the invading forces brought with them, then the disbanding of the Iraqi army. Faced with the widespread lawlessness that is common after violent regime change, the United States lacked the troop numbers to control the situation.[29] In February 2003, in the run-up to war, Army Chief of Staff Eric Shinseki called for 'something in the order of several hundred thousand soldiers' to guarantee post-war order. James Dobbins, in a widely cited study on state-building published in the run-up to the invasion, compared US interventions in other states since the Second World War. Dobbins concluded that occupying forces would need 20 security personnel, police and troops per thousand people. Translated into American personnel, US forces should have had between 400,000 and 500,000 soldiers to impose order on Iraq.[30] In May 2003, the total strength of coalition forces was 173,000. This figured dropped to as low as 139,000 in 2004, and only significantly increased after Bush announced the 'surge' at the start of 2007.[31] Bremer's decision to disband the Iraqi Army in May 2003 forced 400,000 armed, trained and alienated ex-soldiers out onto the streets, facing unemployment. Of even greater significance, Bremer's decision meant that the Iraqi armed forces had to be rebuilt from scratch, a process that by its very nature was bound to take several years. Thus, the violence that shook Iraq after 2003 was a direct result of the security vacuum created by the lack of troops to impose order.

The civilian institutional capacity of the state in 2003 was in a similarly perilous condition. Iraq had staggered through two wars from 1980 to 1990 and was then subjected to the harshest and longest-running international sanctions ever imposed. The sanctions regime was specifically designed to break the government's ability to deliver services and, with the notable exception of the rationing system, it was effective.[32] The civilian capacity of the state was dismantled by the looting that spread across Baghdad after the fall of the Ba'athist regime in April 2003. The first three weeks of violence and theft that followed severely damaged the state's administrative capacity: 17 of Baghdad's 23 ministry buildings were completely gutted.[33] Looters initially took portable items of value such as computers, before turning to furniture and fittings. They then systematically stripped the electric wiring from the walls to sell for scrap. This practice was so widespread that copper and aluminium prices in the neighbouring countries of Iran and Kuwait dramatically dropped as a result of the massive illicit outflow of stolen scrap metal from Iraq.[34] Overall, the looting is estimated to have cost as much as US$12bn, equal to one-third of Iraq's annual GDP.[35]

Following the destruction of government infrastructure across the country, the de-Ba'athification pursued by the US occupation purged the civil service of its top layer of management, making between 20,000 and 120,000 people unemployed and removing what was left of the state and its institutional memory.[36] (The large variation in estimates indicates the paucity of reliable intelligence on the ramifications of such an important policy decision.) After 2003, not only did the state's ability to impose order on Iraq disintegrate, but the coherence and capacity of its civil institutions also fell away. The population was bereft of order or state-delivered services.

Against this background of war, sanctions, inadequate occupying forces and resultant looting, Iraq in 2003 became a collapsed state. As William Zartman has put it:

> State collapse is a deeper phenomenon than mere rebellion, coup, or riot. It refers to a situation where the structure, authority (legitimate power), law, and political order have fallen apart and must be reconstituted in some form, old or new.[37]

In the aftermath of state failure, authoritative institutions, both societal and governmental, quickly lose their capacity and legitimacy.[38] The geographic boundaries within which national politics and economics have been historically enacted simultaneously expand and contract. On one level, because the state has lost its administrative and coercive capacity, the country's borders become increasingly meaningless. Decision-making power leaks out across the boundaries of the country to neighbouring capitals – in Iraq's case, Amman, Damascus and Tehran (as well as distant Washington). As this process accelerates, regional and international actors are drawn into the conflict, for good or ill. More damaging, however, is the fact that power drains into what is left of society, away from the state capital, down to a local level, where limited organisational capacity begins to be rebuilt. The dynamics associated with state collapse mean that politics becomes simultaneously international and highly local.[39] In the aftermath of state failure, individuals struggle to find public goods, services and economic subsistence. They physically survive any way they can, usually through ad hoc and informal channels:

> When state authority crumbles, individuals not only lose the protection normally supplied by public offices, but are also freed from institutional restraints. In response, they often seek safety, profit or both. Their motives become more complex than when they could depend on the state.[40]

This is exactly the situation that Iraqis found themselves in from 2003 onwards. The state suddenly ceased functioning, leaving a security vacuum across Iraq. Iraqi society was initially overrun by opportunist criminals, then by the diffuse forces fighting in the insurgency and finally by a full-blown civil war.

Elite bargains and post-invasion politics in Iraq

The political system put in place after regime change was built around what can best be described as an exclusive elite bargain. This inflamed Iraq's communal conflict and helped transform the insurgency into a sectarian war. Elite bargains are often placed at the centre of negotiations to move a country from dictatorship to democracy, or from civil war to a peace settlement. Such bargains are 'often unarticulated, understandings between elites that bring about the conditions to end conflict, but which also in most states prevent violent conflict from occurring'.[41] The elites involved must be the 'principal decision makers', politically, economically and militarily, and must have the ability to deliver leadership of the dominant groups within a society.[42] The bargain between them involves building a consensus around 'the basic procedures and norms by which politics will henceforth be played'.[43] An elite settlement is likely to be arrived at either because the costs of an ongoing conflict are becoming too great for those leading the fighting, 'elite fratricide with no clear victor', or because the resumption of violence may well have a similar outcome.[44]

However, elite bargains do not always move politics away from conflict towards stable coexistence. Applying the notion of elite bargains to conflict-prone states in Africa, Stefan Lindemann makes the distinction between elite bargains that are inclusive and hence promote stability, and those that are exclusive and prone to drive countries back into conflict.[45] Inclusive settlements integrate a broad section of the existing national elites into a ruling coalition. This gives the organisations they represent access to the state's institutions, jobs and largesse. The politicians can then use state resources, rents and employment opportunities as patronage to sustain a strong base of support within society.[46] Exclusive bargains, on the other hand, involve a much narrower set of elites. They exclude a number of key politicians and their followers, fostering 'antagonism and violent conflict'.[47] In Iraq, the political settlement created by the United States after the invasion, institutionalised by the new constitution and legitimatised by two national elections in 2005, was undoubtedly an elite bargain of the exclusive variety. It played a major role in triggering the insurgency and driving the country into civil war. The settlement was designed to exclude key indigenous political elites from any role in government.

The elite bargain that dominated Iraqi politics has its origins in the formation of the Iraqi Governing Council (IGC) in 2003. The IGC was created after Sérgio Vieira de Mello, the senior UN representative in Baghdad after the invasion, convinced the United States that some form of receptacle was needed for

Iraq's abrogated sovereignty. He persuaded the civilian head of the occupation authorities, Paul Bremer, to form an Iraqi leadership group.[48] However, the IGC became the domain of a small number of formerly exiled political parties, which used it as a platform to solidify their grip on the Iraqi state. Members of the IGC were not chosen in an open or indeed consultative process, but after a period of extended negotiations between Bremer, de Mello and the six dominant, formerly exiled parties: the Iraqi National Alliance (INA), the Iraqi National Congress (INC), the Islamic Dawa Party, the Islamic Supreme Council of Iraq (ISCI), the Kurdistan Democratic Party (KDP) and the Patriotic Union of Kurdistan (PUK). The CPA, run by Bremer, claimed that the politicians chosen represented the ethnically and religiously divided nature of Iraqi society: 13 Shi'ites, five Sunnis, a Turkoman and a Christian. However, the forced and rather bizarre nature of this arrangement was highlighted by the inclusion of Hamid Majid Mousa, the Iraqi Communist Party's representative, in the 'Shia block' of 13. In reality, the political parties that in exile had done so much to encourage the invasion quickly monopolised the mechanics of Iraqi politics once they were delivered back to Baghdad by the American military.

Unsurprisingly, the manner of the IGC's selection caused consternation across Iraq's newly empowered civil society. Criticism focused firstly on the divisive nature of the selection process, which was seen to have introduced an overt sectarianism that had not hitherto been central to Iraqi political discourse.[49] Secondly, debate centred on the possible damage the selection process would do to government efficiency, with complaints that council members were chosen for their party political allegiances and not for their technical skills.

The IGC's membership is a telling indicator of the elite bargain that prevailed within Iraqi politics after 2003. Firstly, the six parties that gained prominence in exile by allying themselves with the United States, the INC, INA, Dawa, ISCI, KDP and PUK, controlled the council. Secondly, only 28% of the IGC's membership could be termed 'insiders'; those who had lived in south and central Iraq under the Ba'ath regime.[50] The rest were either long-term exiles or had lived in the Kurdish Regional Government enclave, which had been beyond Iraqi state control since 1991. Finally, of the five members of the IGC identified as Arab 'Sunni', only two, Naseer al-Chaderchi and Mohsen Abdel Hamid, were members of organised political parties.[51] This made it very difficult for them to deliver the support of their supposed constituencies. Al-Chaderchi's party had been set up by his father in 1946 but quickly lapsed into political irrelevance after regime change.[52] Hamid, conversely, was secretary-general of the Iraqi Islamic Party (IIP). Under the elite bargain, the IIP's role in the IGC, and every government it has served in since, was to deliver the 'Sunni vote', or in other words to bring the section of the population from which the former ruling elite originated back into the new post-war political settlement. From 2003 onwards, there is a great deal of evidence to suggest that it singularly failed to do this since the IIP was not representative of its supposed social constituency. The IIP's close association with the US occupation and the governing structures it erected meant that it was repeatedly outflanked by more radical political forces in the struggle to mobilise the Sunni section of Iraqi society.[53]

It was US domestic concerns that led to the exclusive elite bargain that allowed the IGC to seize control of the whole of the Iraqi state. On 11 November 2003, in the face of increasing violence in Iraq, Bremer was unceremoniously hauled back to Washington, where it was decided that sovereignty would be handed back to Iraqis no later than June 2004. What became known as the November 15 Agreement (the date the IGC was told about the plan and gave its assent) handed interim power to a new government ahead of national elections. The premiership was given to Ayad Allawi, a long-term exile and head of the INA, and the vice-presidencies went to Ibrahim al-Jaafari, the head of the Dawa Party, and Rowsch Shaways, a senior member of the KDP. Ministerial posts were then liberally divided among the other leading parties on the IGC. Thus, the parties at the centre of the exclusive elite bargain negotiated in July 2003 had successfully secured their grip on power.

Attempts followed, during 2005, to gain democratic legitimacy for this exclusive elite bargain. This involved anointing Iraq's new political elite with two electoral mandates and a constitution approved by a popular referendum. However, the nature of the electoral system that was chosen, the way the parties decided to fight the elections, and the manner in which the constitution was drafted all combined to exacerbate the exclusive nature of the post-war settlement and alienate a major section of the Iraqi population.

The democratic process was inaugurated by the election of 30 January 2005, which selected an interim government to rule for a year. The vote itself was held within one nationwide electoral constituency due to security and logistical concerns.[54] This removed local issues and personalities from the campaign and marshalled the politicians and parties that controlled the IGC into large coalitions,[55] most of which played to the lowest common denominator, deploying ethnic and sectarian rhetoric to maximise their vote.

This dynamic was exacerbated by the exclusion of the Sunni community, which in 2005 lacked the organisational capacity to mobilise effectively because the IIP was heavily tainted by its association with the US occupation. The party was challenged by a loose coalition of mosques, the Hayat al-Ulama al-Muslimin (Association of Muslim Scholars, or AMS), which emerged to give voice to excluded Sunnis.[56]

The AMS channelled the widespread outrage against the US military assault on the town of Fallujah in April 2004. The popular anger caused by this operation was such that even the IIP was forced to partially join an election boycott in the wake of the assault.[57]

Eight-and-a-half million Iraqis voted in the first set of post-invasion elections, 58% of those eligible.[58] However, turnout varied dramatically across the country and amongst Iraq's different ethnic and religious communities. In the northern areas with a predominately Kurdish population, turnout was 82%–92%. In the southern districts, where the majority of the population is Shia, 61%–71% voted. In Anbar province, an area of northwestern Iraq with a high concentration of Sunnis, only 2% voted, reflecting their anger and alienation.[59]

The United Iraqi Alliance (UIA), the multiparty list designed to maximise Shia support, won 48% of the vote and 140 seats in the 275-member assembly. The Kurdish Alliance took 27% and 77 seats. Allawi and his nationalist and secular Iraqi List – damaged by his decision to authorise the attack on Fallujah and a military confrontation with Moqtada al-Sadr, a radical Shia Islamist – only managed 14.5% of the vote and 40 seats.

The unbalanced government that the election created had a severe impact on the drafting of Iraq's new constitution, which was the main role of the newly elected parliament. In the aftermath of the elections, a 55-member Constitutional Drafting Committee was formed from the members of the assembly. However, the assembly and the committee were sidelined by early August. To quote Jonathan Morrow, who was involved in the process as an adviser in Baghdad, 'the Iraqi constitutional process was remarkable in the way in which members of the assembly, though legally charged with responsibility for writing the draft, were not involved'.[60] In their place, the parties at the centre of the exclusive elite bargain took control. These parties created a 'leadership council' consisting of Jaafari, Abdul Aziz al-Hakim, the leader of the other main Shia party, the Islamic Supreme Council of Iraq, and the two Kurdish leaders, Iraqi President Jalal Talabani and Masoud Barzani –which then wrote the constitution.

This high-handed, opaque and undemocratic drafting of the constitution caused resentment not only in the excluded parliament, but also across Iraq. It raised the very real possibility that the document would be rejected in the nationwide referendum needed to make it legal. In a last-minute compromise to avoid this, the then US-Ambassador, Zalmay Khalilzad, brokered a deal to secure the vote needed to make the document law. Khalilzad's compromise mandated a new committee of the Iraqi parliament to review and possibly redraft the constitution's most divisive aspects after the referendum had taken place. This was enough to gain the IIP's support.[61] In the short term, this gambit worked and the constitution passed the referendum with 78.4% voting in its favour. However, provinces with a high Sunni population once again voted overwhelmingly against it.[62] Unsurprisingly, no redrafting of the constitution's contentious aspects ever took place and both the election of January 2005 and the constitution became the encapsulation of the exclusive elite bargain around which Iraqi politics were organised.

A second nationwide ballot for a full-term government took place on 15 December 2005. Following on from the legacy of the first elections, this poll was again controlled by three broad coalitions. This time voter turnout reached 76%. The most important of the coalitions was again the UIA, with 46.5% of the vote and 128 candidates elected to parliament. The ISCI and Dawa dominated the alliance, but they widened their appeal by joining forces with Sadr, whose Mahdi Army had twice led uprisings against the American occupation, across south and central Iraq in April and June 2004 and in Najaf in August 2004. The Kurdish Alliance won 19.27% of the vote and took 53 seats.

The rise in voter turnout reflected increased Sunni participation in the election. The coalition that gained the majority of the Sunni vote was the Tawafuq, or Accord Front, put together by the IIP. This coalition took 16% of the vote and 44 seats. A more radical grouping, the Iraqi Dialogue Front, took 4% and 11 seats. Once again the main losers were those attempting to rally a secular nationalist vote. This time Allawi built an even broader coalition to form the National Iraqi List, but it secured just over 9% of the vote and 25 seats.[63] The Tawafuq was 'rewarded' for its vote by being given the largely ceremonial posts of vice president and deputy prime minister. It was also awarded several minor cabinet posts but none with sufficient employment or resource possibilities to tie the constituencies it was meant to represent into the state. The weakness of the Tawafuq's position within government was reflected when its members walked out of the cabinet in August 2007 and spent a year boycotting the government. The Tawafuq's demand that the government crack-down on militia killings as the price of its return to government had little or no effect on state policy.[64]

From July 2003 onwards, the Iraqi political parties that had gained prominence during their long exile successfully leveraged their alliance with the United States to control government. This, in combination with the radical de-Ba'athification pursued by both the United States and the new Iraqi government, created an exclusive elite bargain that consciously excluded, and indeed demonised, not only the old ruling elite, but also the whole Sunni section of Iraqi society from which that elite had largely come. This exclusive elite bargain brutalised Iraqi politics by dividing society into religious and ethnic groups. Within this rubric, the IIP was meant to deliver the Sunni community. However, it faced a series of difficulties in playing this role. Firstly, its close association with the US occupation and the new government severely limited its ability to mobilise the Sunnis, who were deeply antithetical to the US presence and the political structures it had created. The IIP, in an attempt to stay within the post-war political settlement, agreed to a series of compromises, exemplified by its support for the constitutional referendum, which further damaged its ability to represent the Sunni community. Finally, within government, the IIP's rewards for collaboration were scant, undermining the party's capacity to deploy the resources needed to tie an already alienated constituency to the state.

Conclusion

The violent instability that drove Iraq into civil war after 2003 clearly had multiple, interdependent causes. Firstly, in a highly armed society deeply traumatised by sanctions, war and 35 years of brutal dictatorship organised violence was comparatively easy to deploy. Secondly, although Iraq's cultural and ethnic cleavages were not the cause of the violence, they acted as a ready-made excuse for those perpetrating mass killings and for those coercive and ethnic entrepreneurs seeking to mobilise sections of the population for financial and political gain. The political settlement, an exclusive elite bargain built after regime change, exacerbated sectarian tensions, placing at the heart of the state a group of formerly exiled politicians who legitimised their hold on power through the exclusion of others from government by reference to sectarian imagery.

At the centre of the conflict sat the profound weakness of the Iraqi state after regime change. The disbanding of the Iraqi Army and the lack of troops available to the occupation forces created a security vacuum across the whole of south and central

Iraq. Into this vacuum stepped those groups responsible for the Iraqi civil war, those fighting to drive the Americans out of the country, the militias and death squads, the radical Islamists that organised under the banner of al-Qaeda in Mesopotamia (see pp. 58–9) and finally, politicians within the institutions of the state itself. All deployed extreme levels of violence in an attempt to impose their vision of Iraq on the rest of the country. For Iraq's future to be sustainable, these sources of conflict have to be curtailed, if not altogether removed.

Notes

1 Suhrke, 'Introduction', in Berdal and Suhrke (eds), *The Peace in Between*.

2 See *ibid.*; and Stathis N. Kalyvas, *The Logic of Violence in Civil War* (Cambridge: Cambridge University Press, 2006), p. 57.

3 Isam al-Khafaji, 'War as a Vehicle for the Rise and Decline of a State-controlled Society: The Case of Ba'athist Iraq', in Steven Heydemann (ed.), *War, Institutions and Social Change in the Middle East* (Berkeley, CA: University of Californian Press, 2000), p. 260.

4 See, for example, Neil MacFarquar, 'Crime Engulfs Iraq', *International Herald Tribune*, 21 October 1996.

5 David M. Malone, *The International Struggle Over Iraq: Politics in the UN Security Council, 1980–2005* (Oxford: Oxford University Press, 2006), p. 136.

6 Zuhair al-Jezairy, *The Devil You Don't Know: Going Back to Iraq* (London: Saqi, 2009), pp. 162–3.

7 Graduate Institute for International Studies, *Small Arms Survey 2004: Rights at Risk* (Oxford: Oxford University Press, 2004), pp. 45–7.

8 *Ibid.*, p. 47.

9 James D. Fearon and David D. Laitin, 'Ethnicity, Insurgency, and Civil War', *American Political Science Review*, vol. 97, no. 1, February 2003, p. 75; Kalyvas, *The Logic of Violence in Civil War*, p. 75.

10 Fanar Haddad, *Sectarianism in Iraq: Antagonistic Visions of Unity* (London: Hurst & Co., 2011), p. 1.

11 Nir Rosen, 'Anatomy of a Civil War; Iraq's Descent into Chaos', *Boston Review*, November/December 2006, http://bostonreview.net/BR31.6/rosen.php.

12 Joseph Rothschild, *Ethnopolitics: A Conceptual Framework* (New York: Columbia University Press, 1981), p. 61.

13 Haddad, *Sectarianism in Iraq*, p. 25.

14 See Rothschild, *Ethnopolitics*, p. 29.

15 Andrea Kathryn Talentino, 'The Two Faces of Nation-building: Developing Function and Identity', *Cambridge Review of International Affairs*, vol. 17, no. 3, October 2004, p. 569.

16 David Laitin, *The Russian-speaking Populations in the Near Abroad* (Ithaca, NY: Cornell University Press, 1998), p. 16.

17 Andreas Wimmer, 'Democracy and Ethno-religious Conflict in Iraq', *Survival*, vol. 45, no. 4, Winter 2003–04, p. 120.

18 On this distinction, see Sudipta Kaviraj, 'On the Construction of

Colonial Power, Structure, Discourse, Hegemony', in Dagmar Engels and Shula Marks (eds), *Contesting Colonial Hegemony: State and Society in Africa and India* (London: British Academic Press, 1994), pp. 21–32.

19 Haddad, *Sectarianism in Iraq*, p. 33.

20 Nir Rosen, *Aftermath: Following the Bloodshed of America's Wars in the Muslim World* (New York: Nation Books, 2010), p. 30.

21 Anthony Shadid, 'A Tradition of Faith Is Reclaimed on Blistered Feet', *Washington Post*, 23 April 2003, p. A01; Glenn Kessler and Dana Priest, 'US Planners Surprised by Strength of Iraqi Shiites', *Washington Post*, 23 April 2003, p. A03; and Faleh A. Jabar, 'The Worldly Roots of Religiosity in Post-Saddam Iraq', *Middle East Report*, no. 227, Summer 2003, p. 13.

22 International Crisis Group, 'Iraq's Shiites Under Occupation', *Middle East Briefing*, Baghdad/Brussels, 9 September 2003, p. 8.

23 Mohammed M. Hafez, *Suicide Bombers in Iraq: The Strategy and Ideology of Martyrdom* (Washington DC: United States Institute of Peace, 2007), p. 35.

24 Fearon and Laitin, 'Ethnicity, Insurgency, and Civil War', pp. 75–6.

25 For the classic definition see Max Weber, 'Politics as a Vocation', in H.H. Gerth and C. Wright Mills (eds), *From Max Weber: Essays in Sociology* (London: Routledge, 1991), pp. 78–9.

26 Michael Mann, 'The Autonomous Power of the State: Its Origins, Mechanisms and Results', in Michael Mann (ed.), *States, War and Capitalism: Studies in Political Sociology* (Oxford: Blackwell, 1988), p. 4.

27 See Joel S. Migdal, *Strong Societies and Weak States. State-Society Relations and State Capabilities in the Third World* (Princeton, NJ: Princeton University Press, 1988).

28 See Antonio Gramsci, *Selections from the Prison Notebooks* (London: Lawrence and Wishart, 1998), p. 145; and Christine Buci-Glucksmann, *Gramsci and the State* (London: Lawrence and Wishart, 1980). On the lack of hegemony in the developing world see Nazih N. Ayubi, *Over-stating the Arab State: Politics and Society in the Middle East* (London: I.B. Tauris, 1995), Chapter One.

29 On post-regime change violence see Simon Chesterman, *You, the People. The United Nations, Transitional Administration, and State-Building* (Oxford: Oxford University Press, 2004) pp. 100, 112. On the estimated number of troops needed to impose order on Iraq see James Dobbins et al., *America's Role in Nation-Building: From Germany to Iraq* (Santa Monica, CA: RAND Corporation, 2003), p. 197.

30 See *ibid*.

31 Michael E. O'Hanlon and Ian Livingston, *Iraq Index: Tracking Variables of Reconstruction and Security in Post-Saddam Iraq*, 31 October 2010, p. 18, downloadable via http://www.brookings.edu/iraqindex .

32 On the sanctions regime and its effects on the Iraqi state and society, see Toby Dodge, 'The Failure of Sanctions and the Evolution of International Policy Towards Iraq 1990–2003', *Contemporary Arab Affairs*, vol. 3, no. 1, January 2010, pp. 82–90.

33 David L. Phillips, *Losing Iraq: Inside the Post-war Reconstruction Fiasco* (New York: Basic Books, 2005), p. 135.

34 Ali A. Allawi, *The Occupation of Iraq: Winning the War, Losing the Peace* (New Haven, CT: Yale University Press, 2007), p. 116.

35 James Dobbins et al., *Occupying Iraq; A History of the Coalition Provisional Authority* (Santa Monica, CA: RAND Corporation, 2009), p. 111.

36 Phillips estimates that the purge made 120,000 unemployed out of a total party membership of 2m. Paul Bremer cites intelligence estimates that the purge affected 1% of the party membership, or 20,000 people. George Packer estimates 'at least thirty-five thousand'. See Phillips, *Losing Iraq*, pp. 145–46; L. Paul Bremer III with Malcolm McConnell, *My Year in Iraq: The Struggle to Build a Future of Hope* (New York: Simon and Schuster, 2006), p. 40; and George Packer, *Assassins' Gate: America in Iraq* (New York: Farrar, Straus and Giroux, 2005), p. 191.

37 I. William Zartman, 'Posing the Problem of State Collapse', in I. William Zartman (ed.), *Collapsed States: The Disintegration and Restoration of Legitimate Authority* (Boulder, CO: Lynne Rienner, 1995), p. 1.

38 *Ibid.*, p. 6.

39 *Ibid.*, p. 5.

40 Nelson Kasfir, 'Domestic Anarchy, Security Dilemmas, and Violent Predation', in Robert I. Rotberg (ed.), *When States Fail: Causes and Consequences* (Princeton, NJ: Princeton University Press, 2004), p. 55.

41 Alan Whaites, *States in Development: Understanding State-building* (London: DFID, 2008), p. 7, http://www.dfid.gov.uk/Documents/publications/State-in-Development-Wkg-Paper.pdf.

42 Michael Burton, Richard Gunther and John Higley, 'Introduction', in John Higley and Richard Gunther (eds), *Elites and Democratic Consolidation in Latin America and Southern Europe* (Cambridge: Cambridge University Press, 1992), p. 8.

43 John Higley and Richard Gunther, 'Preface', in *ibid.*, p. xi,

44 See Burton, Gunther and Higley, 'Introduction', in *ibid.*, p. 14.

45 Stefan Lindemann, 'Do Inclusive Elite Bargains Matter? A Research Framework for Understanding the Causes of Civil War in Sub-Saharan Africa', Crisis States Discussion Paper 15, Crisis States Research Centre, London School of Economics and Political Science, February 2008, http://www.crisisstates.com/download/dp/dp15.pdf.

46 *Ibid.*, pp. 2, 10.

47 *Ibid.*, pp. 2, 21.

48 Edward Mortimer, 'Iraq's Future Lies Beyond Conquest', *Financial Times*, 22 August 2003, p. 17; and Samantha Power, *Chasing the Flame; Sergio Vieira de Mello and the Fight to Save the World* (London: Penguin, 2008), p. 418.

49 Rend Rahim Francke, 'Iraq Democracy Watch: On the Situation in Iraq', The Iraq Foundation, September 2003, http://www.iraqfoundation.org/news/2003/isept/26_democracy_watch.html.

50 Phebe Marr, 'Who Are Iraq's New Leaders? What Do They Want?', Special Report 160, United States Institute of Peace, March 2006, p. 11.

51 See 'The Iraqi Governing Council', BBC News, 14 July 2003, http://news.bbc.co.uk/1/hi/world/middle_east/3062897.stm.

52 Hanna Batatu, *The Old Social Classes and the Revolutionary Movements of Iraq. A Study of Iraq's Old Landed and Commercial Classes and of its Communists, Ba'athists and Free Officers*, (Princeton, NJ: Princeton University Press, 1978), p. 305.

53 Anthony Shadid, *Night Draws Near: Iraq's People in the Shadow of America's*

War (New York: Henry Holt, 2005), p. 312.

54 Mark Turner, 'Poll Planning on Track But No Room for Hitches', *Financial Times*, 14 October 2004.

55 Adeed Dawisha and Larry Diamond, 'Iraq's Year of Voting Dangerously', *Journal of Democracy*, vol. 17, no. 2, April 2006, p. 93.

56 Roel Meijer, 'The Sunni Resistance and the "Political Process"', in Markus E. Bouillon, David M. Malone and Ben Rowswell (eds), *Iraq: Preventing Another Generation of Conflict* (Boulder, CO: Lynne Rienner, 2007), p. 7.

57 Edward Wong, 'Sunni Party Leaves Iraqi Government over Fallujah Attack', *New York Times*, 10 November 2004; and Steve Negus, 'Attack on City Fails To Shake Sunni Stance on Polls', *Financial Times*, 11 November 2004.

58 For electoral data, see Independent Electoral Commission of Iraq, http://www.ieciraq.org/English/Frameset_english.htm; and Phebe Marr, 'Iraq's Identity Crisis', in Bouillon, Malone and Rowsell (eds), *Preventing Another Generation of Conflict*.

59 John F. Burns and James Glanz, 'Iraqi Shiites Win, But Margin Is Less Than Projections', *New York Times*, 14 February 2005.

60 Jonathan Morrow, 'Iraq's Constitutional Process II. An Opportunity Lost', United States Institute of Peace, Special Report 155, November 2005, p. 15.

61 Marina Ottaway, 'Back From the Brink: A Strategy for Iraq', *Carnegie Endowment Policy Brief*, no. 43, November 2005.

62 Anbar Province voted 96.96% against, Salahhuddin 81.75% and Nineva 55.08%. See Marr, 'Iraq's Identity Crisis'.

63 Larry Diamond, 'Slide Rules: What Civil War Looks Like.', *New Republic*, 13 March 2006, p. 12.

64 Campbell Robertson and Sabrina Tavernise, 'Sunnis End Boycott and Rejoin Iraqi Government', *New York Times*, 20 July 2008.

CHAPTER TWO

From insurgency to civil war: the purveyors of violence in Iraq

The violent struggle that began in 2003 with a rising insurgency against the US occupation can be understood as a conflict between two very different visions of what Iraq's future should be and who was going to rule the country. In effect, the civil war was an attempt by those empowered by regime change to impose a political settlement on the country that guaranteed their own dominance of the state and their ability to control society, in a victor's peace. Pitted against them were those fighting in the insurgency. They deployed violence to overturn the post-war settlement and bring Iraq back to a political system more in line with the wider Arab Middle East. These forces were fighting to reverse the political transformation put in place by the invasion and its immediate aftermath. Throughout 2005 and 2006, this conflict took on an overtly sectarian tone as both sides increasingly deployed religious imagery to justify the struggle. Those now in charge of the state rallied their supporters and demonised their enemies through appeals to Shia religious imagery and the defence of their community, defined in terms of religious exclusion. Those battling to remove them from power deployed a radicalised

Sunni Islamism to justify their own use of violence, claiming to defend their community from those forces wishing to drive them into the political wilderness.

The winners and losers of regime change both deployed violence. One side used it to solidify and make permanent their dominance, the other to overturn the post-war settlement. The conflict arising from this conflict was perceived by its protagonists in totality, a moral struggle between good and evil where success could only be achieved through total victory. Once the initial military struggle was over, state power was deployed to violently 'cleanse' society of the vanquished immoral foe, purging the societal and political organisations associated with the old bankrupt order.[1] The insurgency was marked by an upsurge of grassroots, non-state asymmetrical violence. Here local and national elites, marginalised by the exclusive elite bargain put in place at the end of the war, deployed violence in an attempt either to demand a place at the governing table, or to overthrow the whole settlement. In Iraq after 2003, organised violence was deployed on both sides: by those who now controlled the state, and sought to ensure a victor's peace, and those excluded from power, who sought to destroy that peace.

This increasingly violent struggle was triggered by the collapse in state capacity in 2003 and the resultant security vacuum. This vacuum created a lawless arena into which those fighting to impose the post-regime-change order and those seeking to overturn it quickly stepped. Once a state has lost its institutional and coercive capacity, the population is forced to seek new ways to gain some degree of day-to-day predictability, to meet their everyday needs for food, shelter and water, and to obtain some form of rough-and-ready security. This quest occupied the majority of the population in central and southern Iraq, especially those in Baghdad, for over five years.

At a time when the state's presence within Iraqi society was negligible, the quality of individual Iraqis' lives depended on the discipline, organisational coherence and central control of the militias that dominated the streets, neighbourhoods and towns. The vacuum created by the invasion and the collapse of the Iraqi state in its aftermath are among the central causes that drove Iraq's descent into civil war. The socio-cultural factors that would have made violence more likely had been present within Iraqi society since at least the 1980s.[2] The space for ethno-sectarian politics rapidly expanded after regime change, and was certainly used to explain and justify the activities of the militias as they fanned out across society. However, the socio-cultural causes of violence, from 2003 onwards, are secondary and dependent upon the collapse of the state's coercive and institutional capacity.

The cycle of violence: 2003–07

What began in April 2003 as a lawless celebration of the demise of Saddam's regime grew into three weeks of uncontrolled looting and violence. There was a growing perception amongst Iraqis that, after the removal of the Ba'athist regime, US troops were not in full control of the situation. This understanding helped turn criminal violence and looting into an organised and politically motivated insurgency. Rising disenchantment with the occupation fuelled the increase in politically motivated violence. Ex-members of the security services, Ba'ath Party loyalists and those close to Saddam's family regrouped as the occupation failed to capitalise on regime change and impose order on the country. Initially, these disparate and disorganised groups saw the chance to overturn the nascent post-war order by driving American troops from the country. Taking advantage of the coalition's vulnerability, they launched hit-and-run attacks on US troops with increasing frequency and skill. In a classic case of asymmetrical warfare, small bands of highly mobile assailants, making use of their local knowledge, inflicted rising fatalities on US forces. The insurgency gathered increasing momentum during the first four months of the American occupation, using technical innovation that increased their ability to kill US personnel.[3] In 2003, fewer than 12 American soldiers were killed by roadside bombs; by 2004, at least 20 US soldiers were being killed per month.[4]

Mohammed Hafez argues that, from an early stage, those fighting for the insurgency could be clearly divided along ideological lines into two distinct groups: one more radically Islamist and sectarian, the other pro-nationalist.[5] The more nationalist forces were fighting to overturn the political settlement imposed after regime change. However, the radical Islamist arm of the insurgency was fighting for broader sectarian goals. This arm of the insurgency deployed suicide bombing as one of their main weapons. Between 2003 and 2006, more than 500 suicide attacks were used to devastating effect.[6] Regional and international organisations were targeted to reduce the likelihood of the United States being able to make the occupation a multilateral operation. The Jordanian Embassy and the United Nations were attacked in August 2003, and the International Committee of the Red Cross (ICRC) bombed in October.[7] Following the deadly attack on the UN's Canal Hotel headquarters, severe limits were placed on the organisation's involvement in Iraq that would last for years. Likewise, the attack on the ICRC drove many humanitarian NGOs from the country.

The second strategic use of suicide bombers, to target senior politicians, mosques and geographic areas associated with Shia Islam and its followers, had a much greater destructive effect, driving Iraq into civil war. In August 2003, this campaign was heralded by the assassination of Muhammed Baqir al-Hakim, a senior member of the Shia *ulama* and the leader of the Supreme Council for the Islamic Revolution in Iraq. Al-Hakim was killed by a large car bomb that exploded after Friday prayers outside the Imam Ali Mosque in Najaf. By March 2004, the campaign was targeting Shia mosques and religious ceremonies in Kadhimiya, the Shia religious shrine in Baghdad and the holy city of Kerbala.[8] Finally, from May 2004 onwards, radical Islamist groups began kidnapping and beheading both Iraqis and foreign workers.

The two trends within the insurgency, the pro-Islamist and the nationalist, were geographically united in the battle between US forces and insurgents in the northwestern city of Fallujah. Before regime change, Fallujah, 50 kilometres west of Baghdad, had been so renowned for its conservative adherence to Sunni Islam that it was nicknamed *medinat al-masajid*, the city of mosques. Conversely, it also had a reputation, along with the neighbouring city of Ramadi, as a place of lawlessness, where Saddam's influence was at its weakest. The revolt that broke out in the city was triggered by the killing of 17 demonstrators by US troops in April 2003.[9] It caused a spiral of violence and revenge that destabilised the whole northwest of Iraq. Four Americans working for a private US security contractor were murdered in March 2004, leading to a bloody month-long siege by US marines and finally an all-out ground and air assault on the city in October.

The assault decimated Fallujah and forced the majority of the city's 300,000 inhabitants to flee.[10] Nir Rosen argues that the sectarian cleansing that dominated Baghdad in 2005 and 2006 has its origins in the aftermath of the assault on Fallujah in 2004. Radicalised Sunni refugees who fled the city began to settle in the western areas of Baghdad with Sunni majorities. As they did so, Shia residents of these formerly mixed areas were driven out. 'It was in the al-Amriya neighbourhood of Baghdad in the last months of 2004 that violence by Sunnis against Shi'as became widespread.'[11]

If violent population transfers started at the end of 2004, by May 2005 there is little doubt that Baghdad and the surrounding area was in the midst of a civil war justified by its protagonists in sectarian religious terms. In March 2005, the central mortuary in Baghdad estimated that 60% of the murder victims it dealt with had nothing to do with the insurgency, but were consequences of 'religious rivalries'.[12] Al-Qaeda in Mesopotamia launched repeated mass-casualty attacks using car bombs or suicide bombers aimed at Shia neighbourhoods and mosques. In the wake of these attacks, militias claiming to represent the Shia community would retaliate, abducting and murdering Sunni men. During the first six months of 2005, an estimated 130 suicide bombs were detonated, the vast majority against sectarian targets.[13]

Sectarian violence increased further in the 12 months after the destruction of the al-Askariyya Mosque in Samarra on 22 February 2006.[14] The destruction of the mosque, one of Shia Islam's most revered shrines, was an act calculated to outrage Shia opinion. The most senior and respected member of the Shia *ulama* in Iraq, Grand Ayatollah Ali al-Sistani, had expressly forbidden retaliation against the rising tide of sectarian violence, acting as a major brake on organised sectarian retribution. In the aftermath of the destruction of the al-Askariyya Mosque, however, he called for seven days of mourning and national demonstrations. He added that, if the government was unable to protect religious sites, then 'the believers will do it, with the help of God'. A source close to Sistani was quoted as saying 'he feels that the situation has become unbearable and says it has become too hard to control the streets'.[15]

In retaliation for the attack on the al-Askariyya Mosque, Sunni mosques across Baghdad became targets. Of even greater concern were the shifting demographics of the population, triggered by intimidation and the threat of sectarian violence. The Iraqi government estimated the numbers of displaced people in the wake of the bombing could have been as high as 365,000, the majority coming from in and around Baghdad.[16] Military sources estimated that Baghdad's homicide rate tripled from 11 to 33 deaths a day.[17] United Nations statistics indicate that 34,452 civilians were killed in 2006.[18]

The sectarian violence that unfolded in 2005 and 2006 left Baghdad a deeply fractured city, with people from each side of the sectarian divide seeing themselves as the victims.[19] The city's inhabitants retreated into their respective neighbourhoods and erected makeshift barriers in an attempt to hinder the work of the death squads and suicide bombers. Those neighbourhoods that were not already controlled by established militias, organised or had imposed upon them ad hoc military groupings. These extracted money from the communities they were claiming to protect, justifying this in terms of sectarian identity. By the end of 2006, Baghdad had been transformed into a series of fortified ghettos, where rising violence had reorganised the city's population along sectarian lines.

The perpetrators of violence

The future stability of Iraq is based upon the extent to which those fighting on each side of the civil war have been beaten, or have been convinced to give up their violent struggle. To make such an assessment, the main groups perpetrating organised violence need to be identified and their respective capacities examined. These groups can be divided into those fighting to overturn the new political order, largely non-state grassroots groups specialising in asymmetrical violence, and those fighting to both secure and extend the post-invasion political settlement. These groups include militias but also state-employed members of the police force.

The insurgents

Organising a low-level, diffuse and fractured military campaign against US forces was relatively straightforward. The military collapse of Saddam's regime allowed thousands of Iraqi troops to make their own way home. Untroubled by a managed demobilisation or disarmament, they simply merged back into their communities. The stockpiling of weapons by the Ba'athist regime in numerous dumps across the country meant that small arms and explosives were readily available for anyone with a criminal or political purpose. This encouraged an insurgency that was born in a quick, reactive and highly localised fashion, as the US military proved unable to control Iraq. A number of small fighting units were established around personal ties of trust, cemented by family, locality or friendship.[20] Through a process of trial and error, these groups grew in size and competence throughout 2003 and 2004. From 2005 onwards, however, the insurgency began to consolidate around a small number of larger, better-organised and better-funded groups.[21] The four groups that became the main protagonists in the fighting were the Islamic Army in Iraq, the Partisans of the Sunna Army, the Islamic Front of the Iraqi Resistance and al-Qaeda in Mesopotamia.[22] As the names suggest, political violence was increasingly justified by 2005 in terms of a militant, violent and sectarian political Islam. This was a reaction to the solidification of the victor's peace, the exclusive elite bargain that deliberately demonised those who were associated with the old regime and celebrated the Shia identity of the new state. In opposition to this settlement, the main insurgent groups found ideological coherence by fusing a powerful appeal to Iraqi nationalism with an austere and extreme Salafism, which in turn became increasingly sectarian.[23]

The increased ideological and organisational coherence of the insurgency allowed the Jordanian Islamist Abu Musab al-Zarqawi, the head of al-Qaeda in Mesopotamia, to gain influence over its radical Islamist wing. It was Zarqawi's organisation that was responsible for the spectacular attacks in 2003 on the Jordanian Embassy and the United Nations, and the bomb that killed Hakim.[24] His organisation represented no more than 10% of the total numbers involved in the insurgency.[25] However, it had a very clear strategic aim, to drag Iraq into the midst of a prolonged and bloody civil war. This is revealed in its targeting strategy, where the organisation was responsible for only 15% of the attacks on Americans but 90% of all suicide bombings.[26] Zarqawi's superior financial backing, his organisation's propaganda skills and its sheer brutality allowed it to shape the ideological direction of those fighting in the insurgency. By 2006, the radical Islamist wing of the insurgency, despite driving Iraq into civil war, was also claiming that it was the only thing that stood between the embattled Sunni community in Baghdad and the northwest of Iraq and that community's complete defeat and subjugation by a government and armed forces run by the Shia Islamist parties and their Kurdish allies.[27]

Violence and the victor's peace in Iraq

The evolution of the insurgency, from a struggle fought by small units using violence to drive out the US into a sectarian civil war carried out by highly organised and coherent groups who justified their struggle in increasingly communalistic terms, was matched on the other side by those fighting to impose and defend a victor's peace. The imposition of a victor's peace in Iraq was heralded by the de-Ba'athification edict announced by the US occupation authorities in May 2003. This saw the top four layers of the Ba'ath Party driven out of government employment in the name of cleansing society, and assuring that Saddam's dictatorship could not be reinstated. De-Ba'athification was accelerated once the process was handed over to the new Iraqi governing authorities.[28]

Running parallel to the political purging of former Ba'ath Party members was a more covert campaign of extrajudicial assassinations, building up to a mass campaign of terror carried out against the Sunni population of central and southern Iraq from 2005 to 2007. The campaign began in 2003 with the murder of former senior Ba'athists in and around Baghdad.[29] It was seen at the time to be either haphazard retribution or the work of the two largest militias associated with the Shia Islamist parties, the Badr Brigade and the Jaish al-Mahdi. However, as the insurgency evolved there is strong evidence that the campaign of sectarian violence was supported by key political parties who held ministerial power. This elite deployed its coercive and institutional capacity to drive Sunni residents from Baghdad. Brigadier General H.R. McMaster, a senior adviser to the head of US forces, David Petraeus, argues that, by 2006: 'Many of these activities were war crimes. These were war crimes that were planned and organised by various leaders within the Iraqi government and security services.'[30]

In the run-up to the first set of post-invasion elections in January 2005, the coalition seeking to represent the Shia community, the UIA, drew up its plans for government after the vote. Ali Allawi, who was to serve in that government, describes its aims:

> The first and most vital was the 'security' file. The UIA called for a thorough spring-cleaning of the security forces and asked that elements from outside, obviously meaning the Badr Organization, join the security forces en masse.[31]

At the time, the Ministry of Defence and the Iraqi Army were perceived by Iraqi politicians in government to be under close American control. The Ministry of Interior, however, appeared to be independent of US scrutiny and controlled the Special Police Commandos (later renamed the National Police). This organisation was judged to be the most effective fighting force in the country. Furthermore, since it had been established by ministerial order, it was not subject to legal, parliamentary or cabinet oversight.[32] After its victory in the 2005 elections, the UIA appointed Bayan Jabr as interior minister. Jabr was a senior member of the ISCI and a former commander in its militia, the Badr Brigade. He now had complete control of the Special Police Commandos.[33] His first move to 'spring clean' the ministry consisted of widespread dismissals and then a 'frenetic hiring', employing as many militiamen from his Badr organisation as possible.[34]

Throughout 2005 and into 2006, the Special Police Commandos/National Police, controlled from the Ministry of Interior, acted as a major sectarian death squad, frequently resorting to extrajudicial execution and torture.[35] Reports began to circulate that these forces were involved in the religious cleansing of formerly mixed areas of Baghdad.[36] Their modus operandi was summed up by James Danley, who witnessed their actions while he was an American troop commander in the Sunni-majority Baghdad suburb of Dora:

> The national police were sectarian murderers. They were there to kill people who lived there. You had what could only be described as liquidation missions in which they would go into a Sunni neighbourhood like ours and this National Police Unit would simply shoot everything they could. They would simply fire in every direction. It was called the death blossom … straight into buildings and shooting people.[37]

Complaints about the ministry reached their peak in November 2005, when US forces raided an unofficial Ministry of Interior detention facility and found 170 detainees (166 of whom were Sunnis) 'who had been held in appalling conditions'.[38] Following this, a number of confirmed cases of secret detention facilities and the widespread use of torture came to light.[39] Even after such a public scandal and direct evidence of endemic abuse in the Ministry of Interior, Jabr's ISCI party was so powerful within the government, and its support of Jabr so strong, that he did not leave the ministry until there was a complete change in government in 2006. Even then he was moved to the arguably more influential post of finance minister.

Beyond the Ministry of Interior, there was sustained evidence that other arms of the state were being used to drive the Sunni population from Baghdad. For example, during 2005 and 2006, the Ministry of Finance appears to have systematically withdrawn banking services from communities on the west bank of the Tigris, the area of Baghdad with the largest concentration of Sunnis. In 2006, the nearest bank a resident of western Baghdad could get to without straying into areas on the other side of the river dominated by Shia militias was in Anbar.[40] In comparison, 95% of banks in areas of Baghdad with a majority Shia population remained open.[41] Clearly, during 2005 and 2006, state resources were being deployed to drive Sunnis out of Baghdad, in what Allawi has described as a 'death squad culture under official sanction'.[42]

Even more damage was done and greater levels of violence and destruction were deployed by militias operating outside the formal employment of the state. Estimates of how many people the militias had under arms in 2006 vary. However, at its peak the Jaish al-Mahdi, run by Sadr, could mobilise 60,000 fighters, while the better-organised, -funded and -trained Badr Brigade had 15,000.[43] The Badr Brigade was created, funded and trained by the Iranian Revolutionary Guard, who also comprised its officer corps until its entry into Iraq in 2003. The Badr Brigade's integration into the National Police meant that it became less visible in sectarian killings than the Jaish al-Mahdi, as its militiamen adopted police uniforms to carry out their work.

The Jaish al-Mahdi was the most destructive non-state organisation striving to impose a victor's peace on Iraq. Sadr inherited the basis of his organisation and its legitimacy from his father, Ayatollah Muhammad Sadeq al-Sadr. Under Saddam's rule, Sadr senior had initially allowed himself to be co-opted by the Ba'athist government. However, he was also able to build a radical, nationalist Shia organisation that, in the 1990s, posed the greatest threat to the regime. This led to his assassination in 1999, and his organisation disappeared underground until the change of regime. In 2003, Sadr quickly reconstituted the organisation, now named the Office of the Martyr al-Sadr in honour of his father. Sadr, like his father, anchored the movement's legitimacy in an assertive Iraqi Shia identity, a militant nationalism largely aimed at the '*ibn al-Balad*', the sons of the soil, the poor, marginalised urban youth who were easily mobilised by his radical rhetoric and aggressive anti-occupation message.[44]

Sadr gathered around him the former followers of his father, men like Riad al-Nouri, Mustafa al-Yacoubi, Mohammed Tabatabai and Qais al-Khazali.[45] These men were to form the core leadership of a radical, violent, Shia-themed rebellion. Initially, the movement directed its attacks at the American occupation, but then increasingly engaged in the violent sectarian fighting now at the centre of the civil war. By 2006, although Sadr's sermons were still addressed to the *mustadafin*, the dispossessed, and demanded resistance against the American occupiers in the name of Muslim unity, a distinctly sectarian rhetoric was also deployed, identifying the *nawasib*, 'those who do not accept the Shia imams and hate the family of the prophet', as legitimate targets.[46] To his movement, it was clear that the *nawasib* were Iraqi Sunni Muslims.

Sadr's movement gained momentum in 2003 as a direct consequence of state collapse after regime change; as he himself said: 'I found a vacuum, and no one filled that vacuum.'[47] He quickly capitalised on what was left of his father's movement, giving him a loose network of clerics across south and central Iraq. Using Najaf as his base, Sadr controlled his organisation through weekly meetings with senior figures, and by writing orders and sermons which were posted on the walls of mosques across the country.[48] By September 2003, Sadr's organisation had consolidated its grip over what was to become its main power base, a slum in eastern Baghdad containing more than two million people, many of who had migrated to the capital from the rural south after sanctions were imposed in 1990. This area, called *al-Thawra* or Revolution City when it was built in the 1950s, was renamed Saddam City under the Ba'ath and Sadr City in 2003, in honour of Moqtada's father. By September, Sadr was thought to control 90% of the mosques in the area.[49]

However, Sadr was too junior a cleric within Shia Islam to call for the devout to follow him in his own right, so he aligned himself with the Iranian-based Ayatollah Kadhim Husseini Haeri. This gave Sadr's organisation the right to collect US$65,000 a month in charitable donations from Haeri's followers across Iraq.[50] The movement increased its power by seizing command of the four largest petrol stations in Sadr City and controlling the supply of heating and cooking oil in large parts of Baghdad.[51]

The speed with which the militia was built after regime change gave Sadr a great advantage during 2003 and into 2004. However, the movement's two prolonged conflicts with the US military in 2004 took a toll on its organisational coherence and on Sadr's ability to control his subordinates. Haeri withdrew his support after the second clash with the US military, depriving the organisation of stable revenue.[52] Meanwhile disagreements over tactics during the fighting forced key lieutenants like Khazali to leave the organisation in pursuit of a more radical strategy. Concurrently, Mahdi Army commanders profiting from intimidation became financially independent of Sadr's headquarters in Najaf as they embarked on hostage-taking, ransom and the smuggling of antiquities and petroleum. Sadr repeatedly tried to instil discipline, but as one of his own commanders admitted: 'Even when Sadr fires the brigade commanders, their soldiers follow them and not Sadr. Now Sadr fires commanders every month, so their fighters will not become too loyal to them.'[53]

It was this radical, violent, non-hierarchical and diffuse organisation that entered the civil war in 2005. To begin with, Jaish al-Mahdi's goal was to dominate east Baghdad and drive Sunnis out of mixed areas.[54] As the struggle reached its peak, from mid-2006 onwards, Sadr's militia would use the cover of darkness to leave Sadr City, crossing the Tigris river and sweeping across the north and west of Baghdad. These exercises bore all the hallmarks of well-planned operations to attack the Sunni-dominated areas of western Baghdad. These convoys of armed men would move into mixed or predominately Sunni neighbourhoods, and as many as 60 men at a time would be seized and forced into the boots of cars. Their bodies, bearing the signs of extensive torture before their murder, would be found dumped the next morning on the peripheries of Sadr City.[55]

The ultimate aim of this campaign was to drastically reduce the numbers of Sunni residents in Baghdad. The Sunni population was increasingly corralled into a shrinking enclave in western Baghdad and gradually pushed out into Anbar province to the northwest of the capital. In 2005 and 2006, previously affluent suburbs on the western side of the Tigris, including Mansour and Yarmouk, were targeted for violent population transfers. By early 2007, these suburbs, along with Ameriya and Ghazaliya, had become largely deserted, their markets and shops closed and their remaining residents trapped in their homes. The militia campaigns of murder and intimidation coincided with the withdrawal of banking services and healthcare provision from the Sunni residential areas on the west bank of the river. There is strong evidence to suggest that these services were withdrawn from targeted areas in coordination with the violent campaign to drive Sunnis from Baghdad.[56]

A further dimension was added to the conflict after the second national election of December 2005. Following prolonged negotiations, Maliki was chosen as the new prime minister because of the strong backing he received from the Sadrists. The Sadrists were rewarded for their decisive support of Maliki with several ministerial portfolios, including health and transport. They used these ministerial positions not only to fill their own party coffers through corruption and payrolls stacked with party loyalists (something of which all of the parties in the Iraqi cabinet remain guilty), but also to pursue the religious cleansing of Baghdad. This policy reached its peak in the Ministry of Health. Jaish al-Mahdi fighters were employed in large numbers in the Facilities Protections Service of the ministries they controlled.[57] This allowed them to turn hospitals and other medical facilities into military outposts in the civil war.[58] Doctors and senior officials opposing the Sadrists were murdered or driven out.[59] More sinisterly, there is strong evidence that wounded or ill Sunni were murdered.[60]

Conclusion

The years 2005 and 2006 saw the unfolding of the Iraqi civil war, as insurgents and militias fought to impose or overturn the victor's peace that structured Iraqi politics after the invasion. The civil war caused mayhem and destruction, with thousands of civilians murdered each month as a direct result of three intertwined dynamics. The state was simply not strong enough to impose order on Iraqi society. The armed forces were in disarray and incapable of suppressing the militias or insurgents. The most coherent military force, the National Police controlled by the Ministry of Interior, was a tool in the hands of one side of the conflict, and as such was deployed to cleanse Baghdad of its Sunni population. Ethnic and religious symbolism was increasingly deployed throughout 2005 and 2006 to justify the growing barbarity that flourished in Baghdad. Militias used communalist rhetoric to justify the extortion of money from residents who had little choice but to offer their allegiance to the only organisations that promised a semblance of stability. Each side, the militias and the insurgents, claimed to be protecting their communities from certain annihilation by the other. Overshadowing this was an elite pact that deliberately excluded a section of Iraqi society from the state, and by implication from the right to be protected by that state. The future stability of Iraq depends on the extent to which the dynamics driving violence forward in 2005 and 2006 and the organisations perpetuating it have been removed from Iraqi politics.

Notes

1 This analytical concept is taken from Suhrke's understanding of victor's and loser's peace in 'Introduction', in Berdal and Suhrke (eds), *The Peace in Between* (Abingdon: Routledge, 2011).

2 Faleh A. Jabar, 'The War Generation in Iraq: A Case of Failed Statist Nationalism', in Lawrence G. Potter and Gary G. Sick (eds), *Iran, Iraq and the Lessons of War* (New York: Palgrave MacMillan, 2004).

3 Bruce Hoffman, *Insurgency and Counterinsurgency in Iraq* (Santa Monica, CA: RAND, 2004), p. 8.

4 Jason Burke, *The 9/11 Wars* (London: Allen Lane, 2011), p. 129.

5 Mohammed M. Hafez, *Suicide Bombers in Iraq: The Strategy and Ideology of Martyrdom* (Washington DC: United States Institute of Peace, 2007), p. 25.

6 *Ibid.*, p. 3.

7 See International Crisis Group, 'In Their Own Words: Reading the Iraqi Insurgency', *Middle East Report*, no. 50, 15 February 2006, fn. 41.

8 Patrick Cockburn, *Moqtada al Sadr and the Fall of Iraq* (London: Faber and Faber, 2008), pp. 21, 223.

9 Jonathan Steele, 'To the US Troops It Was Self-defence. To the Iraqis It Was Murder', *The Guardian*, 30 April 2003, http://www.guardian.co.uk/world/2003/apr/30/iraq.jonathansteele.

10 Rory McCarthy and Michael Howard, 'New Insurgency Confronts US Forces', *The Guardian.*, 12 November 2004, http://www.guardian.co.uk/world/2004/nov/12/iraq.rorymccarthy1.

11 See Nir Rosen, 'Anatomy of a Civil War', *The Boston Review*, November/December 2006.

12 Monte Morin, 'Crime as Lethal as Warfare in Iraq', *Los Angeles Times*, 20 March 2005, http://articles.latimes.com/2005/mar/20/world/fg-crime20/2.

13 Oliver Poole, 'Nerves Stretched to Breaking Point as Baghdad Clings to Normal Life', *Daily Telegraph*, 20 July 2005, http://www.telegraph.co.uk/news/worldnews/middleeast/iraq/1494449/Nerves-stretched-to-breaking-point-as-Baghdad-clings-to-normal-life.html.

14 On the increase in violence during 2006, see Kimberly Kagan, *The Surge: A Military History* (New York: Encounter Books, 2009), pp. 8–9.

15 Bobby Gosh, 'An Eye For an Eye', *Time*, 26 February 2006, http://www.time.com/time/magazine/article/0,9171,1167741,00.html.

16 Based on interviews and Fareed Zakaria, 'Rethinking Iraq: the Way Forward', *Newsweek*, 6 November 2006, p. 26, http://www.worldaffairsboard.com/sw-asia-iraqi-campaign-iranian-question-africa/22808-rethinking-iraq-way-forward.html.

17 Jeffrey Gettleman, 'Iraqis Bound, Blindfolded and Dead', *New York Times*, 2 April 2006, http://www.nytimes.com/2006/03/26/international/middleeast/26bodies.html.

18 Sabrina Tavernise, 'UN Puts '06 Iraq Toll of Civilians at 34,000', *New York Times.*, 16 January 2007, http://

www.nytimes.com/2007/01/16/world/middleeast/16cnd-iraq.html; Associated Press, 'Iraq Sets Toll of Civilians at 12,000 for 2006', *New York Times.*, 3 January 2007, http://www.nytimes.com/2007/01/03/world/middleeast/03Casualties.html.

19 Cockburn, *Moqtada al Sadr and the Fall of Iraq*, p. 226.

20 Ahmed S. Hashim, 'The Sunni Insurgency', *Middle East Institute Perspective*, 15 August 2003, p. 8.

21 Hafez, *Suicide Bombers in Iraq*, p. 52.

22 International Crisis Group, 'In Their Own Words', pp. 1–3.

23 For this point, see Roel Meijer, 'The Sunni Resistance and the Political Process' in Markus Bouillion, David Malone and Ben Rowsell (eds), *Preventing A New Generation of Conflict* (Boulder, CO: Lynne Rienner Publishers, 2007).

24 Ali A. Allawi, *The Occupation of Iraq: Winning the War, Losing the Peace* (New Haven, CT: Yale University Press, 2007), p. 181.

25 Peter Beaumont, 'Al-Qaeda's Slaughter Has One Aim: Civil War', *The Observer*, 18 September 2005, http://www.guardian.co.uk/world/2005/sep/18/iraq.alqaida.

26 General James L. Jones, *The Report of the Independent Commission on the Security Forces of Iraq*, 6 September 2007, p. 27.

27 David Kilcullen, *The Accidental Guerrilla: Fighting Small Wars in the Midst of a Big One* (London: Hurst & Co., 2009), p. 177.

28 James Dobbins et al., *Occupying Iraq: A History of the Coalition Provisional Authority* (Santa Monica, CA: RAND Corporation, 2009).

29 Allawi, *The Occupation of Iraq*, p. 145.

30 Quoted in 'Secret Iraq', Part 2, BBC 2, 6 October 2010.

31 Allawi, *The Occupation of Iraq*, p. 394.

32 See PBS interview with Matthew Sherman, deputy senior adviser to the Iraqi Ministry of Interior from December 2003 to January 2006, conducted on 4 October, 2006, http://www.pbs.org/wgbh/pages/frontline/gangsofiraq/interviews/sherman.html; and Matt Sherman and Roger D. Carstens, *Independent Task Force on Progress and Reform*, Institute for the Theory and Practice of International Relations at the College of William and Mary, Williamsburg, VA, 14 November 2008, p. 2.

33 Dexter Filkins, 'Armed Groups Propel Iraq Toward Chaos', *New York Times*, 24 May 2006, http://www.nytimes.com/2006/05/24/world/middleeast/24security.html; Andrew Buncombe and Patrick Cockburn, 'Iraq's Death Squads', *Independent on Sunday*, 26 February 2006, http://www.independent.co.uk/news/world/middle-east/iraqs-death-squads-on-the-brink-of-civil-war-467784.html.

34 Michael Moss, David Rohde, Max Becherer and Christopher Drew, 'How Iraq Police Reform Became Casualty of War', *New York Times*, 22 May 2006, http://www.nytimes.com/2006/05/22/world/middleeast/22security.html; Andrew Rathmell, *Fixing Iraq's Internal Security Forces: Why Is Reform of the Ministry of Interior so Hard?*, Post Conflict Reconstruction Project Special Briefing, Center for Strategic and International Studies, Washington DC, November 2007, p. 7, http://csis.org/files/media/csis/pubs/071113_fixingiraq.pdf.

35 See for example Hannah Allam, 'Wolf Brigade the Most Loved and Feared of Iraqi Security Forces', *Knight Ridder Newspapers*, 21 May 2005, http://www.

mcclatchydc.com/2005/05/21/11687/wolf-brigade-the-most-loved-and.html; Sabrina Tavernise, Qais Mizher, Omar al-Naemi and Sahar Nageeb, 'Alarmed by Raids, Neighbors Stand Guard in Iraq', *New York Times*, 10 May 2006, http://www.nytimes.com/2006/05/10/world/middleeast/10patrols.html.

36 See for example Moss et al., 'How Iraq Police Reform Became Casualty of War'.

37 James Danley, quoted in 'Secret Iraq'.

38 Amnesty International, *Beyond Abu Ghraib: Detention and torture in Iraq*, March 2006, p. 4.

39 See PBS interview with Matthew Sherman.

40 Information gained from interviews in Baghdad March and April 2007.

41 Kilcullen, *The Accidental Guerrilla*, p. 126.

42 Allawi, *The Occupation of Iraq*, p. 319.

43 Jones, *The Report of the Independent Commission on the Security Forces of Iraq*, p. 30.

44 Anthony Shadid, *Night Draws Near: Iraq's People in the Shadow of America's War* (London: Picador, 2006), p. 180.

45 Marisa Cochrane, *The Fragmentation of the Sadrist Movement*, Iraq Report No. 12 (Washington DC: Institute for the Study of War, 2009), p. 11; and Shadid, *Night Draws Near*, p. 172.

46 Rosen, 'Anatomy of a Civil War'.

47 Shadid, *Night Draws Near*, p. 173.

48 *Ibid.*

49 International Crisis Group, 'Iraq's Shiites Under Occupation', p. 17.

50 Cochrane, *The Fragmentation of the Sadrist Movement*, p. 12; Shadid, *Night Draws Near*, p. 186.

51 Burke, *The 9/11 Wars*, p. 274.

52 Cochrane, *The Fragmentation of the Sadrist Movement*, p. 15.

53 Quoted by Solomon Moore, 'Iraqi Militias Seen as Spinning Out Of Control', *Los Angeles Times*, 12 September 2006 http://articles.latimes.com/2006/sep/12/world/fg-militias12. Also see Ghaith Abdul-Ahad, 'Tea and Kidnapping–Behind the Lines of a Civil War', *The Guardian*, 28 October 2006, http://www.guardian.co.uk/world/2006/oct/28/iraq-middleeast and Peter Beaumont, 'Inside Baghdad: Last Battle of a Stricken City', *The Observer*, 17 September 2006, http://www.guardian.co.uk/world/2006/sep/17/iraq.

54 Kagan, *The Surge*, p. 16.

55 Patrick J. McDonnell, 'Following a Death Trail to Sadr City', *Los Angeles Times*, 24 October 2006, http://articles.latimes.com/2006/oct/24/world/fg-sadr24.

56 See Kilcullen, *The Accidental Guerrilla*, p. 126.

57 Michael Mason, 'Iraq's Medical Meltdown', *Discover Magazine*, August 2007, http://discovermagazine.com/2007/aug/iraq2019s.

58 Melissa McNamara, 'Intelligence Seen By CBS News Says Hospitals Are Command Centers for Shiite Militia', CBS News, 4 October 2006, http://www.cbsnews.com/stories/2006/10/04/eveningnews/main2064668.shtml.

59 Ali al-Saffar, 'Iraq's Elected Criminals', *Foreign Policy*, 4 March 2010, http://www.foreignpolicy.com/articles/2010/03/04/iraqs_elected_criminals.

60 See Lara Logan, Reporter's Notebook, CBS News, 4 October 2006, http://www.cbsnews.com/stories/2006/10/05/notebook/main2064892.shtml; Amit R. Paley, 'Iraqi Hospitals Are War's New "Killing Fields"', *Washington Post*, 30 August 2006, http://www.washingtonpost.com/wp-dyn/content/

article/2006/08/29/AR2006082901680.html; and Nir Rosen, 'Killing Fields', *Washington Post,* 28 May 2006, http://www.washingtonpost.com/wp-dyn/content/article/2006/05/26/AR2006052601578.html.

CHAPTER THREE

Iraq, US policy and the rebirth of counter-insurgency doctrine

On 10 January 2007, George W. Bush addressed the United States in a nationwide television broadcast. Faced with spiralling communal violence across south and central Iraq, the US administration had come to the realisation that a dramatic change in policy was necessary to avoid a major strategic defeat.[1] At the centre of the speech was the president's announcement of the 'surge', a temporary increase in US troops posted to Iraq and their aggressive deployment amongst Iraq's warring parties.[2] Bush justified the escalation of American commitment by arguing: 'We'll have the force levels we need to hold the areas that have been cleared.'[3] By unambiguously placing the 'clear, hold and build' rhetoric at the centre of his new strategy for Iraq, Bush declared his support for America's application of counter-insurgency doctrine. This commitment was reinforced when he nominated General David Petraeus, the chief proponent of counter-insurgency doctrine within the US military, to take charge of the administration's new approach in Iraq.

The change in US Iraq policy was specifically designed to shore up the Bush legacy. There was a hope that, if the increase in troop numbers could stop the civil war, then American–Iraqi relations could be stabilised before Bush left office. This would allow the president to draw a line under the single issue that had come to both dog and define his time in office. However, to achieve this goal, one that the Bush administration had singularly failed to resolve during the first four years of the war, the main drivers of the conflict would need to be tackled. When announcing the surge in early 2007, Bush hoped that his investment in counter-insurgency doctrine would allow US forces and the Iraqi government to remove the perpetrators of violence from Iraq's streets, rebuild state capacity, rework the elite settlement shaping Iraq's politics and find a way to reduce the sectarian tensions that had ensnared Iraqi political discourse since 2005. These were clearly extremely ambitious, if not impossible, goals.

The US military's rediscovery of counter-insurgency doctrine was primarily driven by the cumulative failures of the American presence in Iraq after 2003. Petraeus and his assistants, when drafting the army's new approach, burrowed deep into the history of counter-insurgency campaigns, disinterring largely forgotten practitioners of this lost strategic art. Petraeus produced a new military doctrine that claimed to shift the focus from finding and killing the enemy to protecting the population. The military also stressed cultural awareness, knowing whom US troops were meant to be protecting within society and how they were organised, reconstructing governance and bringing the state's institutions back into society. Finally, a greater unity of command was stressed, with the merging of the civilian and military arms of the occupation and much greater coherence in developing strategy and deploying force.

The US policy in Iraq before counter-insurgency

The start of the surge in 2007 triggered a passionate debate among American military veterans of the Iraq campaign about the responsibility that pre-2007 US policy had for driving Iraq into civil war.[4] The genesis of US military policy before the surge has its origins in the handover of sovereignty to the interim Iraqi government in April 2004. In June 2004, General George Casey took over command of the Multi-National Force–Iraq, working in tandem with his immediate superior, General John Abizaid, head of the US military's Central Command. Abizaid's approach to Iraq was shaped by what he termed his 'antibody theory'. This argued that societies, especially Arab and Muslim ones, will inevitably reject a foreign presence in their midst. Under this rubric, the comparative size of US troop deployments would be directly responsible for the level of resentment and violent resistance they faced.[5] Both Casey and Abizaid had been generals during the US mission in Bosnia-Herzegovina from 1996 to 1997, and had drawn their conclusions about troop levels from this experience. They reasoned that having US troops stationed in heavily fortified bases away from major population centres minimised friction and possible conflict with their host societies. Extra weight was given to this policy in Iraq when then-Secretary of Defense Donald Rumsfeld stressed the need for the US military to step back and allow the Iraqi armed forces to take control.[6] Bush gave his public blessing to this decision in June 2005, when he first used his oft-repeated statement that 'as the Iraqis stand up, we will stand down'.[7]

Casey sought to draw these competing pressures together in a new campaign plan, agreed by the administration in mid-June 2006. The new plan, dubbed by Casey 'the leave-to-win strategy', mandated a three-stage transfer of power: 'stabilisation to early 2007, restoration of civilian authority to mid-2008, and support to self-reliance through to 2009'.[8] Throughout 2006, Casey's strategy doggedly focused on reducing the number of US troops in the country.[9] Mirroring the experience in Bosnia, those left would be redeployed to large fortified bases, safely stationed away from urban areas. In June 2006, Casey drew up a three-stage schedule for the complete handover of military responsibility to the Iraqi government. The first stage would see US troop numbers drop by 30,000 to 100,000 by the end of 2006.[10] In the follow-up, the Iraqi government's authority over the military would be restored by mid-2008. The final stage would end in 2009, when the Iraqi armed forces became self-reliant. The drawdown would be accompanied by a reduction of US bases across the country from 69 to 11 by the end of 2007.[11]

Under Casey's plan, the potential dangers of this drawdown would be met by the rapid training of the Iraqi Army. CPA head Paul Bremer had ordered the disbanding of the Iraqi military in May 2003. The US military did not embark on a rapid expansion of the new Iraqi Army until 2004. Yet it was this army, only two years old, that was to take the place of the American soldiers as they redeployed back to their heavily fortified bases. In May 2006, the Iraqi Army was said by the US military to be in command of 50% of the battle-space across the south and centre of the country, with plans for this figure to rise to 100% by the end of the year.[12] However, as the security situation deteriorated during 2006, even Casey's militant optimism began to wane. In August he revised his timetable, stating that it would now take another 18 months for the Iraqi Army to become self-sufficient. This caution did not, however, stop the formal command of Iraq's military being handed over to the government in September, while regional responsibility for security was handed back to provincial governors. By October 2006, in the midst of civil war, Casey claimed the coalition was three-quarters of the way through its mission to train the army.[13]

Casey's transition plan was drafted to meet the needs of his political superiors in Washington, not the realities of the situation on the ground in Baghdad. It focused on reducing US forces and hence, casualties, as quickly as possible. There is little doubt that this policy was a major contributing factor to Iraq's slide into civil war during 2006. The Iraqi Army was not ready to fill the security vacuum created by the reduction and repositioning of US troops. In the aftermath of Bush's speech setting out the indigenisation policy in June 2005, Iraqi civilian fatalities steadily increased, reaching a peak in 2006. This coincided with Casey's plans for reducing or redeploying the US military.[14] The Iraqi forces meant to fill the security void were simply not ready to fulfil their task. By 2007, the approach had been scurrilously labelled 'Casification', the abdication of American responsibility for security whatever the costs for Iraq. It was a policy that exacerbated an already deteriorating situation in Baghdad, across southern and central Iraq and on the fringes of the northern provinces that were handed back to the Iraqi military.

In the midst of the American military's attempt to reduce its troop numbers and dramatically lower the profile of its forces, another approach, almost completely at odds with Casey's policy, was being pioneered in a small town in the far northwest of Iraq. It was the key points of this approach to counter-insurgency, applied by the 3rd Army Cavalry Regiment to the city of Tal Afar in 2005, that shaped the US Army's approach after 2007. The 3rd Army Cavalry Regiment arrived in Tal Afar in May 2005 with a clear mission to 'secure the population'.[15] It set about sealing off the city by establishing checkpoints on all roads in and out. It then engaged in 14 days of intense combat with the insurgent forces that up until that point had controlled the area largely untroubled by either US or Iraqi forces. In the aftermath of this operation, the commander, Colonel H.R.

McMaster, set up 29 small outposts across the city where his own forces, jointly stationed with the Iraqi Army, would guarantee that insurgents could not return to the areas they had been driven from.[16]

The rediscovery of counter-insurgency doctrine

As McMaster's forces were finishing the most intense period of their operation in Tal Afar, Petraeus, recently returned from his second tour in Iraq, began drafting the US military's new counter-insurgency doctrine.[17] The drafting of the new manual, at a time when the Iraqi insurgency was mutating into all-out civil war, 'amounted to a huge and public self-criticism session for the American military'.[18] Although Petraeus's aim may well have been to change not only how the military was fighting in Iraq, but also the structure of the whole institution itself, he chose to do this by anchoring the army's new approach to counter-insurgency firmly in existing doctrines with origins in the 1960s.[19] 'Classic' approaches to counter-insurgency have remained fairly constant since the end of the Second World War, and stress the primacy of the political over the military, with a need for close coordination between the civilian and military wings of the campaign, intelligence-led operations and the separation of the insurgent from the wider population.[20] For Petraeus, the obvious point of departure from the classic approach was that the cases he was wrestling with, Iraq and later Afghanistan, were initiated by invasion and regime change rather than the defence of an existing government.[21] This quasi-imperial form of expeditionary warfare clearly raised profound questions as to whether an external force could ever be seen as legitimate by the population it was committing itself to 'protect'.

In writing the US Army's new manual on counter-insurgency (COIN), Petraeus overtly deployed the work of the most influential COIN theorist, David Galula. This stressed the need to rebuild both the capacity and the legitimacy of the state, the 'machine for the control of the population'.[22] In this conception, weak or illegitimate government is perceived to be at the root cause of rebellion, as it allows space for violent opposition to organise and alienate the population from the state. Galula and Petraeus's approach to counter-insurgency looks a lot like 'competitive state-building', with both sides of the conflict engaging in a struggle to increase the power and reach of their coercive and civil institutions as they compete with each other to gain control over the largest section of society.[23] For the US military, recognisable legitimacy would be delivered through the 'provision of basic economic needs', 'essential services' and the 'sustainment of key social and cultural institutions'.[24]

The second idea taken from classic counter-insurgency doctrine was a need for 'a unity of effort … at every echelon of the COIN operation'.[25] Practically, this means centralising managerial responsibility for all aspects of the civilian and military effort in 'the hands of a single "supremo"'.[26] Ultimate power and oversight is vested in one commander, who has the authority and the resources to meld the tactical and strategic, the civilian and the military, into one cohesive policy with a clear objective. In Iraq from 2007 onwards, Petraeus, partly because of the backing he was given from Bush and partly due to his own reputation and political skills, managed to accrue unrivalled authority to develop and apply his own policies.

Although the new doctrine claimed affinity with Galula's work, and stressed the primacy of the political and the need for unity of effort, the US military's approach to counter-insurgency and its application to Iraq actually represented a major reworking of classic approaches. On the ground, it shifted strategic emphasis away from the costly and time-consuming business of state-building. Instead, it invested a great deal of time and energy in what could be termed 'sociological', as opposed to political, approaches to conflict resolution. One of the key innovations at the centre of the Army's new COIN manual was the almost anthropological focus on the culture of the populations among whom US forces were now operating.[27] As the manual states: 'Cultural knowledge is essential to waging a successful counterinsurgency. American ideas of what is "normal" or "rational" are not universal.'[28] The authors of the manual argued that this cultural knowledge was crucial to understanding how societies were organised, how they gained security and how insurgents sought to mobilise them in support of their campaigns against the United States. Critics have identified this approach to culture as having at least two problematic aspects. Kalyvas has argued that the manual understands culture as being 'malleable', that the application of US military, political and economic power can change identities and attitudes, making the population more amenable to the American presence.[29] This, he infers, underestimates the depth of feeling and ideological motivation driving both the violence and the indigenous hostility to an extended US occupation. Laleh Khalili argues that the manual's approach focuses on a specific type of divisive culture, the sects, clans and tribes that can be used to splinter a society and more easily align a minority within it to the occupation.[30]

Closely aligned with the counter-insurgency manual's stress on cultural knowledge is the strategy it promotes for gaining the quiescence of the population. Here the manual closely follows the strategy pioneered by Galula. Galula argued that one of the central 'laws' of counter-insurgency is that 'support is gained through an active minority'. This minority has to be identified, organised and then used as a vehicle to mobilise the rest of society.[31] This process cannot begin until the threat of insurgent violence has been removed. Support from the population will then be mobilised by convincing them that their security is more likely to be assured by the counter-insurgents and their government than the insurgents.[32] The protection of the population should then become the first priority in a counter-insurgency campaign. As with McMaster's approach in Tal Afar, protection of the population was to be supplied by 'a grid of embedded units' which 'should live in the neighbourhood' and give the population '24-hour access to the counterinsurgent force'.[33]

The application of counter-insurgency doctrine to Iraq

Before leaving for Baghdad in February 2007, Petraeus indicated that he was well aware that, for a sustainable end to the Iraqi civil war, the Americans needed to tackle the underlying causes of the violence, not just remove its perpetrators. He asserted that: 'It was vital that there be a surge in four areas: not just the military, but also the civilian side of the US government, the Iraqi forces, and Iraqi political will.'[34]

Despite this aim, US policy in Iraq during 2007 was embroiled in a two-stage military campaign. The first stage was the Baghdad Security Plan, known in Arabic as *Fard al-Qanoon* or 'enforcing the law'. This saw the direct application of the army's counter-insurgency manual, focusing on the security of the population in and around Baghdad. The second phase of operations, labelled *Phantom Thunder* and *Phantom Strike*, focused on Baghdad's suburbs and hinterland, and looked much more like conventional military search-and-destroy missions, where large numbers of US troops and Special Forces were deployed to hunt down Sunni radical groups.[35]

The start of a civilian 'surge' that focused on state-building was frequently heralded throughout 2007 and 2008, as were moves to reform the settlement regulating Iraqi politics. Although these civilian-focused policies were often discussed, the major change in US policy towards Iraq, launched in 2007, was dominated by military campaigns to the exclusion of all else.

The surge itself technically began on 14 February 2007. As Emma Sky, a key adviser to Petraeus's second-in-command Ray Odierno, put it: 'Population protection became the driving mantra of the command environment.'[36] The plan, as outlined by a senior official in Baghdad in April 2007, was to 'deliver high levels of security to small areas of Baghdad and then expand'.[37] Human security would be delivered at a community level by deploying Petraeus's 'grid of embedded units' across the city.[38] Like other key aspects of Petraeus's approach to counter-insurgency, this tactic was taken straight from the history of COIN, in this case the French approach to revolutionary warfare. The *tache d'huile* or 'oil slick' method aimed to build small enclaves of security that could then be expanded through the continued deployment of military power and a demonstration effect.[39] Ultimately, if successful, Baghdad would be pacified by capturing its population within a 'fine mesh' or *quadrillage* of military and civilian power.[40]

At city level, this grid of power saw Baghdad divided into ten military districts and the operational level driven down into small neighbourhoods, or *muhallas*, city districts containing between 50 and 1,500 houses. With Baghdad divided into 474 *muhallas*, Petraeus could focus his forces in those districts that contained the most intense sectarian conflict. The Baghdad Security Plan begun with 'clearing operations' in these targeted areas which, unsurprisingly, led to a sharp increase in American casualties.[41] Once a US military presence had been established, American soldiers were redeployed from the large heavily fortified military bases on the edge of the city and stationed among the population. This was achieved by building a series of compact, heavily fortified bases in the target *muhallas*, each containing between 120 and 150 troops, a mixture of US forces and the Iraqi Army and National Police. In April 2007, 75% of the 2nd Brigade, 2nd Infantry Division operating in the Rusafa security district in eastern Baghdad had been transferred out of their bases into these small forts.[42] By June there were 68 forts scattered across Baghdad's *muhallas*.[43] The logic of the plan was to use these Joint Security Stations as the most visible sign of government capacity in each area. The security these forts provided would tie the population to them, and the forts could then deliver state services to the areas under their control.

After a designated area had been cleared and the Joint Security Station set up, the *muhalla* was then turned into a 'gated community'. This involved deploying large concrete barriers or 'T walls' to separate the *muhalla* from the surrounding area. Each *muhalla* would only have two access points for traffic, which were easily guarded. The flow of traffic in and out could be monitored, stopping the movement of death squads and suicide bombers. Once an area had been cleared and walled off, US and Iraqi forces issued identity cards and conducted a census so that they could better understand who was resident within their area and who was moving through it. After specific areas had been secured, barriers built and security stations staffed, American battalion commanders used their Commander's Emergency Response Programme (CERP) funds to begin rebuilding government services in the areas they now controlled. Local councils were empowered to hire street cleaners, sewage systems were renovated, schools redecorated and reopened and electricity sub-stations repaired. Micro-grants were handed out to small businesses in an attempt to rejuvenate the local economy. By August 2008, $2.8bn had been spent in CERP funds.[44]

The second stage of the surge was launched in June 2007, using a more conventional mass-military operation. Odierno deployed his troops in two concentric rings around Baghdad in an attempt to stop insurgent groups simply fleeing the city and regrouping elsewhere. Then, in the largest military operation since the invasion itself, *Phantom Thunder* and *Phantom Strike* were launched to break insurgent organisations operating outside the capital. In conjunction with these two campaigns, US Special Forces targeted senior insurgent leaders, breaking the coherence of their organisations and their ability to coordinate their operations and regroup.[45]

Across Iraq and especially in Baghdad, 2007 saw a steep and sustained drop in the number of civilians killed each month. Numbers that stood at 3,500 in January had dropped to 1,950 by June and 600 in December.[46] However, what is much less clear is the link between the Baghdad Security Plan, *Operation Phantom Thunder, Operation Phantom Strike* and the steep decline in the death rate. Until this has been clarified, the sustainability of the reduction in violence in 2007–2008 remains open to question. The walling-off of specific *muhallas* was deeply resented by the communities involved, who suffered the petty humiliations involved in entering and leaving their gated communities through police checkpoints. This triggered demonstrations in the areas affected.[47] More worryingly, there was evidence that the walls themselves were intensifying the violence inside these communities.[48] There is also an argument that walling off *muhallas* subject to the most intense sectarian violence actually aided the cleansing of Baghdad by separating communities that had already been purged of one religious group or the other, thus solidifying the sectarian division of the city.[49]

Overall, it became clear that the reduction in violence in the first three-quarters of 2007 was based upon two dynamics, the delivery of highly local security and increased precision in targeting senior militia and death-squad leaders. However, the accompanying improvements in security, infrastructure and economic activity linked to the surge remained dependent upon US funds, delivered through the American battalions that controlled each *muhalla*. When the local organisations and services either empowered or created by the US military attempted to forge meaningful relationships with the state they found it almost impossible. The central ministries were unwilling or unable to form institutional links with the highly local capacity created by the American military. US army colonels who were responsible for these areas took to driving Iraqi representatives into the Green Zone to lobby the national government and individual minsters for financial support, usually to no avail.[50] The inability of the national ministries in the centre of Baghdad to integrate and further develop local governance initiatives in the capital's most strife-torn areas leaves the continued success of the surge in doubt.

A US assessment of Baghdad carried out in late May 2007 estimated that American and Iraqi forces were only able to protect the population and 'maintain physical influence' over 146 of Baghdad's 457 neighbourhoods.[51] By the end of September, Major General Joseph Fil, the US Army commander responsible for Baghdad, claimed that that figure had risen to 56%. Either way, explanations for the dramatic reduction in violence from February 2007 onwards have to look beyond the activities of the US military in selected *muhallas* and the ability of *Phantom Thunder* and *Phantom Strike* to disrupt militia activity and kill senior militia group members. The 'surge' announced by Bush in January 2007 and implemented in February and June certainly delivered local security to some parts of Baghdad and killed hundreds of 'high-value' purveyors of violence. However, during the first 12 months of the policy it did little, if anything, to tackle the causes of the violence that drove Iraq into civil war.

The 'Anbar Awakening', Sons of Iraq and the 'tribal revolt'

Beyond the three military operations that dominated Baghdad and its hinterlands during 2007, those promoting US counter-insurgency doctrine and its application to Iraq have pointed to events in Anbar in 2006 and 2007 and their influence across the country as the second pillar of a successful policy. Although these events have their genesis before the surge, one of the key innovations in Petraeus's approach to counter-insurgency was the attention given to the anthropology of the societies in which US forces were operating. Societies are examined in order to identify internal divisions, selecting minorities who could be brought into alliance with the occupation, as the start of a search for widespread compliance.[52] The successful identification of allies who could fight against the radical extremists of the insurgency is precisely what happened in the northwestern province of Anbar.

The so-called 'Anbar Awakening' had its origins in an attempt at restructuring the political formula at the centre of the 'victor's peace' that came to dominate Iraqi politics after 2003. The US ambassador to Iraq, Khalilzad, correctly identified the deliberate exclusion from the political process of a large section of the Sunni population as one of the key drivers of the conflict. To address this he persuaded the US government to curb its anti-Ba'athist rhetoric and cajoled Sunni politicians into taking an active part in the December 2005 elections. Meanwhile, the

United States began tentative negotiations with key insurgent groups.[53]

The US diplomatic opening to the Sunni section of Iraqi society coincided with the start of a political dialogue within the ranks of those who were fighting to drive American forces from the country. Their boycott of the January 2005 elections had left them completely disenfranchised, excluded from power but also subject to violent retribution by the new political elite, who used the National Police and their own militias to pursue a victor's peace. As the civil war deepened and the cleansing of Sunnis from Baghdad gathered momentum, a political rethink emerged among nationalist and Sunni groups that had previously advocated and utilised violence.

In the first instance this process centred on the province of Anbar. Geography and sociology make Anbar unique in Iraq. The province has long borders with the Sunni-majority states of Saudi Arabia, Jordan and Syria. These extended borders have long made it a transit point for goods and people crossing into Iraq. After 2003, these trading networks were readily transformed to smuggle foreign fighters, weapons and money into Iraq in support of the insurgency. Anbar is also unique for being 95% Sunni.[54] After 2003, these two factors made it a key contender for the epicentre of the insurgency. The US military's clumsy handling of a demonstration in Fallujah in April 2003 and the resultant killing of 17 civilians acted as a trigger for retaliatory violence across the province.[55] The US Army's assault on Fallujah in 2004 may well have driven the jihadists based there out of the city. However, instead of breaking their capacity for action, it simply spread them across Anbar's other major cities, making Ramadi the new centre of gravity for the insurgency.

From 2003 to 2004, groups that were active in Anbar's insurgency mirrored the rest of the country, as former army officers,

Ba'athists and Iraqi nationalists created an alliance of convenience with foreign jihadists who brought with them money, weaponry and a steady supply of willing recruits for suicide missions. However, from 2005 onwards the insurgency gradually cohered around a small number of larger, better-organised and more radical groups. These groups also became more ideologically coherent, deploying an austere, sectarian and extreme Salafism to unify their membership. This organisational and ideological coherence facilitated al-Qaeda in Mesopotamia's increasing dominance of the insurgency and the societies it operated in and recruited from.

The growing influence of al-Qaeda raised the possibility of far-reaching change in Anbar. The group's organisational structure used Iraqis as the foot soldiers of the movement, but placed foreign jihadists in leadership roles. This ran counter to existing Anbar society, where power and influence were vested in those with historical, social and economic status. This meant that, 'bereft of traditional sources of social or spiritual legitimacy, [al-Qaeda's] power was grounded in the most ruthless and primitive version of Salafist Islam'.[56] In addition, the killing of al-Qaeda in Mesopotamia's leader, Zarqawi, in June 2006 removed a key focus of loyalty and coherence for the group. As US forces improved their targeting of the leadership, the organisation's middle and upper ranks were increasingly filled with younger, less experienced and more brutal figures who had little or no status in Anbar's wider society.[57]

Against this background, the indigenous revolt against al-Qaeda's stranglehold on Anbar society can be explained. Firstly, as mentioned above, from 2005 onwards America's diplomatic policy in Iraq shifted to encouraging Sunni groups to pursue a greater involvement in politics. This, together with the costs of the January 2005 election boycott, led to much greater Sunni mobilisation by the time of the December 2005 election. This political participation put the people of Anbar at odds with the jihadist radicals in their midst who rejected all forms of political participation. Secondly, by 2005 the religious cleansing of Baghdad was forcing an increasing number of displaced Sunni refugees into the towns and cities of Anbar on their way to exile in Jordan and Syria. Clearly, the civil war now raging in Baghdad was causing the Sunni population of the city a great deal of hardship. Against this background, US forces no longer appeared to be the main enemy, but a possible ally and source of protection from the Iraqi government and its allied militias. Finally, the ambition of al-Qaeda itself forced a large section of Anbar's population to reject it. As the ideological zeal of its leaders became more intense, the organisation tried to enforce its own austere version of Salafist Islam on the wider society of Anbar. This quickly alienated al-Qaeda members religiously and culturally from their hosts. Anbar's own Islamic traditions are diverse, with a substantial number of Anbaris following Sufi approaches to Islam and venerating their ancestors' tombs. Al-Qaeda in Mesopotamia tried to enforce and police much more austere rules of religious conduct, banning, for example, cigarettes and music.[58] Finally, in October 2006, al-Qaeda declared an independent Islamic emirate in Iraq. This exacerbated existing tensions between it and wider Anbari society, highlighting what had become increasingly evident, namely that the organisation's aims of fighting the global jihad and propagating an austere form of Salafist Islam set it against the majority of the population in Anbar.[59]

The first indications of a serious division between the population of Anbar and al-Qaeda in Mesopotamia emerged between the two elections of January and December 2005, in the far northwest of Anbar. In the small town of al-Qa'im on the Syrian border, resentment towards al-Qaeda operatives grew, inflamed by their 'treatment of civilians, importation of foreign fighters, and encroachment on ... control of the black market'.[60] In mid-2005, this led to the formation of a local militia, the Hamza battalion, established solely to drive al-Qaeda from al-Qa'im.[61] The failure of this early attempt at an 'awakening' indicates the dynamics surrounding 'tribal' revolts against al-Qaeda, US support and the attitude of the Iraqi government. The US marines who were responsible for the area were aware of the actions of the Hamza battalion and eventually gave it air support in its fight against al-Qaeda. However, the Iraqi government was openly hostile, seeing the Hamza battalion as little more than 'vigilantes', 'who had no place in Iraq'.[62] The marines had insufficient troop numbers to offer sustained support[63] and the Hamza battalion, lacking the internal cohesion or capacity to win, was overwhelmed by al-Qaeda, whose forces were better organised, more determined and able to call on support from a wider set of actors. A similar dynamic took place in Ramadi in late 2005: without sustained US military intervention, al-Qaeda's deployment of violence and intimidation broke the revolt.[64]

However, US policy in Anbar changed in June 2006, with the arrival of the 1st Brigade Combat Team, 1st Armoured Division, which was redeployed from Tal Afar. Colonel Sean MacFarland used the tactics pioneered in Tal Afar and moved into the centre of Ramadi, setting up 19 small combat outposts across the city.[65] This encouraged a number of figures of influence within the city to work alongside the US military. Al-Qaeda's response was predictable, but when it killed a US ally, Abu Ali Jassim, in August 2006, it triggered a backlash that resulted in the formation of the Anbar Awakening Council.[66] Abdul Sittar Eftikhan al-Rishawi took command of this new council and quickly claimed tribal legitimacy for the movement. This proved to be an effective ploy. It associated the Anbar Awakening Council with 'tribal' values and organisations, thus drawing a distinction between an indigenous Anbari movement and the exogenous al-Qaeda. It anchored Sittar's collaboration with US forces in what could be viewed as a local Iraqi conservative cultural ethos, juxtaposed against the radical and innovative Salafist Islam of al-Qaeda's organisation.

Interestingly, the veracity of Sittar's claim to be the son of a chief of the Albu Risha tribe of the Dulaim confederation is doubtful.[67] Anthropological and historical studies of tribal structures in Anbar agree that they began to atrophy during Ottoman rule of what was to become Iraq in the late 1800s. The British occupation's attempts to utilise the power of the Dulaim tribal federation in the 1920s ended in failure, as it was increasingly apparent that their Dulaim 'Paramount Sheikh', Ali Suleiman, had little or no power or legitimacy among 'his' tribespeople in Anbar.[68] In 2006, beyond the use of tribal lineages and organisation to give legitimacy to the movement, a major cause of the revolt was the challenge al-Qaeda posed to Sittar's long-standing source of revenue, robbing cars using the Amman to Baghdad highway.[69]

Whatever the origins of the Anbar Awakening and the source of its organisational cohesion, the US military in Ramadi encouraged this second revolt against al-Qaeda. MacFarland himself estimated that US$2m was dispensed in 2006 and early 2007 to individuals on the council in return for a guarantee of security in their areas. Sittar complained to MacFarland 'that he had several thousand volunteers who didn't qualify for the police, because they were illiterate, underage, or overweight'. To meet this complaint, MacFarland gave permission for Sittar to set up an 'emergency brigade' and gave the recruits a week's training.[70]

Thus the 'Anbar model' was born. Individuals who claimed that they had local influence would be paid by US forces and co-opted to fight against the insurgency. In return for intelligence they would be allowed to form their own militias, which would be given wages from the Commander's Emergency Response Programme. The US military rarely, if ever, gave the wages directly to individual militiamen, nor did they dispute the numbers claimed by the militia's leaders.[71] So, although the Anbar Awakening certainly bought the loyalty of former members of the insurgency, it also delivered a cash bonanza into the hands of Awakening Council members, allowing them to go out and buy the services of as many Anbaris as they could. Initially, the US military had hoped the Anbar Awakening would see irregular Iraqi forces take the lead in fighting al-Qaeda in the province. There is indeed some evidence that members of the Awakening did covertly kill a number of al-Qaeda operatives.[72] However, as events in al-Qa'im in 2005 indicate, the Anbaris lacked the military organisation and social cohesion necessary to fight against their better-organised and more determined adversaries. Instead, the Anbar Awakening was more useful in supplying intelligence and offering local support to US troops. Effective fighting by the Awakening forces against al-Qaeda was only feasible when closely supported by American soldiers and airpower.

Petraeus placed the Anbar Awakening at the centre of his testimony before Congress in September 2007, detailing the progress the surge had made during its first nine months. The Awakening, he argued, 'may be the most significant development of the past eight months'. Monthly attacks against US forces in Anbar had dropped from 1,350 in October 2006 to just over 200 in August 2007.[73] Given the success of the Anbar Awakening, it is little surprise that Petraeus tried to reproduce it across the rest of south and central Iraq, using it as 'a model for exploiting the rift between insurgent groups and the population'.[74] He placed 'local security bargains', deals between neighbourhood militias and the US military, at the centre of consolidating and expanding the security gains made by US military operations since the start of the surge.

Given that the Anbar Awakening was described by Petraeus's advisers as a 'tribal revolt', the US military's understanding of Iraqi tribes was to become crucial in its utilisation of the Anbar experience at a national level.[75] In 2006, the role of the 'tribe' was placed at the centre of the US military's counter-insurgency manual. Tribes are listed as one of eight 'groups that often play critical roles in influencing the outcome of a COIN effort'.[76] The counter-insurgency manual insists that tribes should be closely studied by American military units as part of their pre-deployment training. However, the definition of tribes in the manual as 'autonomous, genealogically structured groups in which the rights of individuals are largely determined by their ancestry and membership in a particular lineage' is factually problematic.[77]

Although placed at the centre of the US Army's counter-insurgentcy manual, current best anthropological practice would be very uneasy about placing such a solid meaning on the term tribe; 'few anthropologists today would consider using the term "tribe" as an analytical category, or even as a concept for practical application'.[78] In contemporary Iraq, tribes were so heavily and instrumentally used by the Ba'athist government from 1968 to 2003 that the word has multiple meanings. It is best understood as a fluid and subjective term, deployed by individuals to understand a small part of their changing personal identities.[79] This analytical complexity did not stop one of Petraeus's advisers from stating categorically that 'more than 85% of Iraqis claim some form of tribal affiliation; tribal identity is a parallel, informal but powerful sphere of influence in the community'.[80] The danger inherent in such blanket statements is that the US military utilised a social grouping that was almost certainly much more fluid than it thought. In doing so it created groups and power relations that had not previously existed. The outcome of such approaches is not to anchor 'local security bargains' into social realities, but instead to create temporary and unstable alliances which funnelled US money and patronage through entrepreneurial middlemen, enabling them to buy the indigenous support and manpower they needed.

However, the sociological complexities of Iraqi society were swept aside as the successes derived from the 'tribal revolt' in Anbar were rolled out across the south and centre of the country. The countrywide application of the Anbar model began in June 2007 and saw US$370m spent on 'local security bargains'. In total the United States signed agreements with 779 local militias and put 103,000 men under arms.[81] The money spent on the Awakening movements represented 10% of all the money spent under the CERP. This money was dispensed without a 'comprehensive plan', or 'specific goals, metrics or milestones from which to measure the individual or collective impact of the effort'.[82] The overall aim of the approach appears to have been to achieve a balancing act between 'competing armed interest groups' in the middle of a civil war that the Americans were having difficulty controlling.[83] To quote Petraeus's second-in-command, Odierno:

> If we are able to buy time from the bottom up, that is a start. That will help us buy time for the government of Iraq to continue to mature. As those pockets of security get larger and larger, and we stitch them together, that buys time.[84]

Despite the reactive and ad hoc nature of the Awakening policy, the US military's interaction with these new local militias was regulated by a common approach. Militia leaders were paid US$350 per month in wages for each individual they recruited. These recruits were meant to be vetted locally, but more importantly they were photographed, fingerprinted and their biometric data was taken. The US military was not required to supply either weapons or ammunition to the new groups, and it was assumed that its role would be limited to specific areas, and involve static defence and checkpoint work.[85]

One of the earliest groups of 'concerned local citizens' to be formed in Baghdad was the 'Ameriya Knights', led by a former Iraqi soldier and insurgent, Saif Sa'ad Ahmed al-Ubaydi or 'Abu Abid'. Once Ameriya, an area in western Baghdad on the road to the airport, had been walled off in line with the Baghdad Security Plan, Abu Abid stepped forward with a scheme to fight al-Qaeda in the area. He quickly recruited 227 men to serve in his militia, and was successful in killing, rounding up or driving out people he claimed were affiliated with al-Qaeda. However, along with the relative calm that the Ameriya Knights brought to the area, there were repeated allegations of brutality, corruption and murder.[86]

Those in favour of the national application of the Awakening model stressed that it acted as 'an amazing force multiplier that denied the enemy freedom of movement in a manner we [the US] could not'.[87] Through the wages militiamen were paid, it brought financial aid into previously war-torn areas and dramatically shrank the recruitment pool that insurgents could draw on. Following on from what could be termed Khalilzad's 2005 policy of 'Sunni outreach', it went some way to rebalancing US policy in Iraq, stepping away from the outright backing of the new ruling elite and their imposition of the 'victor's peace' that had driven policy until then. This directive offered some form of rough-and-ready security to the Sunni communities of Baghdad. However, those critical of the policy warned that the United States ran the risk of creating yet another set of militias, thus further weakening the power of the central state in Iraq and exacerbating the ongoing civil war.[88] Although, for reasons detailed below, this temporary tactical expediency did not increase the number of militias in Iraq or indeed contribute to a long-term weakening of the Iraqi state, it did clearly empower a number of ungoverned armed groupings, which were guilty of lawlessness, murder and human-rights abuses.

Once it became aware of the extent to which the United States was bankrolling the Awakening movement and its geographical reach, the Iraqi government was determined to stifle it. This is not a surprise given that senior members of the government were actively enforcing a 'victor's peace' in Iraq, and were, at the very least, complicit in the civil war and accompanying religious cleansing of Baghdad. In the initial stages, as the US military encouraged the movement in Anbar and later sought to apply it nationally, it simply neglected to notify the Iraqi government that it was involved in the mass hiring of former insurgents.[89] But as the size and extent of the policy became apparent, senior members of the Iraqi government, from Maliki down, began to express their deep opposition to the policy. By December 2007, the scheme had placed 75,000 people on the US military's payroll, 80% of whom were Sunnis. The threat to the 'victor's peace' and the exclusive elite bargain at the centre of Iraqi politics was clear.[90] The suspicions of Iraq's governing elite were expressed by Sami al-Askari, a member of parliament close to Maliki: 'When the US leaves, what we'll have are two armies … One who's loyal to the government and one not loyal.'[91]

In a bid to recover control, Maliki's government obtained as much intelligence about the movement as possible. It wanted to manage its funding, disband it and arrest its key leaders. Firstly, Maliki set up the 'Implementation and Follow-Up Committee for National Reconciliation' to coordinate the government's response to the Awakening movement. The committee then collected from the US military the fingerprint and biometric data each member of the Awakening had submitted.[92] This gave the Iraqi government a vast amount of detailed and personal intelligence about those involved in the Awakening, in effect making it impossible for its members to avoid the authority of the Iraqi state. Maliki then informed the United States that he wanted management of the whole Awakening programme handed over to the Iraqi government as soon as possible.[93] When this occurred in October 2008, more than 103,000 men were registered on the programme.[94]

The threat posed by the Awakening movement to the post-invasion political order, and the government's response to this threat, was clearly illustrated in Diyala province, north-east of Baghdad. Diyala has a religiously mixed population, and levels of communal violence remained high throughout 2007. Diyala is also strategically important in that it acts as a land bridge between the strongholds of the Kurdish members of the exclusive elite pact, the KDP and PUK, and those of the ISCI in the south of the country. In 2007, the US military successfully drew Sunni residents of Diyala into an Awakening council in the province, thus reducing the potential recruiting pool for al-Qaeda and increasing intelligence-gathering. The main promise these recruits were given was a chance to rejoin the provincial police force, which had been purged of Sunnis by a police chief affiliated to the ISCI, who had then used the police as a tool for violently cleansing the province.[95] When these Awakening members were not rehired by the police force they staged demonstrations, threatened to leave the Awakening and lobbied Iraqi Islamic Party members on the local council to sack the police chief. Maliki's response was to launch a deadly assault on the local government headquarters to arrest officials sympathetic to the Awakening members' demands.[96]

The assault was a harbinger of how Maliki would demobilise the Awakening movement and remove the threat it posed to the elite pact. As the date for the handover of the Awakening movement to the Iraqi government approached, the Iraqi Army began to arrest and imprison the leaders of each local force. They were sometimes accused of brutality and murder when they were in charge of the Awakening groups; others found old charges about links to the insurgency were revisited. Either way, prominent Awakening leaders, especially in Baghdad, Diyala and Anbar, were either forced to flee into exile or arrested. Those arrested were frequently tortured or died in unexplained circumstances.[97] Although there were brief localised rebellions in the face of this policy, the Iraqi government continued to arrest the Awakening's leaders, broke its organisational capacity and demobilised its rank and file through intimidation, without a noticeable increase in insurgent violence. As Rosen notes:

> There is nothing the Awakening groups can do. As guerrillas and insurgents they were only effective when they operated covertly, underground, blending in among a Sunni population that has now mostly been dispersed. Now the former resistance fighters-turned-paid guards are publicly known, and their names, addresses and biometric data are in the hands of American and Iraqi forces. They cannot return to an

> underground that has been cleared, and they still face the wrath of radical Sunnis who view them as traitors.[98]

During an interview with a senior US military adviser to Petraeus in Baghdad in April 2007, the Sons of Iraq Programme was described as an exercise in 'funky DDR' (disarmament, demobilisation and reintegration of armed forces). The collection of biometric data from former insurgents in return for payment made them simultaneously visible and vulnerable to whatever organisation had access to that information. Once the US military handed over the data to the Iraqi government, the government wasted little time in breaking what it saw as the organisational threat the Awakening posed to the continued rule of the current governing elite. The ease with which the leaders of the Awakening were rounded up without a sustained return to insurgent violence suggests that the movement itself had fairly shallow organisational or popular roots. The US military had in fact paid a disparate group of desperate individuals to temporarily organise themselves. In return they gained a great deal of useful intelligence about al-Qaeda in Mesopotamia's organisation and activities. However, because the Awakening movement was so weakly organised it was easily targeted by the Iraqi government. It also proved an unsustainable vehicle from which the Sunni community could re-enter national politics.

Moqtada al-Sadr, the targeting of the 'special groups' and the rebranding of Jaish al-Mahdi

The second major drivers of the civil war from 2005 to 2007 were the disparate radical groups loosely organised under the leadership of Moqtada al-Sadr. With the ability to mobilise up to 60,000 men and an increasingly sectarian agenda, the Jaish al-Mahdi was the most destructive non-state organisation striving to impose the victor's peace on Iraq. Sadr's ability to capitalise on his late father's ideological legitimacy and what was left of the mass organisation he built up under Ba'athist rule made the Jaish al-Mahdi one of the most formidable military forces during the civil war, and the main vehicle for the violent religious cleansing of Baghdad's Sunni community. However, the speed with which the organisation mobilised its mass following, the two prolonged conflicts it had with the US military in 2004 and Sadr's own style of leadership caused it to fracture as the civil war progressed.

The US military's attempt to target Jaish al-Mahdi at the onset of the surge faced a number of problems. Sadr was a skilled, if mercurial, politician who, much like his father, successfully aimed his populist rhetoric at a wide and growing constituency, the '*ibn al-Balad*', the sons of the soil, poor, marginalised urban Iraqi youth.[99] Learning from the two unresolved conflicts it had with Jaish al-Mahdi in 2004, the US military recognised that the application of brute force would neither tame nor destroy Sadr's wider constituency. Furthermore, Sadr's support had been crucial in bringing Maliki to power. Throughout 2007, Maliki placed very real constraints on the US military's ability to operate against Sadr, putting a number of his key lieutenants on a 'no-lift list', banning operations against them or their arrest without his express prior knowledge and consent.

In an attempt to minimise these constraints, a key aim of the first two stages of the surge, the Baghdad Security Plan and *Phantom Thunder* and *Phantom Strike* in the suburbs, was to target the Mahdi Army's key nodes, support zones, and capabilities without raising the political ire of the prime minister or triggering a renewed all-out offensive by the Jaish al-Mahdi. The US arrested an estimated 1,000 Jaish al-Mahdi activists per month from the start of the surge to August 2007.[100] However, in both tactical and propaganda terms, the United States sought to exploit the fractured nature of Sadr's movement by claiming that it only targeted rogue operators or 'special groups' that no longer recognised Sadr's authority. The empirical veracity of such a division may be hard to establish, particularly in those areas of high Sadr support targeted by the US military, but the distinction pacified Maliki as key areas of the organisation were dismantled by US forces, and dissuaded the Jaish al-Mahdi from going back on the offensive.[101]

Fearing that he would be targeted by the surge, Sadr left Iraq for Iran after Bush had announced the new approach, but before it was implemented. In the aftermath of his departure, the Jaish al-Mahdi removed its forces from the streets of Baghdad, reducing both its operations and visibility in order to avoid confrontation with the US military. This tactical decision to withdraw its forces from US-dominated areas meant that there was no mass disarmament of those responsible for the previous upsurge in killings. Instead, the Jaish al-Mahdi, learning from the confrontations of 2004, took a tactical decision not to fight the US directly, merging back into its host communities and retaining the majority of its weapons and its organisational capacity. As Sadr's absence became more noticeable, a senior aide, Salah al-Ubaidi, announced that Sadr had indeed left Iraq and gone to the Iranian holy city of Qom, belatedly following his father's instructions 'to pay more attention to learning and studying'.[102]

Sadr's organisation, realising that the civil war had, at the very least, been put on hold by the surge, took the opportunity to reorganise after four years of relentless expansion driven by violent conflict. The Jaish al-Mahdi had been so successful in seizing territory across Baghdad that it now controlled areas well beyond its core *'ibn al-Balad'* constituency. This brought it into extended contact with a much wider group of Shia Baghdadis. In 2007, as security in the capital stabilised, found it more difficult to justify its use of violence, and the extortion of money to pay for it, in terms of protecting the Shia population against insurgent and jihadist violence.[103] To meet these new circumstances, this diffuse and disparate movement now had to impose centralised discipline on its foot soldiers, who counted among their ranks not only loyal followers of Sadr but also criminals and murderers. To overcome increasing criticism from within the Shia community, hundreds of ill-disciplined members of the militia were expelled. A 'Golden Brigade' was set also up in Najaf and sent to Baghdad to impose discipline, including murder, on those who refused to accept the new centralised organisation.

This attempt at rebuilding Sadr's organisation reached its peak in late August 2007. As sectarian violence declined, intra-Shi'a tensions increased over the summer. The primary cause of this violence was the Jaish al-Mahdi's struggle with its rival militia, the Badr Brigade, for control of the Shia population across southern Iraq. This represented the larger and longer-running competition between Sadr's organisation and the other party which claimed to represent mainstream Shia opinion, the ISCI. The ISCI governors of two southern provinces, Qadisiya and Muthanna, were both killed by car bombs in August 2007. At that time there here was clear potential for violent conflict between the ISCI's militia, Badr and Jaish al-Mahdi to escalate into an intra-Shia civil war. This reached its peak on 27 August 2007 when Jaish al-Mahdi and Badr gunmen fought a running battle in the holy city of Karbala, which was crowded with pilgrims for a religious festival. Fifty-two people were killed, outraging Shia public opinion and forcing Sadr to declare an unambiguous six-month ceasefire. This was permanently extended as he strove to impose discipline on his movement and rebuild its legitimacy with its core constituency. Over the next 12 months Sadr attempted to rebrand his movement, stressing its political and charitable work, and in August 2008 he announced that:

> This army is cultural, religious, social and is in charge of a cultural and scientific jihad to liberate minds, hearts and souls from the secular Western tide and which forbids using weapons, ever.[104]

The US counter-insurgency campaign had a direct and indirect effect on the Sadrist movement. By targeting its members, whether those in the 'special groups' or the more lowly foot soldiers, it clearly reduced the Jaish al-Mahdi's ability to mobilise, arm and deploy the number of fighters it had used during the height of the civil war. The greater presence of US and Iraqi troops on the streets of Baghdad, the erection of concrete barriers and the establishment of Joint Security Stations along the frontlines of the sectarian conflict reduced the Jaish al-Mahdi's operating range. Beyond this, however, the slowly increasing levels of security indirectly impacted upon Sadr's *raison d'être.* During 2005 and 2006, using the justification of sectarian violence, it imposed its authority on areas of Baghdad well beyond its traditional working-class heartlands in the east of the city. It used violence and intimidation to drive out the Sunni populations who had inhabited these districts and continued a campaign of intimidation and extortion to maintain control once they had been cleansed. When general levels of communal violence declined, Sadr's anti-occupation rhetoric was not enough to legitimise the role Jaish al-Mahdi now played in Baghdad. Sadr made concerted attempts, accelerated after the violent clashes in Najaf in August 2007, to turn his sectarian militia into something more institutionalised, legitimate and sustainable.

The theory and practice of classic counter-insurgency in Iraq

What did the US counter-insurgency campaign in Iraq achieve after 2007 and how? The greatest and most influential success of the redoubled military efforts was, by its very nature, the least visible: the targeting of senior militia leaders, both Sunni and Shia, involved in the funding and organisation of the civil war. This was carried out by American Special Forces under the command of General Stanley McChrystal. This command was set up in July 2004, but integrated by Petraeus into his 'Anaconda strategy' on his arrival.[105] Special Forces were deployed to kill 'high-value targets' as part of a wider comprehensive plan.[106] The intelligence needed to carry out these killings had been inadequate during the first years of the occupation, when the US military remained ignorant about its opponents. However, its great breakthrough came with the arrival in Iraq of mobile phone networks in 2004. This provided an almost limitless supply of signals intelligence for McChrystal's team to work with. By 2009, five years after the first networks were set up, there were 20m subscribers in a population then estimated to be around 27m.[107] By seizing the mobile phones of known militia leaders, a comprehensive map of key players could be constructed, delivering high-quality real-time intelligence to McChrystal's Joint Special Operations Command. This allowed the US military to target key high- and mid-level operatives, the very people who had driven the civil war forward in 2005 and 2006. The rapid expansion of mobile phone-networks and ownership in Iraq from 2004 onwards may well have been one of the most important aids to US operations since the invasion.

Conclusion

The use of the intelligence the mobile phones provided was a successful innovation, in what was the tactical deployment of coercion. This is indicative of the wider use of counter-insurgency doctrine by the US in Iraq after 2007. As he travelled to Iraq in February 2007, Petraeus made it clear, as he did on numerous occasions during his term in Baghdad, that the conflict in Iraq would be brought to a sustainable end politically, not militarily. This echoed Petraeus's counter-insurgency guru, Galula, who stressed that rebuilding the capacity and legitimacy of the state was the *only* way to win a sustainable victory against an insurgency. The campaign launched in 2007 was very successful in removing the key perpetrators of violence from Iraq's streets and provided security to enough areas of Baghdad to stop the spiralling cycle of violence that had driven Iraq into civil war.

For lasting stability however this new approach needed to address the main drivers of the conflict: the chronic weakness of Iraqi state capacity, both institutional and coercive; and the exclusive elite settlement that had shaped Iraq's politics since 2003, which excluded the Sunni section of society. In his tenure as American ambassador, Khalilzad tried to integrate politicians seeking to represent the Sunni population into the government. This certainly helped trigger the 'Anbar Awakening', but it failed to rework the post-invasion political settlement to the extent needed to bring sustainable peace. Instead, the Awakening delivered intelligence and the tactical passivity of sections of the Sunni community. Once the Iraqi government took control of the Awakening in October 2008, it systematically broke the Awakening's ability to become a viable vehicle for political representation. Against this background, the sustainability of the reduction in violence achieved in 2007 and 2008 is now dependent upon the rebuilding of the Iraqi state's coercive and institutional capacity, and on a reworking of the political settlement that followed regime change.

Notes

1 See Toby Dodge, 'The Ideological Roots of Failure: The Application of Kinetic Neo-Liberalism to Iraq', *International Affairs*, vol. 86, no. 6, November 2010, pp. 1,269–86.

2 In the speech, Bush said that 20,000 extra troops would be sent. However, at its peak, in October 2007, 39,000 additional US troops were deployed to Iraq as part of the surge.

3 George W. Bush, 'President's Address to the Nation', 10 January 2007, http://georgewbush-whitehouse.archives.gov/news/releases/2007/01/20070110-7.html.

4 See for example Andrew Bacevich, 'The Petraeus Doctrine', *The Atlantic*, October 2008, http://www.theatlantic.com/doc/200810/petraeus-doctrine; *Gian P. Gentile*, 'Misreading the Surge Threatens US Army's Conventional Capabilities', *World Politics Review*, 4 March 2008, http://www.worldpoliticsreview.com/article.aspx?id=1715; Pete Mansoor, 'Misreading the History of the Iraq War', *Small Wars Journal* blog, 10 March 2008, http://smallwarsjournal.com/blog/2008/03/misreading-the-history-of-the-iraq-war.

5 Jason Burke, *The 9/11 Wars* (London: Penguin, 2012), pp. 243–4.

6 Bob Woodward, *The War Within: A Secret White House History, 2006–2008* (New York: Simon and Schuster, 2008), p. 15.

7 'President Addresses Nation, Discusses Iraq, War on Terror', 28 June 2005, Fort Bragg, North Carolina, http://www.whitehouse.gov/news/releases/2005/06/20050628-7.html.

8 The joint campaign plan quoted in Woodward, *The War Within*, p. 7.

9 John Koopman, 'Putting an Iraqi Face on the Fight', *San Francisco Chronicle*, 21 May 2006, http://articles.sfgate.com/2006-05-21/news/17295730_1_iraqi-officers-iraqi-security-forces-iraqi-face.

10 Louise Roug and Julian E. Barnes, 'Iraqi Forces Not Ready Yet, US General Says', *Los Angeles Times*, 31 August 2006, http://articles.latimes.com/2006/aug/31/world/fg-iraq31; Julian Borger, 'Iraq Crisis: The US View of Iraq: We Can Pull Out in a Year, the View on the Ground: Unbridled Savagery', *The Guardian*, 31 August 2006, http://www.guardian.co.uk/world/2006/aug/31/iraq.julianborger.

11 Michael R. Gordon, 'Iran Aiding Shiite Attacks Inside Iraq, General Says', *New York Times*, 23 June 2006, http://www.nytimes.com/2006/06/23/world/middleeast/23military.html; Michael R. Gordon, 'Top US General in Iraq Outlines Sharp Troop Cut',

New York Times, 25 June 2006, http://www.nytimes.com/2006/06/25/world/middleeast/25military.html; Borger, 'Iraq Crisis: The US View of Iraq'.

12 Koopman, 'Putting an Iraqi Face on the Fight'.

13 Julian Borger and Richard Norton-Taylor, 'Bush Drops "Stay the Course" Slogan as Political Mood Sours', *The Guardian*, 25 October 2006, http://www.guardian.co.uk/world/2006/oct/25/topstories3.usa.

14 Michael E. O'Hanlon and Ian Livingston, *Iraq Index: Tracking Variables of Reconstruction and Security in Post-Saddam Iraq*, 31 October 2010, p. 4, http://www.brookings.edu/iraqindex.

15 See Army Col. H.R. McMaster, commander of the 3rd Armoured Cavalry Regiment, 'News Transcript Press Briefing on Overview of Operation Restoring Rights in Tal Afar, Iraq', US Department of Defense, Office of the Assistant Secretary of Defense (Public Affairs), 13 September 2005, http://www.defense.gov/transcripts/transcript.aspx?transcriptid=2106.

16 George Packer, 'Letter from Iraq: The Lesson of Tal Afar', *The New Yorker*, 10 April 2006, http://www.newyorker.com/archive/2006/04/10/060410fa_fact2; Thomas E. Ricks, *Fiasco: The American Military Adventure in Iraq* (London: Allen Lane, 2006), pp. 419–23.

17 Linda Robinson, *Tell Me How This Ends: General David Petraeus and the Search for a Way Out of Iraq* (New York: Public Affairs, 2008), p. 76.

18 See Burke, *The 9/11 Wars*, p. 264.

19 Thomas E. Ricks, *The Gamble: General Petraeus and the Untold Story of the American Surge in Iraq, 2006–2008* (London: Allen Lane, 2009), p. 27; Stathis N. Kalyvas, 'The New US Army/Marine Corps Counterinsurgency Field Manual as Political Science and Political Praxis', *Perspectives on Politics*, vol. 6, no. 2, June 2008, p. 351.

20 Ian F.W. Beckett, *Insurgency in Iraq: A Historical Perspective*, January 2005, Strategic Studies Institute, p. 51; http://www.carlisle.army.mil/ssi/, Lorenzo Zambernardi, 'Counterinsurgency's Impossible Trilemma', *Washington Quarterly*, vol. 33, no. 3, p. 21.

21 David Kilcullen, 'Counter-insurgency *Redux*', *Survival*, vol. 48, no. 4, 2006, pp. 112–13.

22 David Galula, *Counter-Insurgency Warfare: Theory and Practice* (London: Pall Mall Press, 1964), p. 27.

23 Kalyvas, 'The New U.S. Army/Marine Corps Counterinsurgency Field Manual', p. 351.

24 Department of the Army, *Counter-insurgency Field Manual*, FM 3-24 (Washington DC: Headquarters, Department of the Army, 2006), Chapter 2, paragraph 6, December 2006, http://www.fas.org/irp/doddir/army/fm3-24.pdf.

25 *Ibid.*

26 David J. Kilcullen, 'Countering Global Insurgency', *Journal of Strategic Studies*, vol. 28, no. 4, August 2005, p. 607.

27 Beatrice Heuser, 'The Cultural Revolution in Counter-Insurgency', *Journal of Strategic Studies*, vol. 30, vo. 1, February 2007, pp. 153–71.

28 Department of the Army, *Counter-insurgency Field Manual*, FM 3-24 (Washington DC: Headquarters Department of the Army, 2006), p. 1, para 80, (1-80).

29 Kalyvas, 'The New US Army/Marine Corps Counterinsurgency Field Manual', p. 352.

30 Laleh Khalili, 'The New (and Old) Classics of Counterinsurgency', *Middle East Report*, no. 255, Summer 2010,

http://www.merip.org/mer/mer255/khalili.html.

31 Galula, *Counter-Insurgency Warfare*, pp. 74–7.

32 See Montgomery McFate and Andrea V. Jackson, 'The Object Beyond War: Counterinsurgency and the Four Tools of Political Competition', *Military Review*, January–February 2006, p. 56.

33 Douglas A. Ollivant and Eric D. Chewning, 'Producing Victory: Rethinking Conventional Forces in COIN Operations', *Military Review*, July–August 2006, pp. 161, 163.

34 Robinson, *Tell Me How This Ends*, pp. 82–3.

35 Kimberly Kagan, *The Surge: A Military History* (New York: Encounter Books, 2009), pp. 196–7.

36 Emma Sky, 'Iraq 2007 – Moving Beyond Counter-Insurgency Doctrine: A First-Hand Perspective', *RUSI Journal*, vol. 153, no. 2, April 2008, p. 31.

37 Interview with senior US official, American Embassy, Baghdad, 1 April 2007.

38 Robinson, *Tell Me How This Ends*, p. 122.

39 Benard B. Fall, *The Two Vietnams: A Political and Military Analysis* (London: Frederick Praeger, 1968), pp. 106–7.

40 Eric R. Wolf, *Peasant Wars of the Twentieth Century* (London: Faber and Faber, 1969), p. 243.

41 See Thomas J. Sills, 'Counterinsurgency Operations in Baghdad: The Actions of 1-4 Cavalry in the East Rashid Security District', *Military Review*, May–June 2009, pp. 97–105; Thomas E. Ricks, 'Understanding the Surge in Iraq and What's Ahead', *E-Notes*, May 2009, http://www.fpri.org/enotes/200905.ricks.understandingsurgeiraq.html.

42 Interviews carried out in Rusafa district, Baghdad, 22 April 2007.

43 O'Hanlon and Campbell, *Iraq Index*, p. 9.

44 Dana Hedgpeth and Sarah Cohen, 'Money as a Weapon', *Washington Post*, 11 August 2008, http://www.washingtonpost.com/wp-dyn/content/article/2008/08/10/AR2008081002512.html.

45 See Kagan, *The Surge*; Mark Urban, *Task Force Black: The Explosive True Story of the SAS and the Secret War in Iraq* (London: Little, Brown, 2010).

46 O'Hanlon and Campbell, *Iraq Index*, p. 4.

47 Alissa J. Rubin, 'Frustration Over Wall Unites Sunni and Shiite', *New York Times*, 24 April 2007, http://www.nytimes.com/2007/04/24/world/middleeast/24iraq.html; Mike Nizza, 'Baghdad's "Great Wall of Adhamiya"', *New York Times* blog, 20 April 2007, http://thelede.blogs.nytimes.com/2007/04/20/baghdads-great-wall-of-adhamiya.

48 Robinson, *Tell Me How This Ends*, p. 230.

49 Nir Rosen, 'The Great Divide', *The National*, 5 June 2008, http://www.thenational.ae/article/20080605/REVIEW/708177227/1043&profile=1043.

50 Interviews carried out in the Kark and Rusafa security districts, Baghdad, April 2007.

51 David S. Cloud and Damien Cave, 'Commanders Say Push in Baghdad Is Short of Goal', *International Herald Tribune*, 4 June 2007, http://www.iht.com/articles/2007/06/04/africa/04surge.php.

52 Kalyvas, 'The New US Army/Marine Corps Counterinsurgency Field Manual'; Khalili, 'The New (and Old) Classics of Counterinsurgency'.

53 Jonathan Steele, 'The Viceroy of Baghdad', *The Observer*, 23 April 2006, http://www.guardian.co.uk/world/2006/apr/23/iraq.jonathansteele; Dana

Priest, 'US Talks with Iraqi Insurgents Confirmed', *Washington Post*, 27 June 2005, http://www.washingtonpost.com/wp-dyn/content/article/2005/06/26/AR2005062600096.html. Also see Allawi, *The Occupation of Iraq*, p. 399.

54 See http://www.sigir.mil/directorates/interactiveMap.html#.

55 See Steele, 'To the US Troops It Was Self-defence'.

56 International Crisis Group, 'Iraq After the Surge I: The New Sunni Landscape', *Middle East Report*, no. 74, 30 April 2008, p. 3.

57 International Crisis Group, 'Iraq After the Surge I', p. 3.

58 Burke, *The 9/11 Wars*, p. 249.

59 International Crisis Group, 'Iraq After the Surge I', p. 4

60 Carter Malkasian, 'Did the Coalition Need More Forces in Iraq? Evidence from Al Anbar', *Joint Force Quarterly*, no. 46, 3rd Quarter 2007, p. 123.

61 Austin Long, 'The Anbar Awakening', *Survival*, vol. 50, no. 2, p. 78.

62 *Ibid.*

63 Malkasian, 'Did the Coalition Need More Forces in Iraq?'.

64 Long, 'The Anbar Awakening', p. 79.

65 Martin Fletcher, 'Fighting Back: The City Determined Not To Become Al-Qaeda's Capital', *The Times*, 20 November 2006, http://www.timesonline.co.uk/tol/news/world/iraq/article642374.ece.

66 Kagan, *The Surge*, p. 67; Ricks, *The Gamble*, p. 64.

67 David, Kilcullen, *The Accidental Guerrilla* (New York: Oxford University Press, 2011), p. 173.

68 See Toby Dodge, *Inventing Iraq: The Failure of Nation Building and a History Denied* (New York and London: Columbia University Press and Hurst & Co., 2003), pp. 87–9.

69 Andrew Phillips, 'How Al Qaeda Lost Iraq', *Australian Journal of International Affairs*, vol. 63, no. 1, p. 73.

70 Ricks, *The Gamble*, p. 66.

71 Office of the Special Inspector General for Iraq Reconstruction, 'Sons of Iraq Program: Results Are Uncertain and Financial Controls Were Weak', *SIGIR Report*, 11-010, 28 January, 2001, p. 11, http://www.sigir.mil/files/audits/11-010.pdf.

72 Urban, *Task Force Black*, p. 185.

73 General David H. Petraeus, 'Report to Congress on the Situation in Iraq', 10–11 September 2007, p. 1, http://www.defense.gov/pubs/pdfs/Petraeus-Testimony20070910.pdf.

74 Office of the Special Inspector General for Iraq Reconstruction, 'Sons of Iraq Program', p. 2.

75 Kilcullen, 'Anatomy of a Tribal Revolt'.

76 *Counterinsurgency Field Manual*, FM 3-24 (Washington DC: Headquarters, Department of the Army, 2006), (2-16).

77 FM 3-24, 3-27.

78 Roberto J. González, 'Going "Tribal": Notes on Pacification in the 21st Century', *Anthropology Today*, vol. 25, no. 2, April 2009, p. 15.

79 See, for example, Faleh A. Jabar, 'Sheikhs and Ideologues: Deconstruction and Reconstruction of Tribes under Patrimonial Totalitarianism in Iraq, 1968–1998', in Faleh A. Jabar and Hosham Dawod (eds), *Tribes and Power: Nationalism and Ethnicity in the Middle East* (London: Saqi, 2003), pp. 69–101.

80 Kilcullen, 'Anatomy of a Tribal Revolt'.

81 Special Inspector General for Iraq Reconstruction, 'Sons of Iraq Program', p. 2; Ricks, *The Gamble*, p. 215.

82 Special Inspector General for Iraq Reconstruction, 'Sons of Iraq Program'.

83 Kilcullen, 'Anatomy of a Tribal Revolt'.

84 Quoted in Michael Gordon, 'The Former-Insurgent Counterinsurgency', *New York Times*, 2 September 2007, http://www.nytimes.com/2007/09/02/magazine/02iraq-t.html.

85 Martin Fletcher, 'Are They Guardians of Ghazaliyah? Or Is the US Giving Guns to a Sectarian Gang?', *The Times*, 6 September 2007, http://www.timesonline.co.uk/tol/news/world/iraq/article2395562.ece; Special Inspector General for Iraq Reconstruction, 'Sons of Iraq Program', p. 2.

86 Ghaith Abdul-Ahad, 'Meet Abu Abed: The US's New Ally Against Al-Qaida', *The Guardian*, 10 November 2007, http://www.guardian.co.uk/world/2007/nov/10/usa-al-qaida; Nir Rosen, *Aftermath: Following the Bloodshed of America's Wars in the Muslim World* (New York: Nation Books, 2010), p. 283; Robinson, *Tell Me How this Ends*, pp. 236–42.

87 Ricks, *The Gamble*, p. 205.

88 Brian Katulis, Peter Juul and Ian Moss, *Awakening to New Dangers in Iraq: Sunni 'Allies' Pose an Emerging Threat* (Washington DC: Center for American Progress, February 2008), http://www.americanprogress.org/issues/2008/02/pdf/new_dangers.pdf.

89 Ricks, *The Gamble*, p. 204.

90 Leila Fadel, 'Shiite Leaders Oppose Expansion of US-backed Citizens Groups', *McClatchy*, 21 December 2007, http://www.mcclatchydc.com/iraq/story/23567.html.

91 Leila Fadel, 'US Sponsorship of Sunni Groups Worries Iraq's Government', *McClatchy*, 29 November 2007, http://www.mcclatchydc.com/iraq/story/22259.html.

92 See Safa Rasul al-Sheikh and Emma Sky, 'Iraq Since 2003: Perspectives on a Divided Society', *Survival*, vol. 53, no. 4, August–September 2011, p. 130; Robinson, *Tell Me How This Ends*, p. 245.

93 Ned Parker, 'Distrusted by the Shiite-led Government, the Sons of Iraq Face arrests and Could Return to Insurgency', *Los Angeles Times*, 23 August 2008, http://www.latimes.com/news/printedition/front/la-fg-sons23-2008aug23,0,2435302.story.

94 O'Hanlon and Livingston, *Iraq Index*, 30 October 2008, p. 12.

95 See Sam Parker, 'Guest Post: Behind the Curtain in Diyala', http://abumuqawama.blogspot.com/2008/08/guest-post-behind-curtain-in-diyala.html, 20 August 2008.

96 Nicholas Spangler, 'US Denounces Chaotic Iraqi Raid', *McClatchy*, 20 August 2008, http://www.mcclatchydc.com/iraq/story/49518.html.

97 See, for example, Richard A Oppel, 'Iraq Takes Aim at US-tied Sunni Groups' Leaders', *New York Times*, 21 August 2008, http://www.nytimes.com/2008/08/22/world/middleeast/22sunni.html; Ned Parker, 'Iraq Seeks Breakup of US-funded Sunni Fighters', *Los Angeles Times*, 23 August 2008, http://www.latimes.com/news/printedition/front/la-fg-sons23-2008aug23,0,2435302.story; Nir Rosen, 'The Big Sleep – Iraq, the Americans, and the Sunni-Shia Civil War', 24 Apr 2009, http://thephora.net/forum/showthread.php?t=49910; *The National*, 24 April 2009, http://thenational.ae/article/20090424/REVIEW/704239996/1008.

98 Rosen, 'The Big Sleep'.

99 Shadid, *Night Draws Near*, p. 180.

100 Rosen, *Aftermath*, p. 236.

101 International Crisis Group, 'Iraq's Civil War, the Sadrists and the Surge',

Middle East Report, no. 72, 7 February 2008, p. 20.

102 Sadr quoted in 'Iraq Cleric Sadr Explains Absence', BBC News, 7 March 2008. http://news.bbc.co.uk/1/hi/world/middle_east/7284211.stm.

103 Rosen, *Aftermath*, p. 271.

104 Quoted in Ali al-Mashakhell and Nick Schifrin 'Anti-US Cleric To Lay Down Weapons; Moqtada al-Sadr Says He'll Turn Iraq Militia into Nonviolent Organization', ABC News, 7 August 2008, http://abcnews.go.com/International/story?id=5536519&page=1.

105 Urban, *Task Force Black*, p. 53.

106 See David H. Petraeus, 'Multi-National Force-Iraq Commanders Counterinsurgency Guidance', *Military Review*, vol. 8, no. 5, September/October 2008, http://nesa-center.org/files/CG%20COIN%20Unclass%20AnacondaGuidance% 2020July08.pdf.

107 See 'Why Iraqis Cherish Their Mobile Phones: Iraq's Mobile-phone Revolution', *The Economist*, 12 November 2009, http://www.economist.com/node/14870118.

CHAPTER FOUR

Rebuilding the civil and military capacity of the Iraqi state

Among the three drivers of conflict and civil war, the major factor was the collapse of state capacity, both civilian and military, after the invasion of 2003. The counter-insurgency doctrine applied to Iraq by the US military after 2007 stressed that the state's 'ability to provide security for the populace' was one of the six key tests of its legitimacy and future stability.[1] Under this rubric, weak or illegitimate government was identified as the root cause of rebellion, as it allowed the space for violent opposition to organise itself and for alienated populations to support it.

From 2003 to 2011, the US government spent an estimated US$61bn trying to rebuild the civil and military institutions of the Iraqi state, in what Stuart Bowen, the Special Inspector General for Iraq Reconstruction, described as 'the largest relief and reconstruction effort for one country in US history'.[2] With the departure of all America's military forces from the country in December 2011, it is the coherence, competence and capacity of these state institutions that will guarantee the future stability of Iraq. Did the US occupation and the ruling elite it empowered build an adequately coherent state with an armed force capable of imposing order and delivering services in return for the Iraqi population's loyalty?

Since Iraq's army and intelligence services were disbanded at the start of the US occupation in May 2003 and then rebuilt from scratch, they are a visible signifier of Iraq's future. From 2009 to 2011, Iraq's security forces took increasing responsibility for guaranteeing order across the country. In June 2009, the American military withdrew from Iraq's towns and cities and was forbidden from operating without Iraqi government permission and oversight. In August 2010, partly to comply with his election manifesto, President Obama ended all US combat missions in the country, leaving primary responsibility for the imposition of order to its new security forces. Finally, all US forces were withdrawn from Iraq at the end of 2011.

The rigid timetable that guided US troop reductions and the resultant responsibilities placed on the Iraqi armed forces were greeted with alarm by some of Baghdad's ruling elite. The aged Iraqi politician Adnan Pachachi, who served as Iraq's foreign minister before the Ba'ath Party seized power in 1968, argued that American politicians were 'deluding themselves' if they thought that Iraq's security forces would be ready to defend the country. Tariq Aziz, former deputy prime minister under Saddam, was even more forthright, declaring from his prison cell that the withdrawal of US troops was 'leaving Iraq to the wolves'. Of greater concern were the comments made by Iraq's then chief of staff, General Babakir Zebari, in May 2010. Zebari, citing the Iraqi Ministry of Defence's own strategic planning, argued that if he had been consulted about a timetable for withdrawal (which he was not), he would have told his political masters that 'the US army must stay until the Iraqi army is fully ready in 2020'.[3]

Are these disparate voices from Iraq's present and previous ruling elite correct? Did the United States, after deliberately destroying Iraq's armed forces and reducing the capacity of its civilian institutions, do enough before 2011 to prevent the country's return to civil war?

The rebuilding of Iraq's armed forces

The head of the Coalition Provisional Authority (CPA), Paul Bremer, and his military adviser, Walter Slocombe, decided to disband the Iraqi Army and the security services shortly after arriving in Baghdad in May 2003, making 400,000 soldiers unemployed.[4] Slocombe then announced that the New Iraqi Army he planned would be built over the next three years. It would consist of only 44,000 men, with no tanks or artillery. Its central role would be to guard Iraq's borders.[5] However, in the face of the rising insurgency and increasing US casualties, the training schedule of the Iraqi Army was condensed and an additional force, the Iraqi Civil Defence Corps, was created to bolster numbers.[6] In February 2004, Major General Karl Eikenberry reported that the CPA was not training enough qualified Iraqi troops and suggested that the US military should take over the role.[7] In April 2004, the United States faced dual rebellions against its occupation; one centred on Fallujah and the other driven by Sadr's militia across the south of the country. In the face of these two revolts, desertion rates 'reached up to 30 percent in northeastern Iraq, 49 percent in Baghdad, 30 percent in the south-central region, and 82 percent in western Iraq'.[8] As a result of both the Eikenberry report and the disastrous performances of 2004, a new institution to train the Iraqi Army, the Multi-National Security Transition Command Iraq (MNSTC-I), was created. The new organisation, run by the US military, was given lavish resources to rebuild the Iraqi security forces. The US government then embarked on a US$5.7bn plan to train 270,000 Iraqi troops and paramilitary police units by 2006.[9] US advisers in ten-man teams were dispersed throughout the new Iraqi Army, with up to 10,000 American troops 'stiffening' the resolve of inexperienced soldiers. By 2008, the United States planned to increase the target size of the Iraqi military to 560,000 men.[10] By 2011, US$24.5bn had been spent in an attempt at rebuilding the country's armed forces.[11]

In January 2012, the Iraqi security forces employed 933,000 people, spread between the Ministry of Defence, the Ministry of Interior and the Prime Minister's Counter-Terrorism Force.[12] Beyond the possibility of a return to civil war, the rapid expansion in the size and strength of this force raises troubling questions over the military's ability to threaten Iraq's fledgling democracy. The disbanding of the Iraqi Army in May 2003 played a central role in the United States' ambitious plans to re-establish Iraq's politics and place clear limits on the power of the state they were rebuilding in Baghdad.[13] Across the post-colonial Middle East, regime change was more likely to be delivered by military coup than political uprising or democratic elections. Iraq suffered the Middle East's first ever post-colonial coup in 1937, only five years after it gained independence. From then on, the officer corps of the army was a major player in the country's politics, violently removing the monarchy in 1958 and triggering a number of coups. From 1968 onwards, however, the Ba'ath Party worked hard to keep the military out of politics, frequently purging the officer corps of those regarded as politically unreliable, creating a series of competing military organisations and using ties of family and clan to break the coherence of the armed forces and tie its upper echelons to the ruling elite.[14] By 1988, Iraq had the fourth-largest military in the world, with 1.7m people mobilised.[15] However, its officer corps was politically neutered, recruited from sections of the population loyal to the Ba'ath Party and fractured in a way that made a successful coup almost impossible.

The US government's disbanding of Iraq's armed services in 2003 was an attempt to end the military's influence on Iraqi politics. This radical approach to exogenous political and social engineering unsurprisingly played a major role in fuelling the insurgency. So, in the face of growing violence, the United States set about rebuilding the Iraqi armed forces as quickly as it could. Caught between the hazards of insurgency, civil war and military coup, there is a danger that the Iraqi armed forces were expanded with such haste and to such a size that they once again pose a threat to Iraq's governing elite.

There has been a lively debate among those who study the causes of military intervention in politics about whether it is the internal organisation of the military itself that drives it into politics, or broader factors within society. Historically, the ultimate defence against intervention has been the opposition the army would face once it has installed itself in power. This in turn depends on the level of political mobilisation, institutionalisation and state legitimacy within society. If the population values the role its government plays, uses state institutions regularly and sees them as legitimate, then military intervention would be viewed as a threat to a central facet of the community's life and hence actively opposed. However, if the state is popularly perceived to be detached from society, failing to deliver services that are valued and dominated by unrepresentative or corrupt elites, then the military, far from being opposed, can be welcomed into power.[16]

The Iraqi state in 2012 certainly has a large and overbearing military. Given the civil war the country experienced between 2005 and 2007, the size of its armed forces is hardly a surprise. However, two other dynamics give cause for concern. Firstly, the state's civilian institutions, key to its legitimacy, are largely perceived to be absent from society. Secondly, the ruling elite is also seen, with good reason, as highly corrupt and increasingly detached from the day-to-day concerns of its population. Both these political dynamics have, in Iraqi and wider post-colonial history, driven the military to enter politics and remove civilian governments.

The Iraqi security services after US withdrawal

The repercussions of the United States' muscular approach to reforming the Iraqi Army are the 930,000 people currently working for the security forces. The fact that these forces are primarily designed to impose order on Iraq's own population, not to protect the country from external aggression, is shown in the discrepancy in size between the Ministry of Interior and the Ministry of Defence, with the former double that of the latter.[17] The remilitarisation of Iraqi society since 2003 is reflected in the total number of people employed by the security forces, who now equal 8% of the country's entire workforce or 12% of the total population of adult males.[18]

The dominant role that rebuilding the coercive capacity of the Iraq state played in Iraqi government policy is likewise represented by the fact that the Ministry of Defence's budget grew annually by 28% between 2005 and 2009, and that of the Ministry of Interior by 45%.[19] This level of defence expenditure makes Iraq the world's biggest defence spender by percentage of GDP.[20] The size, speed and scale of the expansion of the Iraqi armed forces raise two profound questions for the future of the country. Firstly, in light of Iraq's recent civil war, can a force built in haste by an exogenous actor function coherently after the United States reduced its military presence and influence at the end of 2011? If not, then the domestic stability of the country could be in doubt. Secondly, given Iraq's history of military-led regime change, can such a large armed force be kept out of politics, subservient to the civilian arm of government and ultimately to the Iraqi electorate?

Given the ferocity of the communal conflict from 2005 to 2008, the fear that Iraq may revert to civil war is very much in the minds of the population. The rapid increase in troop numbers and the intensity of their operations from the start of the 'surge' in February 2007 clearly broke the capacity of the internecine groups fighting the civil war. The radical Islamist groups surrounding al-Qaeda in Mesopotamia were targeted with much better intelligence, and they saw important sections of their host communities turn against them. Similarly, the US military and Iraqi security forces successfully launched sustained campaigns against Jaish al-Mahdi at a time when its leader, Sadr, had imposed a ceasefire. In parallel with the targeting of al-Qaeda and Jaish al-Mahdi, extensive purges of the Ministry of Interior, in particular the Federal Police, stopped its direct involvement in the mass religious cleansing of Baghdad.

However, those fearing that Iraq could return to civil war after 2012 argue that the three main organisations responsible for the civil war could regroup and drive the country back into more damaging levels of violence and instability. The Iraqi security forces are the main brake on this happening. The overall coherence and capacity of the army, Federal Police and intelligence services make a return to civil war unlikely. The Ministries of Interior and Defence control what is now the most powerful set of coercive forces in Iraq. They operate with enough central control and have enough resources to keep violence at its current levels. There is little chance that a major political crisis or upsurge in communal violence would deliver a systemic shock big enough to break the operating capacity of the army and police force, and create a security vacuum comparable to the one that arose in 2003, and which drew Iraq into civil war.

The post-2007 reforms of the security services have reduced the ability of sectarian actors, those seeking to impose a victor's peace on Iraq, from using the security forces to achieve their goals. But a greater threat is that the military will be used to impose and defend a civilian dictatorship. The strategy that Prime Minister Maliki has employed to tighten his grip over the security services poses a direct threat to the continuation of meaningful democracy in Iraq. In setting up the Office of the Commander in Chief and a number of Provincial Operations Centres, the prime minister has bypassed both parliamentary oversight and the chain of command that should lead from the cabinet ministers responsible for defence and the interior to the soldiers and police involved in operations across Iraq. Maliki's undemocratic and unconstitutional control of the armed forces is at its greatest in his use of Iraqi Special Operations Forces. By creating the Counter-Terrorism Bureau to control it, he has removed this force from ministerial and parliamentary oversight. He has then used these elite troops to arrest politicians who have troubled him and intimidated his political rivals.

The first question regarding the ability of the armed forces to guarantee the stability of the country concerns the internal coherence, management and capacity of these forces. The speed with which the army especially was recruited has given rise to a very varied rank and file. A census of the army carried out in 2009 indicated that 25% of current soldiers did not meet the military's own educational standards, and that roughly 15% were illiterate.[21] There are also persistent reports of increasing drug and alcohol abuse.[22]

There have also been sustained problems at a senior and managerial level. The Ministry of Defence in Baghdad has a well-deserved reputation for bureaucratic inefficiency and complexity, and is unresponsive to requests from the field. This has led to poor management of the ministry's budget, as well as to weaknesses in logistics and strategic planning. This inflexible approach at a leadership level by senior military figures and their reluctance to delegate stifles innovation and independent decision-making further down the hierarchy. In theory, the chain of command in the Iraqi military is clearly institutionalised. The Iraqi Ground Forces Command is in charge of the country's forces in the field and is itself subordinate to the Joint Headquarters/Joint Forces Command, which is in turn managed by the Iraqi National Command Operations Centre.[23] In practice, a leaked memo written in 2009 by the head of the US advisory team to the Baghdad Operations Command summed up the situation as the 'near total ineffectiveness of the Iraq Army and National Police institutional organisations and systems'.[24] This may in part be because the command ethos remains from the pre-regime change army.[25] However, more importantly it is a direct result of sustained political interference from the Prime Minister's Office. This has prevented 'vertical integration and horizontal coordination' across the security forces and led to the 'cellphone management' of the army. The Prime Minister's Office regularly circumvents the chain of command, ringing up mid-ranking officers and issuing orders to them on their mobile phones.[26]

The inefficiency of command and control has been exacerbated by, and has contributed to, widespread corruption at all levels of the armed forces. In 2008, Iraq's government anti-corruption watchdog, the Commission on Public Integrity, opened 736 cases into corruption involving the Ministry of Interior, whose portfolio includes the national and local police.[27] Junior Iraqi officers complain that defence officials demand bribes of US$3,000 for a place at the Officer Training Academy, and the price of promotion to general is reputed to be US$30,000. The costs involved in successfully procuring advancement may partially explain the existence of 'ghost payrolls', full of fictitious soldiers whose names were supplied to defraud the Ministry of Defence of an estimated 25% of its annual wage budget.[28] Corruption also directly impedes the military's ability to deliver security. In the aftermath of a series of devastating truck bombings in the centre of Baghdad in 2009, reports pointed to corrupt military officers taking bribes to let trucks containing the bombs through the security cordon surrounding the government district in Baghdad.

Sectarian politics and the security services

If the quality of rank-and-file soldiers and the weaknesses in the command and control of the armed forces raised doubts about the military's ability to function after a US drawdown, then the size and role of the security forces also raise fears about their commitment to a democratic and civilian leadership for Iraq. The most serious problem is the politicisation of the officer corps since 2003. The struggle to impose a victor's peace on Iraq was played out much more fully in the Ministry of Interior than in the Ministry of Defence. The speed with which the Iraqi Army was reconstituted after 2003 necessitated the re-employment of the Saddam-era officer corps. Today, up to 70% of officers are holdovers from the Ba'athist armed forces. To reduce the influence of these officers on the army, those seeking to impose a victor's peace inserted so-called *dimaj* officers into the senior ranks of the military.[29] These political appointments were either leaders of party-affiliated militias or lacked the necessary military experience. They owe their allegiance to the sectarian political parties that placed them within the chain of command, bypassing the state and its legislature. The struggle between those who gained military experience under the old regime and those inserted into the senior ranks by political appointment has fractured the military and introduced both incoherence and division into its ranks.

Some 75–80% of the army's rank and file are estimated to be Shia, a figure comparable to the sectarian demography of the Saddam-era army. The senior ranks of the army are more ethnically and religiously diverse, with divisional commanders coming from all three of the country's major ethnic and religious communities.[30] The ethnic diversity of specific army divisions and the influence of political parties on them is, to a large extent, dependent upon whether they were enlisted locally or nationally. The 2nd, 3rd, 4th, 15th and 16th divisions of the army include high numbers of Kurdish soldiers and are heavily influenced by the Kurdish Democratic Party (KDP) and the Patriotic Union of Kurdistan (PUK).[31]

Overall, however, the Iraqi Army appears to have largely managed to escape the worst excesses of sectarian infiltration and behaviour. At the height of the civil war, the army, in contrast to the Federal Police, was not used to carry out religious cleansing in and around Baghdad. The mixture of senior officers from the old regime, former leaders of the Peshmerga Kurdish militias and political appointments from the Shia Islamist parties has undermined operational coherence, but has also stopped the army becoming a major tool in the sectarian conflict.

The biggest problem with the security services is the sectarian and political bias of the Ministry of Interior's Federal Police, (formerly named the National Police) who acted as a death squad in 2006 and 2007. Bayan Jabar, a former senior figure in the Badr militia who oversaw the mass integration of his former militia members into the Federal Police during his tenure, left the ministry in 2006. His successor, Jawad al-Bolani, served as interior minister from 2006 until 2010 and oversaw sustained attempts to purge the most egregious sectarian actors from the Federal Police. More than 60,000 men were sacked from the force; seven of the nine commanders of National Police brigades and 17 of 27 of National Police battalions were also removed.[32]

Despite these widespread purges, sustained attempts at restructuring the national police force and an expansion in their numbers, the force is still plagued by corruption and sectarianism. At the end of 2009, after major reforms had been completed, reports indicated that 1,500 recruits had been nominated by Iraq's political parties, signalling political interference not only in hiring and promotion, but also in policy formation.[33] Following the US withdrawal, the Iraqi government is in the midst of a wider transformation of its security forces that will see the Federal Police take responsibility for internal order as the army is moved to the more traditional role of border defence. If the direct influence of sectarian actors and political parties are still present in both the recruitment and policy formation of the Federal Police by the time this transformation is complete in 2020, then it could pose a sustained problem for Iraq's ability to stabilise its politics.

The increasing dominance of Nuri al-Maliki

There is little surprise that a security force hastily reconstituted in the midst of a bloody civil war remains exposed to the continuing influence of the political parties that were the major protagonists of that conflict. However, the speed with which the Iraqi security forces were built, the size that they became, and the dominance they gained over Iraqi society has led them to become extremely susceptible to political influence of a more focused nature. Since his appointment in 2006, Prime Minister Maliki has worked very successfully to subvert the formal chain of command and tie senior army commanders and paramilitary units to him personally. One of the reasons Maliki was appointed as a compromise candidate for the premiership in 2006 was that he was not regarded as a threat to any of the existing parties that were competing for political power. From 2006 until 2008, the US government and all of the major political parties in Iraq damned Maliki for the same reasons as he was appointed: that he was weak, ineffectual and too dependent on the support of his rivals.[34] All of the major players within Iraqi politics toyed with removing him during the first two years of his appointment.

On his appointment, Maliki was the second-in-command of the Shia Islamist Dawa Islamic Party, one of the oldest groups to organise against Ba'athist rule. A major reason why Dawa's first leader after regime change, Jaafari, was chosen as interim prime minister in May 2005 was that his party did not have a militia of its own and therefore was not seen as a military threat to any of its political rivals. When Maliki replaced Jaafari as prime minister in 2006, the political rationale remained the same. However, Maliki's ascendance to the office of prime minister coincided with efforts to increase the coherence, power and reach of the Iraqi security forces. The new Iraqi military had been built with such haste that the institutionalisation of political oversight was fragile. With his political vulnerability in mind, Maliki exploited this and used the Office of the Prime Minister to cement his grip over the army, Special Forces and the intelligence services. The other Shia political parties in government, the Sadrists and the ISCI, had neglected the army in favour of using their militias and influence in the Ministry of Interior to pursue a victor's peace and drive the Sunni population from Baghdad. As Iraq descended into civil war, Maliki quietly moved to take charge of the three arms of the security service least culpable in the sectarian violence.

Since then, Maliki has secured his grip over the Iraqi security forces by creating two extra-constitutional organisations. The first, the Office of the Commander in Chief, was originally envisaged by US advisers to be a coordinating forum for the prime minister to chair. However, Maliki quickly realised its potential importance and increased its staff, influence and reach. He moved the organisation into the Office of the Prime Minister and appointed his close ally, Farouk al-Araji, to run it and staff it with trusted functionaries.[35] The Office of the Commander in Chief then began to issue orders directly to battalion heads, thus circumventing and in effect destroying the army's chain of command.[36] The office then involved itself directly in the appointment and promotion of senior army staff.

> Prime Minister Maliki pushed hard to place his own officials and senior officers in key roles, often by giving them temporary appointments that bypassed the [parliamentary] confirmation process and then keeping them in the role indefinitely. He pushed Kurdish, Sunni, and less loyal Shi'ite officers aside or removed them.[37]

The second extra-constitutional innovation Maliki has deployed to control the security forces is the proliferation of Provisional Command Centres. Beginning in February 2007 with the Baghdad Security Plan, the Baghdad Operational Command was created to coordinate all Iraqi forces, both police and army, in the city.[38] Provincial Command Centres were then set up in unstable areas across south and central Iraq. The centres brought together the command and control of both the police and army under one general in each province. These generals are chosen and directed from a central office in Baghdad under Maliki's control. Thus, the Provincial Command Centres undermine the Ministry of Defence's command and control of the army and give Maliki the power to appoint and direct the most important generals in the most strategically sensitive areas of the country. Unsurprisingly, those generals appointed to run the command centres are politically or personally aligned with the prime minister.

Once Maliki had increased his control over the army through the Office of the Commander in Chief and Provincial

Command Centres, he then undertook direct management of the most effective fighting force in the country, the Iraq Special Operations Forces. Created by the United States, it comprises 4,200 soldiers and is considered the best special-forces organisation in the Middle East.[39] In April 2007, as managerial responsibility was transferred from the US Special Forces to the Iraqi government, Maliki set up a ministerial body, the Counter-Terrorism Bureau, to control it.[40] This effectively removed the force from the oversight of parliament and the control of either the Ministry of Interior or Ministry of Defence. Since then, its size, capacity and reach has grown exponentially. Iraq's Special Forces are, in effect, the personal coercive tool of its prime minister, his Praetorian guard. They have become known across Iraq as the '*Fedayeen al-Maliki*', a reference to their reputation as the prime minister's tool for covert action against his rivals as well as a bleakly ironic comparison to Saddam's militia.[41]

Iraq's intelligence services have similarly been targeted by the prime minister. Initially, the struggle for control of the intelligence services became apparent in the conflict between General Mohammed Abdullah al-Shahwani, the head of the National Intelligence Service, and Sherwan al-Waeli, who was appointed by Maliki in 2006 as minister of state for national security affairs.[42] The National Intelligence Service was established by the CIA, and Shahwani had enjoyed a long and close working relationship with Washington.[43] Waeli, conversely, although close to the prime minister also had longstanding links to the Iranian government. Matters came to a head in August 2009 after major bombings in the centre of Baghdad. Shahwani argued in the Iraqi press that there was clear forensic evidence linking the attacks to Iran. Shahwani was subsequently forced to resign, thus delivering uncontested control over the intelligence services to the prime minister and his allies.[44] The struggle for control of Iraq's intelligence-gathering agencies has led to a proliferation of organisations, with six separate entities spread across different ministries in Baghdad, competing with each other and representing different power centres within the Iraqi state.[45] This competition has undermined the ability of the Iraqi state to gather, process and act upon intelligence. In addition, there is evidence that Maliki has been involved in purging serving intelligence officers not aligned to his party.[46]

The civilian capacity of the Iraqi state

The comparative study of post-colonial democracies indicates that the most effective curb on the dictatorial aspirations of politicians or military officers is the extent to which the state's civilian institutions have a meaningful and valued presence in the population's daily lives. If the state's civilian service provision is seen to be central to people's quality of life, then it accrues legitimacy within society. This in turn means that the population values the state and is prepared to actively mobilise against its takeover by an authoritarian ruling elite. The future of Iraq's democracy could then lie in the capacity of its civilian institutions to deliver much-needed services to its population. So, once a state has imposed order on society and gained control over the monopoly of collective violence across the country, its legitimacy rests on its capacity to deliver services to its population, to become central to their day-to-day 'strategies of survival'.[47] In addition to playing a major role in building support for continued democratic government, the civilian capacity of the state also has a central role in the creation of a unified national identity. By delivering the services a population needs, the state becomes the central vehicle for and focus of a unified national identity. Nationalism follows the creation of the state.[48]

The Iraqi state inherited by the US-led occupation in 2003 had already experienced two major transformations over the previous 30 years. The oil-price rises of the mid 1970s transformed the political economy of Iraq. The Ba'ath Party used this financial windfall to drive a powerful set of institutions, both coercive and civil, into society. These institutions shaped Iraq, breaking organised resistance to Ba'athist rule and effectively atomising the population. By 1990, 21% of the active workforce and 40% of Iraqi households were directly reliant on government payouts.[49] Due to land-reform programmes instigated by the Ba'ath Party, the state also became the largest landowner in the country.[50] The state funnelled a proportion of its new resources into building powerful civil institutions, a social security system and new housing projects, and invested in health and education. By the 1970s, the Iraqi population was increasingly and self-consciously linked directly to the largesse of state institutions funded by oil wealth. By deploying coercion, infrastructural power and patronage in hitherto unheard-of quantities, the Ba'athist regime destroyed any organisational capacity within society that could have been mobilised to threaten it.

The Iraqi invasion of Kuwait in 1990 brought about a second, even more dramatic, transformation of the state. The United Nations placed upon Iraq the harshest and most intrusive sanctions regime in modern diplomatic history. Thirteen years of sanctions caused profound and widespread suffering to the Iraqi population. Iraqi imports fell dramatically in the immediate aftermath of the embargo, from $10.3bn in 1988 to just $0.4bn by 1991. The value of wages across the labour market fell by 90% in 1990–91 and then by another 40% between 1991 and 1996.[51] This 'macroeconomic shock of massive proportions' was estimated by UN Children's Fund (UNICEF) in 1997 to have increased child malnourishment by 73%, and was directly responsible for the deaths of between 5,000 and 6,000 children per month.[52] The most noticeable effect of sanctions was the retreat from society of the official civil institutions of the state, beyond a rationing system set up by the government. This was especially pronounced in the areas of welfare, health and education. Using the excuse of 'self-financing', state agencies from hospitals to schools were hollowed out, starved of funding and encouraged to extract what resources they could from the wider population.[53]

The arrival of US troops in Baghdad in the first week of April 2003 caused the final collapse of state institutions. The removal of the Ba'athist regime was greeted by an explosion of looting that US authorities had neither the troop numbers nor the political will to halt. In the ensuing anarchy, 17 of the Iraqi government's 23 central ministry buildings were destroyed.[54] The total cost of the damage in monetary terms is generally considered to be around US$12bn, equivalent to as much as one-third of Iraq's annual GDP.[55] The CPA contributed to the institutional collapse of the Iraqi state by pursuing a thoroughgoing process of de-Ba'athification from May 2003 onwards. General Order No. 1 disbanded the Ba'ath Party, banned the top four levels of the party's membership from holding government jobs, and barred former members of the Ba'ath from occupying jobs in the top three management levels of any government institution. The de-Ba'athification order purged government ministries of their top layer of management, making between 20,000 and 120,000 people unemployed.[56] For example, one-third of the Ministry of Health's staff stopped coming to work after the order was issued.[57] In an economy that was historically dominated by state employment, legislating for the exclusion of such a large number of people was in effect legalising their enforced penury. The administrative capacity of the state had been destroyed by more than a decade of sanctions, three wars in 20 years and three weeks of uncontrolled looting triggered by the arrival of American troops in Baghdad. The decision to pursue de-Ba'athification at this stage removed what was left of the state: its institutional memory and a large section of its skilled personnel.

In the immediate aftermath of the war, looting and de-Ba'athification, estimates about how much it would cost to rebuild the Iraqi state varied widely. In 2003, the contractor Bechtel estimated that it would cost US$16bn, whilst the United Nations suggested a figure of US$36bn.[58] These figures proved wildly optimistic; by March 2012, the US and Iraqi governments had collectively spent US$200bn trying to reconstruct the state.[59]

Rebuilding the Iraqi state after 2003

The US$200bn spent on reconstruction was channelled through a myriad of different organisations. During 2003–04, the Coalition Provisional Authority was responsible for civilian reconstruction. When sovereignty was handed back to the Iraqi government in April 2004, the US government set up the Iraq Reconstruction Management Office (IRMO) and the Project and Contracting Office to oversee the continuing flow of reconstruction money. IRMO was disbanded in early 2007 and replaced by the Iraq Transition Assistance Office, which was responsible for managing the $3bn of US money left for reconstruction.

The US-led reconstruction effort faced three major obstacles. Firstly, the reconstruction project was incoherent. Beyond the Department of Defense, the State Department and USAID, every arm of the US government had been mandated by Bush to take part in the effort to rebuild Iraq. The effective coordination between American government organisations operating in the sprawling embassy complex in Saddam's former Republican

Palace, proved to be a task beyond the ability of every US ambassador who served in Baghdad between 2004 and 2012. Not only did the coordination of the reconstruction project fail, but no coherent master plan was ever developed. This forced repeated rethinks on the targets, ethos and emphasis of this gargantuan task. A US Government Assessment Team sent to Baghdad in April 2008, to judge the best way that civilian development could capitalise on the progress of the military surge, concluded:

> The United States Government's advisory effort in Iraq is best described as fragmented and incoherent … Coalition efforts have suffered from the lack of a coherent strategy that outlines priorities and assigns lead responsibility to a specific directorate or agency. The ministerial surge that followed the reinforced security effort of 2007 resulted in more advisors arriving in Baghdad, but not in a focused effort.

The report went on to cite a lack of coordination between civilian and military reconstruction efforts, too few Arabic speakers and the restrictive nature of security arrangements as reasons why efforts at rebuilding the Iraqi state had failed.[60]

The second obstacle was insecurity. The increasing levels of politically motivated violence between 2003 and 2007 reduced the emphasis placed on economic reconstruction. John Negroponte, the first US ambassador to Iraq after the CPA had been disbanded, quickly shifted the focus of American funding from reconstruction to security and the political support of the 2005 elections. As a result, the budgets for rebuilding the water and electricity sectors saw cuts of between a quarter and a half.[61] In August 2006, USAID launched the *Tatweer* project, a US$165m training programme focused on the ministries of planning, finance, oil, electricity and water. The commencement of this landmark reconstruction project coincided with the start of the most destructive period of Iraq's civil war. Understandably, the effective training of Iraqi civil servants proved to be impossible as they became prime targets for assassination at the height of the conflict.

The third obstacle was the political system itself: the exclusive elite pact built around the Governing Council in 2003, and then institutionalised after two sets of national elections in 2005, directly hindered reconstruction efforts. The creation of governments of 'national unity' in 2006 and again in 2010 sought to bring all the major electoral winners into the cabinet. In effect, unity was achieved by rewarding the parties who entered government with complete autonomy to use the ministries they were given control of as they saw fit. Ministries were purged of non-aligned civil servants and their payrolls used to buy party loyalty through employment. The technocrats who had survived de-Ba'athification and who understood how government worked were sacked or intimidated into leaving their ministries. In their place friends, followers or faction members aligned to the ministers and their parties were employed. After 2005, as party affiliation dictated government employment, the ability of the newly employed civil servants to do the job they were hired for rapidly declined, reducing government efficiency. Government payrolls meanwhile were increased as the influence of party patronage spread. Statistics suggest that, since 2005, the number of people employed by the state has risen from 1.2m to 2.3m. In 2006, the statistics agency of the Iraqi Ministry of Planning estimated that the state employed 31% of Iraq's labour force and estimated that this would rise to 35% by 2008. This would put state employment just 5% lower than the CIA's estimates for 2003 before Saddam was removed.[62] For the political parties who dominate Iraq today, the primary function of the civilian arms of the state is to provide jobs and resources, political patronage, for their members. The fact that using the state in this way is highly corrosive, directly impeding the government's ability to deliver services to the population, is of secondary concern when compared to the benefits that political sanctioned corruption can deliver to the ruling elite.

The Iraqi state today

Although US financial support for reconstruction rapidly declined at the end of 2011, in conjunction with its troop presence, the Iraqi state does not lack the revenue to continue rebuilding its own institutions. The government budget has increased from US$24.4b in 2005 to US$100.4bn in 2012. In 2012, 32% of this budget was earmarked for rebuilding.[63] However, with 90% of government expenditure derived from oil exports, the budget is conditional upon the international market price of oil and at least maintaining existing levels of oil output. Evidence of the instability this can cause was seen in early 2009, when oil prices dipped below US$50 a barrel, forcing a rapid curtailment in the government's developmental spending.[64]

The cumulative results of draconian sanctions, three wars, looting and civil war ensured sustained neglect of national infrastructure and the state's inability to deliver even basic services to its population. This still remains the case, with the last major water treatment plants to be built before 2003 being finished in the 1980s, with some plants still servicing Baghdad surviving from the 1930s. In 2011, the UN estimated that only 26% of the population was covered by the public sewerage network. This leaves 83% of the country's waste water untreated. Two-thirds of Iraqi households rely directly on the public water supply for drinking water, but in 2012 surveys suggested that up to 25% of them received only two hours of water per day. Overall, UN figures suggest that 7.6m people or 25% of the population lack access to safe drinking water.[65]

From the 1990s onwards, it has been the government's ability to supply electricity to its population that has become the popular benchmark of its efficiency. Iraqi public opinion blames power cuts and the accompanying end of government television transmissions from Baghdad in 1990 as the catalyst for the uprising that spread across the south and north of the country in March that year. If the government could no longer supply electricity it was not considered to be in control. Conversely, when the southern rebellions were violently suppressed in 1991, the re-establishment of the electricity supply across the south and centre of the country became a major propaganda issue for the government to show that Saddam was in control and ministering to his population's needs. In reality, under the Ba'ath electricity was rationed to gain the maximum political benefits for the regime, whereby Baghdad and the regime's heartlands obtained preferential treatment. By the 1990s, the official maximum output of Iraq's electricity industry was 9,000 megawatts of power per year. However in 1991, after the national grid was restored, actual output hovered around 2,325 megawatts. Once the UN-managed Oil-for-Food Programme delivered reconstruction materials, the government was able to push that figure up to 4,000 megawatts by 2002.[66]

Given the centrality of the electricity supply to popular conceptions of government capacity, the CPA made the national grid's reconstruction a key priority after the invasion, earmarking US$5.7bn for the purpose and setting a target of 6,000 megawatts of electricity output.[67] The CPA focused on building a series of gas-turbine plants as the quickest way to boost production. However, Iraq's hydrocarbon sector did not produce enough gas to keep the power plants running and did not have the required technical expertise to service the plants once they were built. By the time the CPA was closed down, it had increased pre-war production levels by just 200 megawatts.[68] In 2012, Iraq's electricity production remained largely dependent on gas, and was still dogged by insufficient supplies.[69] Until the elections of 2010, the oil and electricity ministries found it difficult to work harmoniously together, an outcome of the larger political tensions that had fractured the cabinet into separate and warring ministerial fiefdoms.

By April 2012 output had increased to 7,918 megawatts. However, some of this increase was delivered through importing electricity from Iran and Turkey, and even these increases have not kept pace with consumer demand. Once sanctions were lifted in 2003 and Iraq's borders opened to consumer goods, especially refrigerators and air conditioning units, demand is estimated to have increased by 10% a year.[70] The Ministry of Electricity estimates that its supplies are meeting 60% of demand. Nationwide surveys carried out by the Iraqi Knowledge Network in 2011 found that the average household received just 7.6 hours of electricity from the national grid each day, with 79% of those surveyed rating electricity delivery as bad or very bad.[71]

The popular resentment at the continuing weakness of state institutions and their inability to deliver the level of services required is amplified and exacerbated by the justified perception that widespread corruption amongst the ruling elite is the major cause of state weakness. In August 2011, with temperatures reaching 50 degrees Centigrade, the Minister of Electricity, Ra'ad Shalal al-Ani, was forced to resign when it emerged that he had signed US$1.7bn of suspect contracts for developing Iraq's electricity industry with two dubious companies from Canada and Germany. The pervasive nature of corruption is a major cause of institutional weakness. In both 2010 and 2011, Transparency International's *Corruption*

Perceptions Index placed Iraq at 175th out of 182 countries.[72] The World Bank produced comparable figures in its Worldwide Governance Indicators. It rated countries out of 100 on the basis of the rigour of their anti-corruption institutions. Iraq scored five points.[73] Judge Radhi Hamza al-Radhi, the most senior government figure responsible for pursuing corruption from 2008 to 2011, identified the government's contracting process as 'the father of all corruption issues in Iraq'.[74] Contracts are frequently awarded to companies run by or very close to senior Iraqi politicians. The companies are then given large cash down payments before work is started, but complaints of poor or non-existent work are ignored as the companies are protected by the same politicians who ensured that they won the contracts in the first place.

Two institutions are tasked with tackling corruption. The older of the two is the Board of Supreme Audit, which was set up in 1927. The second, the Commission of Public Integrity (CPI), was created under the US occupation. The Board of Supreme Audit is responsible for auditing all of Iraq's government ministries, whereas the Commission of Public Integrity is mandated to both investigate and help prosecute corruption cases. The CPI has managed some successful prosecutions. In February 2012, it announced that 1,661 people had been convicted for corruption in 2011, an increase of 21% on the previous year. However, a closer examination of these cases indicates that the majority were comparatively small-scale or minor cases of forgery.[75] The distinct lack of major prosecutions is explainable by the intense political pressures the CPI operates under. Two of the four commissioners who have run the CPI since 2007 have resigned citing political interference. Radhi Hamza al-Radhi left his job in 2007 and fled to the United States after his house was attacked and he was warned he was on a death list. Judge Raheem al-Ugaili served in the post from 2008 until 2011. He then handed in his resignation, citing the prime minister's call for his departure in a major public speech as one reason. He went on to argue that senior politicians within the government are effectively immune from prosecution and operate in complete secrecy, spending public money with little oversight.[76] A leaked US Embassy report concluded in 2007 that 'Iraq is not capable of even rudimentary enforcement of anti-corruption laws'. There is no reason to suggest there has been any significant change to the situation since then.

Conclusion

US counter-insurgency doctrine identifies weak or illegitimate government as the root cause of rebellion, as those wishing to deploy violence for political ends operate within the space vacated by state failure and use the alienation of the population to gain support for an insurrection. The coercive arms of the Iraqi state, its army, police and intelligence services, were rebuilt in haste after the US occupation disbanded their predecessors in 2003. Today, after the US military has largely vacated the country, Iraq's security services are on balance probably coherent and powerful enough to impose a rough-and-ready order on the majority of the population. However, in order for the Iraqi state to maintain its current monopoly on the large-scale deployment of violence, its civil institutions need to function in Iraqi society and gain legitimacy from the population by delivering essential services. The weakness of the civilian institutions of the Iraqi state, exacerbated by widespread corruption, means that it is not coherent enough to have a sustained or legitimate presence in Iraqi society. For Iraq's ruling elite this means that the state will remain illegitimate, or at best tolerated as a necessary evil, which provides order but little else. At worst, such a weak and obviously corrupt state could, once again, provide the breeding-ground for increased political violence. The great danger is that Iraq's democracy will be swept aside because its institutions are not valued, or seen as worth defending.

Notes

1 *Counterinsurgency Field Manual,* FM 3-24 (Washington DC: Headquarters, Department of the Army, 2006), page 1, paragraph 166 (1-116).

2 Special Inspector General for Iraq Reconstruction, *Quarterly Report and Semiannual Report to the United States Congress,* 30 April 2012, p. 2, http://www.sigir.mil/files/quarterlyreports/April2012/Report_-_April_2012.pdf#view=fit; Special Inspector General for Iraq Reconstruction, *Hard Lessons: The Iraq Reconstruction Experience* (Washington DC: US Government Printing Office, 2009) , p. vii, http://www.sigir.mil/publications/hardLessons.html.

3 Sam Dagher, 'Iraqis Face Uncertain Future as US Ends Combat Mission', *Wall Street Journal,* 27 August 2010, http://online.wsj.com/article/SB10001424052748704913704575453303215595156.html; Martin Chulov, 'Iraq Tries To Play Down General's Remarks over US Withdrawal', *The Guardian,* 12 August 2010, http://www.guardian.co.uk/world/2010/aug/12/iraq-general-unease-us-withdrawal.

4 See 'Letter from L. Paul Bremer to George W. Bush', 22 May 2003, subsequently published in the *New York Times,* http://www.nytimes.com/ref/washington/04bremer-text1.html?ref=washington.

5 Rajiv Chandrasekaran, *Imperial life in the Emerald City: Inside Baghdad's Green Zone* (London: Bloomsbury, 2007), p. 85.

6 Eric Schmitt, 'US Plans Iraqi Force for Civil Defence', *International Herald Tribune,* 21 July 2003.

7 Special Inspector General for Iraq Reconstruction, *Hard Lessons,* p. 133.

8 *Ibid.,* p. 134.

9 Sabrina Tavernise and John F. Burns, 'As Iraqi Army Trains, Word in the Field Is It May Take Years', *New York Times,* 13 June 2005, http://www.nytimes.com/2005/06/13/international/middleeast/13training.html.

10 Ricks, *The Gamble,* p. 199.

11 Anthony Cordesman, *Iraqi Force Development: A Progress Report, Working Draft,* Center for Strategic and International Studies, Washington DC, 23 August 2007, http://csis.org/files/media/csis/pubs/070823_iraqi_force_development.pdf; Special Inspector General for Iraq Reconstruction, *Quarterly Report and Semiannual Report to the United States Congress,* 30 July 2011, p. 70, http://www.sigir.mil/files/quarterlyreports.

12 Special Inspector General for Iraq Reconstruction, *Quarterly Report and Semiannual Report to the United States Congress,* 30 January 2012 , p. 68, http://www.sigir.mil/files/quarterlyreports/January2012/Report_-_January_2012.pdf.

13 See Dodge, 'The Ideological Roots of Failure', pp. 1,269–86.

14 See Toby Dodge, 'Cake Walk, Coup or Urban Warfare: The Battle for Iraq', in Toby Dodge and Steven Simon (eds), *Iraq at the Crossroads: State*

and Society in the Shadow of Regime Change (London and Oxford: International Institute for Strategic Studies and Oxford University Press, 2003), pp. 59–75.

15 General James L. Jones, *The Report of the Independent Commission on the Security Forces of Iraq*, September 2007 , p. 55, http://csis.org/program/independent-commission-security-forces-iraq.

16 See Samuel Huntington, *Political Order in Changing Societies* (New Haven, CT: Yale University Press, 1968), pp. 192, 216; S.E. Finer, *The Man on Horseback: The Role of the Military in Politics* (Harmondsworth: Penguin, 1976), pp. 104, 200.

17 The Ministry of Defence employs a total of 271,400 personnel, spread between the Iraqi Army (193,421), the Air Force (5,053) and subsidiary organisations. The Ministry of Interior employs 531,000. The Iraqi police service has 302,000 on its payroll, including the Facilities Protection Service 95,000, Border Enforcement 60,000, Iraqi Federal Police 44,000 and Oil Police 30,000, according to the Special Inspector General for Iraq Reconstruction, *Quarterly Report and Semiannual Report to the United States Congress*, p. 75.

18 Anthony H. Cordesman with Adam Mausner and Lena Derby, *Iraq and the United States: Creating a Strategic Partnership* (Washington DC: Centre for Strategic and International Studies, June 2010), p. 312.

19 Special Inspector General for Iraq Reconstruction, *Quarterly Report to the United States Congress*, 30 October 2010, p. 34, http://www.sigir.mil/files/quarterlyreports/October2010/Report_-_October_2010.pdf#view=fit.

20 International Institute for Strategic Studies, *The Military Balance 2013* (forthcoming), p. 41.

21 Jane Arraf, 'Iraqi Army: Almost One-quarter Lacks Minimum Qualifications', *Christian Science Monitor*, 22 May 2009, http://www.csmonitor.com/2009/0522/p06s07-wome.html.

22 Timothy Williams and Oma al Jawoshy, 'Drug and Alcohol Abuse Growing in Iraqi Forces', *New York Times*, 24 October 2010, http://www.nytimes.com/2010/10/25/world/middleeast/25baghdad.html.

23 Barak A. Salmoni, 'Responsible Partnership: The Iraqi National Security Sector after 2011', *Policy Focus*, no. 112, Washington Institute for Near East Policy, May 2011, p. 10, http://www.washingtoninstitute.org/templateC04.php?CID=343.

24 See 'Text of memo from Col. Timothy R. Reese, Chief, Baghdad Operations Command Advisory Team, MND-B, Baghdad, Iraq', 30 July 2009, http://www.nytimes.com/2009/07/31/world/middleeast/31advtext.html.

25 Anthony H. Cordesman, *The US Transition in Iraq: Iraqi Forces and US Military Aid*, 21 October 2010, p. 21, http://csis.org/files/publication/101019_IraqiForcesMilAid.pdf.

26 Salmoni, 'Responsible Partnership', p. 11; Cordesman, Mausner and Derby, *Iraq and the United States*, p. 269.

27 Steven Lee Myers, 'Concerns Mount on Preparedness of Iraq's Forces', *New York Times*, 7 May 2009, http://www.nytimes.com/2009/05/08/world/middleeast/08security.html.

28 Alexandra Zavis, 'Iraq Army Still Needs US Support, Commanders Say', *Los Angeles Times*, 1 September, 2008, http://www.latimes.com/news/nationworld/iraq/complete/la-fg-

army1-2008sep01,0,7199960.story; Ernesto Londoño, 'Lower Oil Prices Put Iraq's Security Forces in Bind at Crucial Time', *Washington Post*, 20 May 2009, http://www.washingtonpost.com/wp-dyn/content/article/2009/05/19/AR2009051903259.html; Nir Rosen, 'Iraq's Fragile Peace Rests on Its Own Forces', *The National*, 9 September 2010, http://thenational.ae/apps/pbcs.dll/article?AID=/20100910/REVIEW/709099998/1008.

29 Michael Knights, 'The Iraqi Security Forces: Local Context and US Assistance', *Policy Notes*, no. 4, Washington Institute for Near East Policy, June 2011, http://www.washingtoninstitute.org/templateC04.php?CID=344, p. 6.

30 Jones, *The Report of the Independent Commission on the Security Forces of Iraq*, p. 45.

31 International Crisis Group, 'Loose Ends: Iraq's Security Forces between US Drawdown and Withdrawal', *Middle East Report*, no. 99, 26 October 2010, p. 18.

32 Jones, *The Report of the Independent Commission on the Security Forces of Iraq*, p. 80, Cordesman, *Iraqi Force Development*, p. 30; Tim Arrango, 'Iraq's Forces Prove Able, But Loyalty Is Uncertain', *New York Times*, 13 April 2010, http://www.nytimes.com/2010/04/14/world/middleeast/14security.html.

33 Nada Bakri, 'In Iraq, Battling an Internal Bane', *Washington Post*, 22 October 2009, http://www.washingtonpost.com/wp-dyn/content/article/2009/10/21/AR2009102103617.html.

34 See, for example, the memo that then National Security Adviser Steven Hadley wrote about Maliki upon returning from Baghdad in November, 2006. 'Text of US Security Adviser's Iraq Memo', *New York Times*, 29 November, 2006, http://www.nytimes.com/2006/11/29/world/middleeast/29mtext.html.

35 Salmoni, 'Responsible Partnership', p. 14.

36 Robinson, *Tell Me How This Ends*, p. 157.

37 Cordesman, Mausner and Derby, *Iraq and the United States*, p. 268.

38 International Crisis Group, 'Loose Ends', p. 7.

39 Shane Bauer, 'Iraq's New Death Squad', *The Nation*, 22 June 2009, http://www.thenation.com/doc/20090622/bauer.

40 Department of Defense, *Measuring Stability and Security in Iraq*, December 2009, p. 66, http://www.defense.gov/pubs/pdfs/Master_9204_29Jan10_FINAL_SIGNED.pdf.

41 Nir Rosen, 'Iraqi Security Forces and the Iraqi Political Mess', *The National*, 3 September 2010, http://www.thenational.ae/news/worldwide/middle-east/iraqs-fragile-peace-rests-on-its-own-forces.

42 International Crisis Group, 'Loose Ends', p. 11.

43 Patrick Cockburn, 'The US Can Quit Iraq, Or It Can Stay, But It Can't Do Both', *The Independent*, 11 November 2008, https://www.commondreams.org/view/2008/11/11-5.

44 David Ignatius 'Behind the Carnage in Baghdad', *Washington Post*, 25 August 2009, http://www.washingtonpost.com/wpdyn/content/article/2009/08/24/AR2009082402491.html.

45 International Crisis Group, 'Loose Ends', pp. 8–10.

46 Shashank Bengali, 'WikiLeaks: Maliki Filled Iraqi Security Services with Shiites', *McClatchy*, 3 December 2010, http://www.mcclatchydc.

com/2010/12/03/104726/us-cables-say-maliki-filled-iraqi.html.

47 Joel S. Migdal, *Strong Societies and Weak States: State-Society Relations and State Capabilities in the Third World* (Princeton, NJ: Princeton University Press, 1988).

48 Andrea Kathryn Talentino, 'The Two Faces of Nation-building: Developing Function and Identity', *Cambridge Review of International Affairs*, vol. 17, no. 3, October 2004, pp. 557, 571.

49 Isam al-Khafaji, 'The Myth of Iraqi Exceptionalism', *Middle East Policy*, vol. 7, no. 4, October, 2000, p. 68.

50 Charles Tripp, *A History of Iraq* (Cambridge: Cambridge University Press, 2000), pp. 205–6.

51 Peter Boone, Haris Gazdar and Athar Hussain, 'Sanctions against Iraq: Costs of Failure', paper delivered at the conference 'Frustrated Development: The Iraqi Economy in War and in Peace', Centre for Gulf Studies, University of Exeter, in collaboration with the Iraqi Economic Forum, 1997, pp. 9, 40.

52 Nikki van der Gaage, 'Iraq: The Pride and the Pain', *New Internationalist*, no. 316, 1999, p. 8.

53 Khafaji, 'The Myth of Iraqi Exceptionalism', p. 82.

54 Phillips, *Losing Iraq*, p. 135.

55 Larry Diamond, *Squandered Victory: The American Occupation and the Bungled Effort To Bring Democracy to Iraq* (New York: Times Books, 2005), p. 282; Packer, *Assassins' Gate*, p. 111.

56 See David L. Phillips, *Losing Iraq: Inside the Post-war Reconstruction Fiasco* (New York: Basic Books, 2005), pp. 145–6; L. Paul Bremer III with Malcolm McConnell, *My Year in Iraq: The Struggle to Build a Future of Hope* (New York: Simon & Schuster, 2006), p. 40; George Packer, *Assassins' Gate: America in Iraq* (New York: Farrar, Straus and Giroux, 2005), p. 191.

57 Chandrasekaran, *Imperial Life in the Emerald City*, pp. 79–80.

58 Special Inspector General for Iraq Reconstruction, *Hard Lessons*, pp. 95–6.

59 Special Inspector General for Iraq Reconstruction, *Quarterly Report*, 30 April 2012, pp. 17, 24.

60 Report of the Government Assessment Team, Baghdad, 24 April, 2008, p. 2.

61 Special Inspector General for Iraq Reconstruction, *Hard Lessons*, p. 170.

62 Campbell Robertson, 'Iraq Private Sector Falters; Rolls of Government Soar', *New York Times*, 10 August, 2008, http://www.nytimes.com/2008/08/11/world/middleeast/11baghdad.html.

63 Joel Wing, '2010 Iraq Budget Passed', 28 January 2010, http://musingsoniraq.blogspot.co.uk/2010/01/2010-iraq-budget-passed.html; Special Inspector General for Iraq Reconstruction, *Quarterly Report*, 30 April 2012, p. 9, http://www.sigir.mil/files/quarterlyreports/April2012/Report_-_April_2012.pdf.

64 Liz Sly, 'Economic Downturn Finally Hits Iraq', *Los Angeles Times*, 11 May 2009, http://www.latimes.com/news/nationworld/world/la-fg-iraq-economy11-2009may11,0,6735436.story.

65 Special Inspector General for Iraq Reconstruction, *Quarterly Report*, 30 January 2011, p. 98, 30 April, p. 119 and 30 January 2012, p. 76.

66 Special Inspector General for Iraq Reconstruction, *Hard Lessons*, p. 146.

67 Allawi, *The Occupation of Iraq*, pp. 257–58.

68 Special Inspector General for Iraq Reconstruction, *Hard Lessons*, p. 152.

69 Ben Lando, 'Power Problems May Continue Through Summer', *Iraq Oil*

Report, 21 January 2011, http://www.iraqoilreport.com/energy/electricity/power-problems-may-continue-through-summer-5296.

70 *Ibid.*

71 Iraq Knowledge Network, 'Essential Services Fact Sheet', December 2011, http://www.iauiraq.org/documents/1583/ServicesFactsheet-English.pdf.

72 Transparency International, *Corruption Perceptions Index 2011*, http://cpi.transparency.org/cpi2011/results.

73 Special Inspector General for Iraq Reconstruction, *Quarterly Report and Semiannual Report to the United States Congress*, 30 January 2012, p. 9, http://www.sigir.mil/files/quarterlyreports/January2012/Report_-_January_2012.pdf.

74 Special Inspector General for Iraq Reconstruction, *Quarterly Report and Semiannual Report to the United States Congress*, 30 July 2011, p. 8, http://www.sigir.mil/files/quarterlyreports/July2011/Report_-_July_2011.pdf.

75 Special Inspector General for Iraq Reconstruction, *Quarterly Report and Semiannual Report to the United States Congress*, 30 April 2012, p. 89. http://www.sigir.mil/publications/quarterlyreports/April2012.html.

76 Special Inspector General for Iraq Reconstruction, *Quarterly Report and Semiannual Report to the United States Congress*, 30 April 2011, pp. 5–6, http://www.sigir.mil/files/quarterlyreports/April2011/Report_-_April_2011.pdf.

CHAPTER FIVE

The politics of Iraq: the exclusive elite bargain and the rise of a new authoritarianism

The final cause of the civil war was political: the elite bargain and exclusive pact that was placed at the core of the new governing system in 2005. The elite bargain was struck between the political parties that had gained dominance in exile by aligning themselves with the United States in the run-up to the invasion. Sovereignty was transferred back to their key representatives in 2004. A 'leadership council', consisting of senior politicians from four of the main parties, then went on to write Iraq's new constitution. The elite bargain, using the justification of de-Ba'athification, set about deliberately excluding key sections of society from government. Those affected were not only senior members of the old ruling elite; the exclusive elite pact also sought to marginalise the wider Sunni section of Iraqi society, and indeed, because of the use of religious and ethnic markers for political mobilisation, secular and nationalist Iraqis as well. This exclusion induced widespread alienation among those who were politically marginalised, and a segment of those excluded deployed violence in an attempt to overturn the new political settlement. For the Iraqi political system to stabilise and become sustainable over the long term, this exclusive elite pact will have to be remodelled. Iraq's Sunni community and those not mobilised along ethnic and religious lines also need to be fully reintegrated into national politics and offered a stake in the new political system.

Attempting to break Iraq's exclusive elite bargain

It was the politics of exclusion that fuelled the cycle of violence that drove Iraq into a communal civil war. By 2006, the conflict was being justified in aggressively divisive sectarian language. Sectarianism was used to justify the imposition of the post-war order and those seeking to overturn it. However, the imposition of counter-insurgency doctrine to Iraq by the US military from February 2007 onwards dramatically reduced the violence. US Special Forces successfully targeted the mid- to top-level civil-war commanders who had been driving the conflict, removing them from the battle. Along with the steady reduction in violence, by 2008 the United States' attempts at rebuilding the Iraqi security forces were finally bearing fruit. The expansion of the Iraqi military progressively reduced the space within which the insurgents could operate.

By 2008–09, the steady improvement in security began to influence public opinion, transforming the rhetoric that shaped Iraqi politics and the voting patterns of the Iraqi population. As the International Crisis Group argued in January 2009:

> Former confessional blocs are fraying, as sectarianism is increasingly challenged by more nationalist sentiment and promises of better governance by political actors seeking to capture the public mood. Competition between communities is joined by competition within them.[1]

The reduction of sectarian mobilisation was aided by changes in the voting system. The first set of national elections, in January 2005 (see Appendix one for full list of election results), were held with one nationwide electoral constituency. This was recommended by the UN as a way to minimise the risks posed by disorganisation and violence.[2] However, it also favoured those parties seeking to maximise their vote through the use of sectarian rhetoric. Local issues and personalities were minimised during the campaign; politicians and parties were marshalled into large coalitions,[3] and candidates played to the lowest common denominator, deploying ethnic and sectarian rhetoric to define and then mobilise their constituencies. The December 2005 elections were conducted through a 'closed list system', where voters chose between the now-dominant national parties mobilised within large coalitions, not individual candidates. These parties coordinated the campaign around the ethnic and religious divisions in Iraqi society. In both sets of elections held in 2005, ethnic and sectarian mobilisation triumphed. The majority of Sunnis who voted backed the Iraqi Accord Front (Tawafuq), which ran a Sunni Islamist campaign. Allawi's National Iraqi List tried to buck the sectarian trend by overtly courting the secular, urban and nationalist middle classes. In a country dominated by state collapse, the flight of the middle class into exile, the onset of a civil war and an atmosphere of profound uncertainty, this electoral platform could only muster about 9% of the vote in December 2005.[4]

The electoral system was changed for the January 2009 provincial elections. A 'modified list' system was used, allowing voters to choose both parties and, more importantly, individual candidates.[5] The effects were dramatic. The provincial election campaign was suffused with arguments about government effectiveness, the competence of the provincial councils elected in 2005 and debates about the best way to run the Iraqi state.

The Islamic Supreme Council of Iraq (ISCI) deliberately set out to recapture the success that an overtly religious approach had given it in 2005. It named its narrow coalition Qaimat Shahid al-Mihrab was al-Quwatt al-Mustaqilla ('The Martyr of Mihrab and Independent Forces List'). This was a name imbued with meaning, referring both to the death in 661 of Ali, the Prophet Muhammad's cousin and son-in-law and founder of the Shia branch of Islam, and the murder of the head of the ISCI, Muhammad Baqir al-Hakim, shortly after his return to Iraq in 2003. The ISCI saw a sharp decline in its share of the vote. The result signalled that its overtly sectarian approach to the elections had badly misjudged the mood of the Iraqi population. The country had recently emerged from one of the worst periods of a civil war that had been largely justified by aggressive sectarian ideology. By 2009, Iraqis were exhausted by division and strife, and used their votes to back parties campaigning on issues of security and government effectiveness.[6]

In the wake of the provincial elections, the ISCI, along with the other two parties that based their main claim to electoral appeal on religious and ethnic identity politics, the Kurdistan Democratic Party (KDP) and the Patriotic Union of Kuridistan (PUK), attempted to block legislation that would have extended the 'modified list' voting system to the 2010 national elections.[7] Intriguingly, Grand Ayatollah Ali al-Sistani, the most senior Shia religious authority in the country, threw his considerable moral weight behind support for the modified list system in the 2010 elections.[8] It was reported at the time that he had become increasingly frustrated with the corruption, sectarianism and government incoherence associated with the existing political system. The stage was now set for the first sustained electoral challenge to the exclusive elite pact that had dominated Iraq since 2003, and which played a major role in driving the country into civil war.

In the run-up to the 2010 national elections (see Appendix one), Allawi set out to capitalise on the decline in sectarian politics. He benefitted from a reduction in the popular acceptance of communalist ideology. From 2003 onwards, the Iraqi Islamic Party (IIP) had played a key role in the exclusive elite pact. It was meant to be the vehicle through which the Sunni section of Iraqi society would be brought into the pact specifically as Sunnis, mobilised and delivered to the ballot box through their religious identity. To do this, the IIP set up Tawafuq, a broader electoral coalition.[9] As violence declined, and with it the assertion of aggressive sectarian politics, tensions amongst the parties within Tawafuq grew as key members sought to distance the organisation from the exclusive assertion of a Sunni identity. These tensions came to a head in 2008, when a number of prominent personalities left the coalition.[10] This allowed Allawi the freedom to build a much broader-based organisation to fight the 2010 national elections. It brought together a coalition built around 18 parties. In addition to his own party, Allawi was joined by two prominent former politicians who had broken with the IIP, Vice-President Tariq al-Hashimi and his party Tajdeed and Rafi al-Issawi, the head of Mustaqbal. Saleh al-Mutlaq also brought his Hiwar Party within the fold. Two other prominent politicians from Mosul, the brothers Usama and Atheel al-Nujaifi, then followed.[11] These moves created an organisation that combined senior politicians enjoying national recognition with local personalities and regional political organisations that could effectively mobilise voters in their communities.

After the disastrous poll results of December 2005, Allawi had adopted a low profile, spending his time largely abroad. As a consequence, his party and coalition were not a major force in parliament. However, by 2010 this gave them a distinct advantage as they were free from the taint in the popular consciousness associated with the civil war, corruption and government incoherence. Allawi the set out to make the Iraqi National Movement (Iraqiyya) as wide and as coherent an electoral coalition as possible. All parties that joined overtly committed themselves to a secular nationalist electoral platform. Allawi then played on his image as a strong man to promote law and order, as well as an anti-Iranian message that promised to reintegrate Iraq into the wider Arab world.[12]

The combination of a united electoral front, the changing ideological parameters within which Iraqi politics were now conducted and strong local organisation delivered a potentially revolutionary result for Iraqiyya. It won 91 seats, compared to 89 for the prime minister's State of Law coalition and 70 for the Iraqi National Alliance (INA). The decline in the attraction of an overtly sectarian platform was reflected in the fact that Tawafuq won just six seats, or 1.8% of the national vote. Iraqiyya took 80% of the Sunni vote, and was the only electoral coalition to secure seats in areas dominated by both Sunni and Shia voters, winning 12 seats in Shia-majority areas.[13] Such a strong, overtly secular vote raised the possibility in March 2010 that Iraq's exclusive elite pact could be swept aside and a new, more inclusive political dispensation built.

The reassertion of the exclusive elite pact in 2010

The potentially revolutionary effects of Iraqiyya's 2010 election campaign and victory triggered an aggressive defence of the existing system by those who had benefitted from it most. This was a blatant attempt to trigger a return to the sectarian politics of the previous five years. Its proponents hoped that this would solidify voting blocs along religious and ethnic lines to deliver the desired election results. To this end, the first steps were taken two months before the vote. In early January 2010, the Justice and Accountability Commission, the government agency charged with implementing the de-Ba'athification process set in motion by the Americans, issued edicts to ban 511 individual candidates and 14 party lists from the elections.[14] The committee's chair, Ahmed Chalabi, and its director general, Ali Faysal al-Lami, were both parliamentary candidates for the INA coalition.[15] This flagrant conflict of interest signified both the political nature of the exclusions and the fragility of the whole political system, in which governmental institutions had been colonised by political parties and run as private fiefdoms. The Iraqi High Electoral Council, the organisation charged with delivering a free and fair election, simply rubber-stamped the de-Ba'athification orders.[16]

The lack of a legal basis for the exclusion of the 511 candidates also reflected how tenuous the rule of law in Iraq remained. Only two pieces of legislation passed by the Iraqi parliament dealt specifically with de-Ba'athification. The first, Article Seven of the Iraqi constitution, simply forbids the glorification or promotion of 'Saddamist Ba'athism' in Iraq. The second piece of relevant legislation is the Justice and Accountability Law of January 2008, which stipulates that high-ranking former Ba'athists are subject to de-Ba'athification.[17] But Lami made it clear in a public statement accompanying the exclusions that the most influential politician to be banned from the elections, Saleh al-Mutlaq and his party, the Iraqi Front for National Dialogue, was not excluded under this legislation. Mutlaq had actually been expelled from the Ba'ath Party in 1977. He had not been prevented from participating in the drafting committee of the new Iraqi constitution in 2005 and had led a party that won 11 seats in the December 2005 elections.[18]

The political aim of the de-Ba'athification orders becomes obvious when examining its effect on Maliki's coalition and the INA, run by the ISCI. Neither coalition was much affected by the ban, and nor were the coalitions seeking to maximise the

Kurdish vote. Overtly Sunni sectarian groups, Tawafuq and the parties seeking to mobilise the Sunni tribes of Anbar involved in the Awakening Movement were also largely unaffected, though they clearly had ex-Ba'athists in their membership.[19] It was the coalitions who sought to build cross-sectarian support – in particular Allawi's Iraqiyya – that saw the largest number of their candidates excluded. This implies that state institutions were being manipulated to increase sectarian tension as an election ploy and to deliberately hinder the evolution of a non-sectarian more inclusive politics in Iraq. More worrying still was that these same institutions were being used to break the political cohesion of those electoral coalitions trying to win votes on a secular, non-sectarian nationalist platform. Those parties and coalitions trying to maximise an exclusively Sunni vote posed no threat to the prime minister and the other Shia coalition, the INA, and were hence left alone.

Although it is hard to tell if Maliki was party to the initial decision to issue the banning edicts, he publicly threw his support behind them, hoping that they would mobilise the Shia section of the electorate, which had become increasingly alienated by corruption and weak government. Those, including the prime minster, who advocated the mass exclusion of candidates from the election, must have known that, at the very least, this would inflame sectarian tensions and encourage politically motivated violence. Despite this danger, in the aftermath of the bans the 'Ba'athist threat' became a key plank of Maliki's election campaign. When faced with an increasingly cynical electorate alienated by his government's continued inability to deliver jobs and services, Maliki chose to conjure up the spectre of Ba'athism, playing to sectarian sentiment in order to solidify his vote.

Given the fractious and unconstitutional nature of the election campaign, the close result and the potentially revolutionary ramifications of the outcome, it is no surprise that the process of government formation was bitter, punctuated by mistrust and very time-consuming. Negotiations lasted 249 days from polling until the formation of the government (compared to 156 days in 2005).

The political deadlock was shaped by two opposing fears. On the one hand, most of Iraq's ruling elite was deeply perturbed that Iraqiyya's election victory could herald far-reaching changes to the whole political system. The rise to prominence of a coalition that won its votes on an overtly secular platform was a direct threat not only to the exclusive elite pact, but also to the political logic of the whole system. Since 2003, and crucially in the aftermath of both elections in 2005, governments of national unity were formed through the application of *muhasasa* (sectarian apportionment), the principle that all of Iraq's sectarian and religious communities should be given cabinet posts as a way of delivering social harmony.[20] The rise of an overtly non-sectarian vote placed the validity of this system in doubt. How was Iraqiyya to be integrated into a system that only recognised parties organised along ethnic and religious lines?

On the other hand, the same ruling elite was also deeply concerned that the centralising ambition of Maliki, witnessed during his first term in office, could lead to dictatorship if he was reappointed in 2010. In the end, with US backing, the status quo and the vested interests it protected won out over fears of Maliki's dictatorial ambitions.

The final breakthrough came in November 2010. Maliki used the threat of Allawi and the potentially far-reaching ramifications of Iraqiyya's vote to impose a rough-and-ready unity on the Kurdish and Shia parties, which had much to lose from an Allawi premiership. Barzani, the head of the KDP and president of the Kurdish Regional Government (KRG) chaired three days of negotiations in Irbil to bring Allawi and Iraqiyya into yet another government of national unity. During these negotiations, key members of Allawi's coalition, Mutlaq and Nujaifi, opened separate discussions with Maliki. After securing positions for themselves in the new government – deputy prime minister and speaker of the parliament, respectively – they forced Allawi into accepting a formal deal by threatening to split Iraqiyya if he rejected it.[21]

The political practice of *muhasasa*, or the division of cabinet posts according to sectarian quotas, with its assertion of religious and ethnic identity, its defence of elite interests and its encouragement of both personal and political corruption and government incoherence, had once again triumphed. Cabinet posts and the resources they brought with them were divided between the victorious electoral coalitions and justified in the name of sectarian quotas. The other concern shaping the 250 days of negotiations – that Maliki had the makings of a dictator if he were allowed to serve another term – was placated by what became known as the 'Irbil Agreement'. Maliki signed a 15-point list of demands designed to place meaningful limits on his ability to exercise personal power while prime minister. These restrictions were meant to include the transfer of the counter-terrorism Special Forces to the Ministry of Defence and strengthening the chains of command over the army and police force. The centrepiece of the agreement was the formation of a National Council for Strategic Policy, which Allawi would chair. All major policy decisions would be sent to this council for approval before they were enacted by parliament.

The agreement struck in Irbil in November 2010 was meant to serve two purposes. By bringing Iraqiyya into another government of national unity on the basis of *muhasasa*, the rest of Iraq's governing elite hoped that the threat it posed to the political system would be curbed. Iraqiyya could now be treated as just another sectarian party, replacing Tawafuq as the representative of the Sunni vote. This would neuter the threat it posed to the political system and integrate it into the exclusive elite pact as a junior member. The threat of de-Ba'athification would be held over it to ensure that it played its allotted role and did not try to use the size and nature of its vote to reform the system as a whole. The second function of the Irbil Agreement was to restrain Maliki. The agreement was meant to remove his control over the armed forces and remove the threat that his increasing power would come to threaten the exclusive elite pact and the politicians within it. The Irbil Agreement certainly realised its first aim of co-opting and weakening Iraqiyya, but it has assuredly not delivered on the second.

The irresistible rise of Maliki

The irony of the 2010 national election saw Maliki fail to win the most votes, yet triumph as the victor. Although his coalition came second in the popular vote, he retained the premiership and skilfully escaped *all* attempts to constrain his power by inserting a number of loyalists into important cabinet positions. A comparison of the situation in 2010 to his first appointment as premier in 2006 reflects the extent to which he has successfully centralised power in his own hands and now dominates government. In the months after he became prime minister in April 2006, Baghdad was awash with rumours about a series of plots to unseat him. In 2006 and 2007, he had few if any institutions at his command. Within the Iraqi government the formal position of prime minister was deliberately weak. In the aftermath of the 2005 elections, the successful political parties divided up ministerial positions and the resources they brought with them as the spoils of electoral success. Against this background, Maliki did not control or even direct his cabinet. Instead, his role was to act as a facilitator, attempting to build a degree of consensus amongst cabinet ministers, their powerful party bosses, the US Embassy and the American military. However, from 2006 onwards Maliki successfully overcame the inherent weakness of the prime minister's position within the Iraqi system. Covertly, but with great skill, he used the fractured nature of the Iraqi cabinet and the state itself to consolidate his power.

Maliki's path to power began when his former boss, Jaafari, the leader of the Islamic Dawa Party, was appointed interim prime minister after the January 2005 elections. Because Dawa had no militia, Jaafari and Maliki were initially not seen as major threats to the other party leaders, who had to choose a compromise candidate to occupy the prime minister's office. Jaafari served as interim prime minister for 12 months. By the time of the elections for the first post-invasion full-term government in December 2005, he had alienated a number of key Iraqi politicians, as well as the British and American governments. The December elections were followed by 156 days of increasingly fractious negotiations. Finally, those involved achieved enough cohesion to remove Jaafari. Maliki, his deputy in the Islamic Dawa Party, was then chosen as a replacement because none of the other competing party bosses saw this grey functionary as a threat to their own power.

On taking office in April 2006, Maliki was confronted by the very issue that had enabled his appointment: he lacked the political power with which to govern. He simply had too few coherent governmental institutions through which to rule. Maliki's first move in his quest to secure his grip on power was to gain control over the political constituency from which he came, the Dawa Party. He succeeded in April 2007, when he sidelined his old boss, Jaafari, and was elected general-secretary of the party. He built a small and cohesive group of functionaries, the *Malikiyoun*, tied personally to him, and used them as a vehicle to consolidate his grip on state power.[22] The *Malikiyoun* comprise two separate groups. The first is composed of close family members, his son, nephews and son-in-law, who occupy sensitive positions in the Office of the Prime Minister.[23] The rest consist of Dawa Party functionaries who aligned themselves with Maliki as he took over the party and consolidated his grip on power. When faced with a fractured political elite, consumed with infighting and self-enrichment, Maliki placed the *Malikiyoun* at the centre of a network of influence and patronage that bypassed the cabinet and linked the prime minister directly to those generals and senior civil servants who were exercising state power below ministerial level. In effect, from 2006 onwards Maliki built a shadow state that circumvented the existing governing elite. It placed the Office of the Prime Minister at the centre of state power, reducing the ability of the cabinet to influence the formation and application of policy. As the networks of influence spread out from the Office of the Prime Minister into the formal institutions of the state, Maliki relied on members of his family and individuals who had allied themselves to him personally from within the ranks of Dawa. He appointed his son, Ahmed Maliki, deputy chief of staff, giving him an oversight role across all of Iraq's security services, and making him personally responsible for his father's security.[24]

Maliki's use of the Iraqi security services to personally and politically protect himself reached a new height at the end of March 2008, when he perceived a coordinated plot to unseat him. He believed that the plot against him would use an upsurge in militia violence in the southern port city of Basra as a pretext to push a vote of no confidence through the parliament in Baghdad and unseat him as prime minister.[25] To outflank this plot, Maliki launched the 'Charge of the Knights'. This operation sent four divisions of the Iraqi Army into Basra to seize control of the city back from the militias that were threatening his rule. The resulting military campaign almost ended in disaster, with defeat only avoided by the intervention of US troops and air support.[26] However, the eventual re-establishment of government authority in Basra struck a widespread popular chord with an Iraqi population long subject to criminality and sectarian violence. Maliki bolstered his new-found popular appeal in May 2008 by imposing state control over the Sadr City area in Baghdad, the huge slum that had until then been run by Jaish al-Mahdi. Maliki used this victory to stamp his authority on the Iraqi government and the armed forces, and to reshape his political image countrywide as an Iraqi nationalist and the saviour of the country.

The prime minister's new nationalist image was unveiled in the provincial election campaign of January 2009. He named his coalition Dawlat al-Qanoun or 'State of Law', in an attempt to convince the population that it was his policies and actions that had brought increased law and order to Iraq. On the campaign trail, Maliki stressed the success of the military operation in Basra and his decision to send troops into Sadr City. He also emphasised his role in challenging the KRG's expansionist policies along its boundary with the rest of Iraq. In a key campaign speech he set himself against the decentralised federal agenda of his main rivals for the Shia vote, the ISCI and its partners within the coalition government, the KDP and the PUK.[27] The prime minister then built on this popular support by portraying himself as an Iraqi nationalist and adopting a tough negotiating stance over the Status of Forces Agreement with the United States. This approach struck a chord with a population that had been mired in a sectarian civil war and endured a long American occupation. The achievements of the campaign were reflected in the election results: Maliki's coalition won the largest slice of the popular vote in nine of the 14 participating provinces.[28]

Maliki attempted to reproduce this vote-winning formula in the March 2010 national elections. He hoped to capitalise on his popularity across the south and centre of the country and on his claim to have been responsible for the drop in communal violence since 2007. However, unlike the 2005 national elections, he refused to join a united Shia coalition, the Iraqi National Alliance, designed to maximise the Shia vote. Instead, he chose to use his own coalition, State of Law, to contest the elections. This, along with the rising current of nationalism, allowed Iraqiyya to gain a slim majority (91 seats to Maliki's 89). In the period following the vote, Maliki became increasingly authoritarian as he faced potential electoral defeat. 'No way we will accept the results,' he stated bluntly, demanding a recount in order to prevent a 'return to violence'.[29] The potentially sinister implications of this statement were exacerbated in light of the fact that he issued it in his role as head of the country's armed forces. In mid-May 2010, after the recount, the electoral commission, backed by the United Nations, announced that it had found no evidence of fraud and that the vote and seat allocation remained unchanged.[30]

However, Maliki's tried-and-tested formula of encouraging divisions amongst the ruling elite, exploiting the lack of rules governing politicians' behaviour and building informal networks across government, allowed him to dismantle any attempts at limiting his power in the post-election Irbil Agreement. For the first seven months after the agreement, Maliki rejected all the candidates proposed by Iraqiyya for the ministries of defence and interior. In June 2011, he appointed his close adviser, Falih al-Fayyad, as acting minister of national security. In August, he chose the minister of culture, Saadoun al-Dulaimi, as acting minister of defence, while retaining the post of acting minister of interior for himself.[31]

By designating weak politicians or members of the *Malikiyoun*, people personally tied to him, as acting ministers, Maliki has retained control over the army, police force and intelligence services. He has successfully circumvented both the Irbil Agreement and the constitutional demand for cabinet posts to be validated by parliament. In addition, as the Irbil Agreement has no constitutional or legal standing, the only possible sanction Maliki faces for breaching it is a vote of no confidence in parliament. A senior parliamentarian, when asked about this option, bleakly commented:

> If we move towards a vote of no confidence do you think he [Maliki] would allow members to reach the chamber and if they did do you really think he would take any notice?[32]

Further concerns about Maliki's plans have been raised by his public statements about how state power will be exercised in the future. A week after US troops left Iraq, he gave a news conference in which he effectively repudiated the Irbil Agreement and threatened to move away from coalition government to majoritarian rule based around the Shia Islamist political parties.[33] The centrepiece of the agreement, the National Council for Strategic Policy, was never established and cannot play the oversight role envisioned for it.

In addition, Maliki has deployed an increasingly pliable judiciary to weaken existing institutional oversights. In January 2011, Chief Justice Medhat al-Mahmoud ruled that a series of previously independent and powerful agencies set up during the American occupation – the Committee of Integrity, the Independent High Electoral Commission (IHEC), the Central Bank of Iraq and the High Commission for Human Rights – were now subject to direct cabinet oversight. Given that the cabinet is fractious and lacks the coherence to act as a unified policymaking body, the ruling clearly increased the influence and reach of the Office of the Prime Minister.[34]

In the aftermath of the judge's ruling, the parliamentary speaker, Usama al-Nujaifi, sent a letter to the cabinet seeking to defend the Central Bank's independence. The widely respected head of the bank, Sinan al-Shabibi, and his deputy, Mudher Saleh, were then indicted on corruption charges. Shabibi was quickly replaced as the head of the Central Bank by Abdelbassit Turki, who had previously been appointed by Maliki as head of the anti-corruption organisation the Board of Supreme Audit.[35] Parliament has also seen its powers undermined by judicial ruling. In 2010, the Higher Judicial Council ruled that new legislation could only be proposed by the cabinet not parliament, thus giving the prime minister, as the dominant voice in cabinet, the ability to control the work of the legislature.[36]

More worrying still, in April 2012 Faraj al-Haidari, the head of the IHEC, was arrested on charges of corruption and then sentenced to a year in jail. The IHEC, which oversees national and provincial elections as well as any referendums, was praised by the United Nations for running a free and fair election in 2010. However, Maliki blamed the organisation when he failed to obtain a majority. The arrest and prosecution of its head and another senior official on minor corruption charges was clearly an attempt to intimidate the commission and puts the transparency and fairness of future elections in doubt.[37]

Fighting against Maliki: attempting to unseat the new strongman

As it became increasingly apparent that the Irbil Agreement had failed to curb Maliki's power, the rest of Iraq's ruling elite looked to the country's constitution for help. Iraq's new constitution was a hurriedly written and controversial document.

In 2005, when it was drafted, it was thought to represent a victory for the two dominant Kurdish parties, the PUK and the KDP. Their aim was to keep the autonomous powers they had amassed since the end of the Gulf War in 1991, while simultaneously constraining the powers of the central state so that it could not once again become a vehicle for the oppression of Iraq's Kurds. To this end, the constitution gave regions the right to exercise executive, legislative and judicial authority and to demand an equitable share of national oil revenues. Beyond the Kurdish Regional Government, the constitution also gave other governorates the right to become regions. A referendum to allow this to happen could be triggered by a provincial council vote.[38]

During 2011, key Iraqiyya politicians, particularly the speaker of the parliament, Nujaifi, and Vice-President Tariq al-Hashimi, came to the conclusion that regional decentralisation was the only way to limit Maliki's domination of Iraq.[39] Maliki's response to this constitutionally mandated challenge shows his willingness to use the state's coercive power against his opponents. He unleashed a wave of arrests across the three provinces north of Baghdad, Anbar, Salahuddin and Diyala, which have a Sunni majority.[40] It was these same three provinces that delivered a large percentage of Iraqiyya's votes in the 2010 election.

Following the crackdown, on 27 October 2011, Salahuddin Council voted to move forward with a referendum. This was followed by Diyala in mid-December, and Anbar Council threatened to follow suit a week later. More worrying still for Maliki, the oil-rich Shia-majority provinces of Wasit and Basra in the south also attempted this move in 2010 and 2011. When faced with constitutionally legitimate attempts to weaken the central state's dominance of the provinces, Maliki unleashed further repression and exerted his influence over Iraq's election commission to ensure that these referendums never took place. Instead, he blamed the moves in Salahuddin on Ba'athists and used them as justification for further waves of repression in those provinces seeking greater autonomy, arguing that 'Power-sharing cannot be the foundation of solving our problems'.[41]

It was Maliki's decisive move against the federalist threat that may have been behind the most startling attack on his political rivals to date. On 15 December 2011, on the same day as the ceremony to mark the final withdrawal of US troops from Iraq, Maliki moved against three of Iraqiyya's most senior politicians. Troops and tanks, led by Maliki's son Ahmed, surrounded the houses of the vice-president, Hashemi, Minister of Finance Rafi al-Issawi and Deputy Prime Minister Saleh al-Mutlaq.[42] That night all three politicians were placed under temporary house arrest. Hashemi was then allowed to fly to the capital of the KRG, Irbil. Three of his bodyguards were arrested. After four days in detention, the trio reappeared on national television and made dramatic confessions denouncing the vice-president for paying them to carry out a series of assassinations and bomb attacks.[43] When an arrest warrant was issued for Hashemi, three more confessions from policemen in the northwestern town of Fallujah were added.[44] They claimed that the vice-president, the minister of finance, Issawi, and senior regional members of their party had set up and run a death squad, Hamas of Iraq, in the town from 2006 onwards.

Soon after these startling confessions were aired, evidence emerged to shed light on the political motivation behind their extraction. As the 'facts' unravelled, those involved in torturing the bodyguards gave a lengthy and detailed interview explaining how they had used extended torture to obtain the confessions, admitting that the confessions themselves were factually 'absurd'.[45] US State Department cables released by

Wikileaks revealed that, as early as 2006, the Iraqi government was using the sustained torture of prisoners in an attempt to produce incriminating evidence against Hashemi.[46] On 15 March, credence was added to the accusations of torture when one of the bodyguards, Amir Sarbut Zaidan al-Batawi, died in custody. Government officials claimed that he had suffered kidney failure but pictures of his corpse showed clear evidence of brutality.[47]

The timing of the move against Hashemi may have been caused by the vice-president's increasingly vocal support for federal decentralisation as a way of limiting Maliki's power. In mid-December, Hashemi threw his public support behind the federalist movements in both the south and northwest of the country, saying the people involved 'are unwilling to accept further injustice, corruption and bad management from the central government'.[48] Two days later, his house was surrounded by Iraqi troops, his bodyguard arrested and he fled into exile. Maliki's move against his own vice-president and Iraqiyya's role in government can be seen as a very public and brutal attempt to stop the most serious threat to his campaign to centralise power in his own hands. It is hard to overstate the political importance of Hashemi's arrest and the accompanying moves against Minister of Finance Issawi and Deputy Prime Minister Mutlaq. Hashemi is not a particularly popular or effective politician. This perhaps made him more vulnerable to persecution than the other senior members of Iraqiyya, who were initially detained with him on the evening of 15 December, but then released.

The arrest, along with the prime minister's successful attempts during 2011 to circumvent the restrictions placed upon his power by the Irbil Agreement, finally brought consensus to the rest of Iraq's ruling elite that Maliki's behaviour posed a greater threat to their power than Iraqiyya's electoral success.

In mid-December, three days prior to Hashemi's arrest, Mutlaq raised the alarm, arguing that, 'America left Iraq with almost no infrastructure. The political process is going in a very wrong direction, going toward a dictatorship.'[49] In the wake of the arrest, the conviction took hold among the ruling elite that Maliki was a clear danger to Iraq's continued democracy. In April, Allawi wrote that; 'The country is slipping back into the clutches of a dangerous new one-man rule, which inevitably will lead to full dictatorship.'[50] It was left to Barzani, the KRG president, to bring that message directly to Washington, where he told the US administration that 'Iraq is facing a serious crisis ... it's coming towards one-man rule'.[51]

Faced with a direct attack on one of its senior leaders and the distinct possibility that this could spread to the whole of the coalition's ruling elite, Iraqiyya launched a boycott of both parliament and the cabinet that lasted from the end of December 2011 until the first week of February 2012.[52] However, this appeared to have little influence on Maliki and simultaneously reduced Iraqiyya's influence on government. After Iraqiyya returned to parliament, Barzani took over the responsibility of constraining, if not removing, Maliki. On 28 April 2012, Barzani hosted a political summit in Irbil attended by Talabani, Allawi, Sadr and Nujaifi. At the end of the meeting they sent the prime minister a letter containing eight demands to be met within a 15-day timetable. If Maliki failed to comply, the other politicians threatened to remove him from office through a parliamentary vote of no confidence.[53]

The leading role that Barzani played in orchestrating the campaign against Maliki reflects the declining relations between Irbil and Baghdad during 2011–12. Maliki's consolidation of power in Baghdad, and his use of the state to silence those Iraqi politicians challenging him, leaves the KRG as one of the few organisations inside Iraq with uncontested political autonomy. It is thus no surprise that Hashimi initially sought sanctuary in Irbil when Maliki sought to arrest him. Barzani then placed himself at the forefront of attempts to constrain Maliki and draw attention to the threat he posed to Iraqi democracy and Kurdish regional autonomy. In a series of speeches and interviews, Barzani focused on the extent to which Maliki had seized control of Iraq's armed forces. In late March 2012, he claimed that the Kurdish chief of staff of the Iraqi Army, Babakir Zebari, had been 'stripped of all authorities'. This was part of a larger process, he argued, whereby Maliki bypassed parliament in direct violation of the constitution and appointed divisional commanders aligned to him as Kurdish members of the Iraqi armed forces were being driven out.[54] He went on to argue that Maliki was planning to use the 36 F-16 fighter jets the Iraqi government had ordered from the United States against the KRG.[55] Ultimately, Barzani claimed, if Iraq did head back into dictatorship the KRG would secede.[56]

There is no doubt that Barzani and the wider Kurdish leadership are justifiably worried about the threat that Maliki's power poses to their continued autonomy. They have been at the forefront of efforts to constrain the prime minister by forcing him to abide by the terms of the Irbil Agreement, negotiated by Barzani himself. However, their ability to influence events in Baghdad, although greater than Iraqiyya's, has distinct limits. The threat of secession is not credible at the moment. The KRG is a net recipient from the Iraqi state budget, receiving 17% of the national budget, approximately US$11bn in 2012.[57] Although its plans to develop its own oil reserves are well advanced, these will not, for many years, give the regional government enough money to replace the resources it currently gets from Baghdad. Likewise, it cannot get its oil to international markets without the agreement of neighbouring Turkey, which has its own domestic reasons to fear Kurdish separatism. The realities of the KRG's continued dependence on Baghdad has led Barzani to explore other ways of dealing with Maliki. However, even if those opposed to the prime minister could stage a vote of no confidence in the Iraqi parliament, it is highly unlikely that they could build the necessary unity to get a majority.

Maliki's governing strategy and the Arab Spring

Maliki's response to the increasingly coherent attempts to remove him has seen the repackaging of the ideological justification for his rule, attempts to divide the political forces arrayed against him and the continued use of violence. Ideologically, the State of Law, in its 2010 election campaign, tried to portray itself as a nationalist and increasingly secular coalition representing the interests of all Iraqis. At the same time, however, the spectre of the Ba'athist threat was used to solidify its core Shia vote. In the aftermath of this election, the duality of Maliki's discourse was dropped. He arranged instead for a parliamentary merger between State of Law and the main coalition seeking to maximise the Shia vote, the INA, building a specifically partisan Shia electoral majority.[58] He then justified his use of the military to lock up his opponents by describing increasingly lurid conspiracies to remove the government as the start of Ba'athist plans for a military coup.[59] Finally, he sought to marginalise Iraqiyya's national influence by portraying it as an exclusively Sunni political force. In addition, he sought to encourage divisions within Iraqiyya by bringing back to Iraq former Sunni members of the insurgency to act as an alternative Sunni sectarian voice within the political arena.[60]

Overall, Maliki calculated that his opponents did not have the unity of effort or vision required to muster the parliamentary majority of 163 votes needed to pass a vote of no confidence. His gamble proved correct and a series of manoeuvres in and around parliament in Baghdad did not come anywhere near delivering the numbers needed.

Since the elections of March 2010, and certainly since the beginning of the political crisis in December 2011, Maliki has shown that he has far greater strategic capacity than any of his rivals for power. He has successfully retained the backing of the United States and Iran, both of whom fear the instability that might be unleashed during any attempt to unseat him. Sadr, although increasingly vocal in his support for Maliki's removal, is constrained in his actions by his Iranian allies and his extended residence in Iran. This leaves the senior politicians running Iraqiyya as the main opposition to Maliki. Both before and since Hashimi was driven into exile, Allawi, Nujaifi and Mutlaq have proven to be strategically inept politicians, unable to act in concert with each other, let alone build the much larger coalition needed to oust Maliki. This has emboldened the prime minister, who has abrogated the constitution, betrayed the promises he made in the Irbil Agreement and continued to centralise power in his own hands. Despite, or indeed because of, this he is as secure in his job now as at any time since his appointment in 2006.

Against a background of intra-elite conflict and conspiracy, popular resentment of the government has grown. Until 2011, the US State Department collected data from all of Iraq's 18 provinces, in an attempt to judge whether the lack of state services was driving political unrest and violence. In July 2011, it judged that 16 of Iraq's provinces were 'very unstable' due to the state's poor delivery of electricity, water, sewerage and transport infrastructure.[61] It is not just a lack of government services, it is also the level of unemployment, which is officially put at 12%, but is estimated by the Iraq Knowledge Network at 26% and by the World Bank at 40%, with an additional 30% of the workforce defined as 'under-employed'.[62] Opinion polls published by two separate organisations in March and April 2012 suggest that Iraqis' frustration with the poor delivery of services and the rate of unemployment is increasing. In April 2012, 89% of Iraqis outside the KRG-administered region believed that job opportunities were declining, with 77% thinking the same about the electricity supply.[63]

In light of events surrounding the Arab Spring, the increasing anger felt towards the government in Iraq became apparent in February 2011, when 1,000 people forced their way into local government offices in the southern provincial capital of Diwaniya.[64] Protests quickly spread across the south of Iraq and up to Baghdad. Maliki attempted to stem the rising tide of protest and react to the regional instability of the Arab Spring by announcing that he would cut his own salary by half. A day later one of the prime minister's advisers went as far as to suggest that Maliki may even not seek a third term in office, although this statement was quickly undermined by a number of caveats and the idea has not been mentioned again.[65] However, these attempts at placating public anger at government inefficiency and corruption were unsuccessful and demonstrations against the government spread across Iraq. Protesters, seeking to emulate the successful demonstrators in Cairo, set up a tented encampment in Baghdad's Tahrir Square, only to see it broken up by plain-clothes government supporters wielding clubs and knives.[66]

Maliki's government then adopted a dual strategy to demobilise popular resentment. At the end of February 2012, the prime minister announced that he had given his cabinet 100 days to improve the performance of their ministries. He also tried to shift the blame for poor services on to the provincial councils and called for new local elections only two years after the previous ones.[67] He temporarily redeployed US$1bn that had been allocated to buy US fighter jets to increase the content of the government-delivered national ration and promised to create 280,000 new jobs.[68] However, while publicly striking a conciliatory tone, Maliki's government also used state power to crush the demonstrations. On 25 February 2012, Iraq's 'Day of Rage', the government banned all cars from Baghdad, forcing protesters to walk to Tahrir Square. Following the demonstrations, 300 intellectuals were arrested and two parties were banned and evicted from their headquarters.[69] Finally, in mid-March, Maliki publicly denounced the demonstrators, claiming that they were out of touch with the popular will, small in number and deliberately trying to sow the seeds of discord.[70]

The extent of popular alienation with both the state and the ruling elite that controls it was revealed when the KRG faced popular protests in the northern cities of Irbil and Suleimaniya greater than any demonstrations in south and central Iraq.[71] The demonstrators denounced the government as corrupt, with power being undemocratically monopolised by the two main Kurdish parties, the KDP and PUK. When protesters threw rocks at party buildings, guards responded with deadly gunfire. Like Baghdad, the KRG deployed state-sponsored violence in the central square of Suleimaniya to break up demonstrations and arrest the organisers.[72]

Although the protesters participating in the 'Iraq Spring' in south, central and northern Iraq are manifestly urban and young, they constitute a large group deeply alienated from the governing elite who have been in power for at least seven years. The government in Baghdad has failed to reduce unemployment and cannot deliver sufficient electricity to meet the country's needs. The KRG is blamed for widespread corruption and for using non-democratic means to facilitate the KDP's continued dominance of government. These problems are not going to go away, and with pervasive political corruption embedded at the centre of the state, the government is unable to increase the delivery of either jobs or electricity. Its legitimacy is likely to remain at best tenuous as alienation continues to spread across the population.

Conclusion

The political system set up in 2003, and anointed by two national elections in 2005, has produced a series of national 'unity' governments. Under this system, both the cabinet and the government as a whole have been fractured, and divided between Iraq's new ruling elite, who are then free to use the resources and payrolls of the ministries they control for party political or personal advantage. This system justifies the division of the Iraqi state through a deliberately sectarian rhetoric, which parties use to claim that they represent the religious and ethnic communities from whom they seek votes. Maliki was appointed prime minister in 2006 because he and his party were seen to pose the least threat to the continuation of this system. However, Maliki quickly exploited the incoherence of this exclusive elite pact, circumventing the divided cabinet and building a shadow system of power that saw his functionaries, the *Malikiyoun*, placed throughout the Iraqi state, centralising power in the Office of the Prime Minister. To date, the rise in the power of the prime minister, although guaranteeing Maliki's continued rule, has not delivered any increase in the coherence of the state or improvement in the delivery of services to Iraq's long-suffering population. This has led to high levels of popular resentment directed towards government inefficiencies which are blamed, for good reason, on elite corruption.

The national election campaign of 2010 saw a sustained organisational and ideological challenge to the exclusive elite pact that had governed Iraqi politics since at least 2005.

Iraqiyya ran a successful campaign that sought to mobilise voters on a secular, nationalist basis. However, the very success of Iraqiyya's campaign threatened the rest of Iraq's ruling elite and the political system they prospered under. The integration of Iraqiyya into another government of national unity, justified in terms of *muhasasa,* was a deliberate ploy to neuter the political challenge they posed. However, the aim of the Irbil Agreement in the aftermath of the elections was a failure, namely the constraint of Maliki's growing power. The agreement appears to have been hastily drawn up and poorly drafted. The fact that the limitations it sought to place on the role of the prime minister have never been fully published, and were neither enshrined in law nor bore reference to the existing constitution, has enabled Maliki to openly flout them. Maliki continues to run the security forces, has direct and increasing influence over the judiciary, and is using his powers to systematically curtail the autonomy of what is left of the independent institutions within the Iraqi state. This does not bode well for the future of free, fair and contested elections.

Beyond the political struggle for power, the elongated negotiations that followed the 2010 elections, the government of national unity that was finally formed and the political crisis triggered by Hashimi's arrest have further weakened Iraq. For two years, senior Iraqi politicians who should have focused on rebuilding the capacity of the government ministries under their jurisdiction from 2010 turned their attention to an increasingly zero-sum struggle, firstly to obtain power for themselves and their coalitions, and then to remove Maliki. This has left Iraq with weak and highly corrupt state institutions, which has in turn bred widespread and growing popular resentment of Iraq's ruling elite.

Notes

1 International Crisis Group, 'Iraq's Provincial Elections: The Stakes', *Middle East Report*, no. 82, 27 January 2009, p. i, http://www.crisisgroup.org/~/media/Files/Middle%20East%20North%20Africa/Iraq%20Syria%20Lebanon/Iraq/82_iraqs_provincial_elections_the_stakes.pdf.

2 Mark Turner, 'Poll Planning on Track But No Room for Hitches', *Financial Times*, 14 October 2004.

3 Adeed Dawisha and Larry Diamond, 'Iraq's Year of Voting Dangerously', *Journal of Democracy*, vol. 17, no. 2, April 2006, p. 93.

4 Juan Cole, 'Civil War? What Civil War?', *Salon*, 23 March 2003, http://www.salon.com/opinion/feature/2006/03/23/civil_war/print.html; Phebe Marr, 'Who Are Iraq's New Leaders? What Do They Want?' United States Institute of Peace, Special Report 160, March 2006, http://www.usip.org/files/resources/sr160.pdf.

5 Juan Cole, 'Iraqi Parliament Passes Electoral Law; Obama Hails Move Toward Independence; Kurdistan Wins on Kirkuk', *Informed Comment*, 9 November 2009, http://www.juancole.com/2009/11/iraqi-parliament-passes-electoral-law.html.

6 Reidar Visser, 'No Longer Supreme: After Local Elections, ISCI Becomes a 10 Per Cent Party South of Baghdad', *Southern Iraq and Iraqi Politics*, 5 February, 2009, http://www.historiae.org/ISCI.asp.

7 Reidar Visser, 'A Closed Assembly Will Produce a Closed List', *Gulf Analysis*, 16 October 2009, http://gulfanalysis.wordpress.com/2009/10/16/a-closed-assembly-will-produce-a-closed-list.

8 Roy Gutman, 'In Najaf, Iraq's Shiite Clerics Push for Direct Elections', *McClatchy*, 19 October 2009, http://www.mcclatchydc.com/world/story/77413.html.

9 See Roel Meijer, 'The Sunni Factions and the "Political Process"', in Mark Bouillon, David M. Malone and Ben Rowswell (eds.), *Iraq: Preventing a New Generation of Conflict* (Boulder, CO: Lynne Riener, 2007), pp. 89–108.

10 Marina Ottaway and Danial Kaysi, 'Sunnis in Iraq, 6 Years After Saddam', Carnegie Middle East Center, 10 December 2009, http://carnegie-mec.org/publications/?fa=24292.

11 International Crisis Group, 'Iraq's Secular Opposition: The Rise and Decline of Al-Iraqiya', *Middle East Report*, no. 127, 31 July 2012, p. 10, http://www.crisisgroup.org/~/media/Files/Middle%20East%20North%20Africa/Iraq%20Syria%20Lebanon/Iraq/127-iraqs-secular-opposition-the-rise-and-decline-of-al-iraqiya.

12 Antony Shadid interviewed in David Kenner (ed.), 'Iraq At Eye Level', *Foreign Policy*, 8 March 2010, http://www.foreignpolicy.com/articles/2010/03/08/iraq_at_eye_level.

13 On the 2010 election results, see International Crisis Group, 'Iraq's Secular Opposition', pp. 12–13; Adeed Dawisha, 'Iraq: A Vote Against Sectarianism', *Journal of Democracy*, vol. 21, no. 3, July 2010, p. 36; Joel Wing, 'Iraq's Politics; Not Much Has Changed by 2010 Elections', *Musings on Iraq*, 21 May 2010, http://musingsoniraq.blogspot.co.uk/2010/05/iraqs-politics-not-much-changed-by-2010.html.

14 Salam Faraj, 'Iraq Election Officials Bar Nearly 500 Candidates from Poll',

Agence France-Presse, 15 January 2010, http://www.google.com/hostednews/afp/article/ALeqM5iq5fJFplxZiPms3wzK1upEolpP1A.

15 Leila Fadel and Ernesto Londoño, 'Sunni Iraqis Fear Disenfranchisement after Hundreds of Candidates Banned', *Washington Post,* 19 January 2010, http://www.washingtonpost.com/wp-dyn/content/article/2010/01/18/AR2010011803475.html.

16 'Iraqi Election Commission Bans 500 Candidates', BBC News, 15 January 2010, http://news.bbc.co.uk/1/hi/8461275.stm.

17 Reidar Visser, 'Mutlak and Ani Are Banned: Miscarriage of Justice in Iraq', *Gulf Analsysis,* 11 February 2010, http://gulfanalysis.wordpress.com/2010/02/11/mutlak-and-ani-are-banned-miscarriage-of-justice-in-iraq.

18 Nada Barki, 'The Rise and Fall of a Sunni in Baghdad', *New York Times,* 18 January 2010, http://www.nytimes.com/2010/01/19/world/middleeast/19sunni.html.

19 Reidar Visser, 'Governorate and Party-level Indicators of De-Ba'athification,Plus Some Breaking News', *Gulf Analysis,* 16 February 2010, http://gulfanalysis.wordpress.com/2010/02/16/governorate-and-party-level-indicators-of-de-baathification-plus-some-breaking-news.

20 Dawisha, 'Iraq: A Vote Against Sectarianism', p. 37.

21 Toby Dodge, 'Iraq's Perilous Political Carve-up', *IISS Voices Blog,* 16 November 2010, http://www.iiss.org/whats-new/iiss-voices/?blogpost=91.

22 Joel D. Rayburn, 'Rise of the Maliki Regime', *Journal of International Security Affairs,* no. 22, Spring/Summer 2012.

23 Hosham Dawod, 'Nouri Al-Maliki: The Construction and Deconstruction of Power in Iraq', *Near East Quarterly,* 30 June 2012, p. 3, http://www.neareastquarterly.com/index.php/2012/06/30/nouri-al-maliki-the-construction-and-deconstruction-of-power-in-iraq.

24 Ned Parker, 'The Iraq We Left Behind; Welcome to the World's Next Failed State', *Foreign Affairs,* vol. 91, no. 2, p. 100.

25 See McMaster, quoted in 'Secret Iraq', Part 2, BBC 2, 6 October 2010.

26 Leila Fadel and Nancy A. Youssef, 'Is "Success"' of US Surge in Iraq About To Unravel'? *McClatchy,* 24 March, 2008, http://www.mcclatchydc.com/iraq/story/31527.html; Seattle Times News Service, 'Fighting Leaves Crucial Truce with Iraq Militia in Shambles', *Seattle Times,* 26 March 2008, http://seattletimes.nwsource.com/html/iraq/2004306601_iraq26.html; Peter Graff, 'US Special Forces Units Working with Iraqi Troops in Basra', Reuters, 30 March 2008, http://www.reuters.com/article/latestCrisis/idUSL30612974.

27 See International Crisis Group, 'Iraq's Provincial Elections', fn. 96.

28 International Institute for Strategic Studies, 'Iraq's Provincial Elections', *Strategic Comments,* vol. 15, no. 1, 2009.

29 Ned Parker and Caesar Ahmed, 'Maliki Seeks Recount in Iraq Elections', *Los Angeles Times,* 22 March 2010, http://www.latimes.com/news/nationworld/world/la-fg-iraq-election22-2010mar22.

30 Gabriel Gatehouse, '"No Fraud Found" as Iraq Election Recount Ends', BBC News, 14 May 2010, http://news.bbc.co.uk/2/hi/middle_east/8684071.stm.

31 Special Inspector General for Iraq Reconstruction, *Quarterly Report*

and Semiannual Report to the United States Congress, July 2011, p. 60; Special Inspector General for Iraq Reconstruction, *Quarterly Report and Semiannual Report to the United States Congress*, October 2011, p. 40.

32 Confidential interview with the author.

33 See Roy Gutman, 'Iraq's Maliki Rebuffs Biden, Signals Move to Shiite Rule', *McClatchy*, 21 December 2011, http://www.mcclatchydc.com/2011/12/21/133802/iraqs-maliki-rebuffs-biden-signals.html.

34 Special Inspector General for Iraq Reconstruction, *Quarterly Report and Semiannual Report to the United States Congress*, April 2011.

35 Ali Latif, 'Iranian Lobby Topples Iraqi Central Bank Governor', *Azzam*, 16 October 2012, republished in *al-Monitor*, http://www.al-monitor.com/pulse/business/2012/10/warrant-issued-for-iraqs-central-bank-governor.html?utm_source=&utm_medium=email&utm_campaign=4858.

36 Special Inspector General for Iraq Reconstruction, *Quarterly Report and Semiannual Report*, April 2013, p. 73.

37 Tim Arango, 'Iraq Election Official's Arrest Casts Doubt on Prospect for Fair Voting', *New York Times*, 16 April 2012, http://www.nytimes.com/2012/04/17/world/middleeast/iraq-arrest-calls-fair-elections-into-question.html; 'Iraq Election Chief Gets Prison Sentence for Graft', Agence France-Presse, 28 August 2012, http://www.google.com/hostednews/afp/article/ALeqM5hGq3HTU-mfYoSGVgSothEHiOsb_w?docId=CNG.682a24f16b365825cf867757eef8144e.d81.

38 See The Constitution of Iraq, Articles 116, 117, 119, 120, 121, http://www.uniraq.org/documents/iraqi_constitution.pdf.

39 Marina Ottaway and Danial Kaysi, *The State of Iraq* (Washington DC: Carnegie Endowment, 2012), pp. 13–14, http://carnegieendowment.org/files/state_of_iraq.pdf.

40 *Ibid.*, p. 14.

41 Dan Morse and Asaad Majeed, 'Iraq Premier Nouri Al-Maliki Challenges Restive Provinces', *Washington Post*, 24 December 2011, http://www.washingtonpost.com/world/middle_east/iraq-premier-nouri-al-maliki-chides-restive-provinces/2011/12/24/gIQAzegYFP_story.html.

42 Marisa Cochrane Sullivan, 'Iraq's Post-withdrawal Crisis, Update 2', Institute for the Study of War, 23 December 2011, http://www.understandingwar.org/backgrounder/iraqs-post-withdrawal-crisis-update.

43 Roy Gutman, 'Iraq Orders Vice President's Arrest after TV "Confessions"', *McClatchy*, 19 December 2011, http://www.miamiherald.com/2011/12/19/2553867/iraq-orders-vice-presidents-arrest.html.

44 Joel Wing, 'Charges Against Iraq's Vice President, and Why They Matter', *Musings on Iraq*, 26 December 2011, http://musingsoniraq.blogspot.com/2011/12/charges-against-iraqs-vice-president.html.

45 Ghaith Abdul-Ahad, 'Corruption in Iraq: "Your Son Is Being Tortured. He Will Die If You Don't Pay"', *The Guardian*, 16 January 2012, http://www.guardian.co.uk/world/2012/jan/16/corruption-iraq-son-tortured-pay.

46 Roy Gutman, 'Iraqi VP Denies Terror Charges as Sectarian Dispute Continues', *McClatchy*, 20 December 2011, http://www.mcclatchydc.com/2011/12/20/133693/iraqi-vp-denies-terror-charges.html#storylink=cpy.

47 'Iraq Vice-President Hashemi's Guards "Die in Custody"', BBC News, 11 April 2012, http://www.bbc.co.uk/news/world-middle-east-17675666.

48 Mustafa Habib, 'Niqash Interview with Iraqi Vice President: US Withdrawal "Nothing To Worry About"', *Niqash*, 13 December 2011, http://www.niqash.org/articles/?id=2953.

49 Arwa Damon and Mohammed Tawfeeq, 'Iraq's Leader Becoming a New "Dictator", Deputy Warns', CNN, 13 December 2011, http://articles.cnn.com/2011-12-13/middleeast/world_meast_iraq-maliki_1_al-maliki-iraqi-prime-minister-nuri-shiite-and-minority-sunni?_s=PM:MIDDLEEAST.

50 Ayad Allawi, 'Iraq's Slide Toward Renewed Violence', *Washington Times*, 9 April 2012, http://www.washingtontimes.com/news/2012/apr/9/iraqs-slide-toward-renewed-violence.

51 Josh Rogin, 'Kurdish Leader: No to Arming the Syrian Opposition', *Foreign Policy*, 5 April 2012, http://thecable.foreignpolicy.com/posts/2012/04/05/kurdish_leader_no_to_arming_the_syrian_opposition.

52 Tim Arango, 'Iraq's Political Crisis Eases as Sunni Ministers Rejoin the Government', *New York Times*, 7 February 2012, http://www.nytimes.com/2012/02/08/world/middleeast/crisis-in-iraq-lulls-as-sunni-ministers-return-to-cabinet.html?ref=iraq.

53 Suadad al-Salhy, 'Iraq's Sadr Meets Kurdish Leader, Aims To End Dispute', Reuters, 26 April 2012, http://uk.reuters.com/article/2012/04/26/iraq-politics-idUKL6E8FQ9QY20120426; Raheem Salman, 'Leading Iraqi Lawmakers Threaten Vote of No Confidence', Reuters, 5 May 2012, http://www.chicagotribune.com/news/sns-rt-us-iraq-politicsbre84409i-20120505,0,5816533.story.

54 See interview with Masoud Barzani, Al-Sharqiyah News Television, 27 March 2012.

55 'Iraqi PM Must Not Obtain F-16s: Kurdistan Chief', Agence France-Presse, 23 April 2012.

56 Lara Jakes, 'Iraqi Kurd Leader Hints at Secession', Associated Press, 26 April 2012, http://www.dailystar.com.lb/News/Middle-East/2012/Apr-26/171467-iraqi-kurd-leader-hints-at-secession.ashx#axzz1tDzoQ05m.

57 Denise Natali, 'Coddling Iraqi Kurds', *Foreign Policy*, 4 April 2012, http://mideast.foreignpolicy.com/posts/2012/04/04/coddling_iraqi_kurds.

58 Feisal al-Istrabadi, 'Is a Democratic, Unified Iraq Viable?', *Near East Quarterly*, March 2012, http://www.neareastquarterly.com/index.php/2012/03/24/is-a-democratic-unified-iraq-viable.

59 Faleh A. Jabar, Renad Mansour and Abir Khaddaj, 'Maliki and the Rest: A Crisis Within a Crisis', *Iraqi Institute for Strategic Studies Iraq Crisis Report – 2012*, p. 17, http://iraqstudies.com/Maliki%20and%20the%20Rest%20-%20A%20Crisis%20within%20a%20Crisis.pdf.

60 International Crisis Group, 'Iraq's Secular Opposition', pp. 11–12.

61 Special Inspector General for Iraq Reconstruction, *Quarterly Report and Semiannual Report to the United States Congress*, July 2011, p. 94.

62 Elliot Wood, 'Iraq: Under Worse Management', *Businessweek*, 18 January 2012, http://www.businessweek.com/magazine/iraq-under-worse-management-01182012.html.

63 Greenberg Quinlan Rosner Research, 'A Major Shift in the Iraqi Political

Landscape; Report on the April 2012 National Survey', http://www.greenbergresearch.com/articles/2763/7271_NDI-Iraq%20-%20April%202012%20National%20Survey%20-%20Report.pdf; Steve Crabtree, 'Opinion Briefing: Discontent and Division in Iraq', 6 March 2012, http://www.gallup.com/poll/153128/Opinion-Briefing-Discontent-Division-Iraq.aspx.

64 Suadad al-Salhy, 'Iraqis Protest Power and Food Shortages; 3 Shot', Reuters, 3 February 2011, http://www.reuters.com/article/2011/02/03/idINIndia-54637220110203.

65 See 'Prime Minister Nouri Al-Maliki Ordered a Fifty Per Cent Reduction in His Monthly Salary as Prime Minister and Have the Remainder Credited to the Treasury', Statement issued by the Prime Minister's Office, 4 February 2011, translated from Arabic by Nathaniel Markowitz, http://www.pmo.iq/ArticleShow.aspx?ID=83; Lara Jakes, 'Iraqi PM Says He Will Not Seek 3rd Term', Associated Press, 5 February 2011, http://www.huffingtonpost.com/2011/02/05/eye-on-unrest-iraqi-pm-sa_n_819118.html.

66 Human Rights Watch, 'Iraq: Police Allow Gangs To Attack Protesters', 24 February 2011, http://www.hrw.org/news/2011/02/24/iraq-police-allow-gangs-attack-protesters.

67 Alice Fordham, 'Up In Arms', *Foreign Policy*, 28 February 2011, http://www.foreignpolicy.com/articles/2011/02/28/up_in_arms.

68 Maria Fantappie, 'Iraq: The Sadrists' Golden Opportunity', *Los Angeles Times*, 1 April, 2011, http://carnegie-mec.org/publications/?fa=43402&lang=en.

69 Stephanie McCrummen, 'After Iraq's Day of Rage, a Crackdown on Intellectuals', *Washington Post*, 27 February 2011, http://www.washingtonpost.com/wp-dyn/content/article/2011/02/26/AR2011022603345.html.

70 Qassim abdul-Zahra and Lara Jakes, 'PM: Protesters Are Out Of Step with Iraq's Will', Associated Press, 12 March 2011, http://www.washingtonpost.com/wp-dyn/content/article/2011/03/12/AR2011031201400.html.

71 Dana Asaad, 'Unrest in Kurdistan', *Niqash*, 21 February 2011, http://www.niqash.org/articles/?id=2786; Zanko Ahmad, 'Iraqi Kurdistan 2011: A Year of Demonstration and Political Debate', *Nigash*, 29 December 2011, http://www.niqash.org/articles/?id=2962.

72 Human Rights Watch, 'Iraq: Widening Crackdown on Protests', 21 April 2011, http://www.hrw.org/news/2011/04/21/iraq-widening-crackdown-protests; Tim Arango and Michael S. Schmidt, 'Anger Lingers in Iraqi Kurdistan After a Crackdown', *New York Times*, 18 May 2011, http://www.nytimes.com/2011/05/19/world/middleeast/19iraq.html.

CHAPTER SIX

From bully to target: Iraq's changing role in the Middle East

The invasion and regime change in 2003 was motivated by a desire in Washington to eradicate the Ba'athist regime, and to curtail the autonomy that Iraq had accumulated since 1968. The Iraqi regime's ability to defy the international community from 1990 until 2003 was rooted in the political and economic autonomy it had developed both domestically and internationally. Politically, the state controlled by Saddam Hussein had brutally broken the majority of organised resistance to it. On the economic front, the nationalisation of its oil industry allowed the regime in Iraq to reap the benefits of the 1973–74 oil price rise, and use this new-found wealth to build a coercively dominant state that became a major driver of regional instability from 1980 onwards.

Ironically, because the United States' invading force in 2003 lacked the manpower to impose order on the country, Iraq became, and remains, highly vulnerable to its neighbours' interference in domestic affairs. In light of this, the United States' ambitions to limit Iraq's regional and international autonomy have gone far beyond what was envisaged. After 2003, the US did not have the troop numbers to effectively seal Iraq's borders. This has allowed Iran and Turkey, in particular, to transgress Iraqi sovereignty almost at will. As the Iraqi state collapsed following the demise of the Ba'athist regime, central authority drained away.[1] This empowered certain sub-state actors, militias and political parties, but also allowed neighbouring states to pursue their own agendas on Iraq's soil, forging alliances with Iraqi actors to realise their own foreign-policy goals. In contemporary Iraq, Turkey, Iran and Saudi Arabia are still funding and exercising control over influential political actors in southern and northern Iraq, but also in Baghdad itself. Iraq, far from retaining the ability to infringe on the sovereignty of its neighbours, cannot even protect itself from interference by the regional powers that surround it.

At the centre of this weak state sits the prime minister, Nuri al-Maliki. It could be said that, for Maliki, foreign policy starts not at the borders of the country, but just outside the close circle of his associates: the *Malikiyoun* and, beyond that, the membership of his party, Dawa. In a system emerging from an extended civil war, in which the rules of permissible political behaviour are still violently contested, the majority of Maliki's time and energy is spent not maximising the interests of Iraq, but seeking to consolidate his own power and increase his personal grip on the institutions of the Iraqi state. In the conduct of Iraq's foreign policy since the restoration of sovereignty, national interests have been defined mainly through the prism of narrow interests of the ruling elite. The principal objective of this foreign policy has been to create a set of internal and external conditions that will guarantee the survival and strengthening of the existing regime in the domestic sphere. There is little sign, as yet, that Iraq aspires to influence the domestic arrangements of neighbouring states, as it has in the past.

Thus, Maliki has successfully obtained support from both Washington and Tehran, but has simultaneously striven to assert his autonomy from both. He understands that their interests in Iraq are not the same as his, and that agendas could rapidly change.

US influence on Iraq

Given Washington's extended investment of troops and money in the country, the United States' ability to shape the actions of its ruling elite has been surprisingly limited. Even at the height of the surge in late 2007 and 2008, General David Petraeus found it difficult to direct Maliki's behaviour. Policy decisions had to be slowly negotiated, and the aspects of Maliki's approach to politics that the United States found troubling required many extended exercises in diplomatic persuasion, rather than dictates handed down from the US commander's office.

The limits of the United States' ability to influence the actions of Maliki and Iraq's ruling elite were highlighted in the negotiations to draft a Status of Forces Agreement (SOFA). The process lasted for well over 12 months. It began with Bush and Maliki committing their respective governments to a legal agreement that would formalise long-term relations between the two countries. In March 2008, the US government sent a large team of lawyers to Baghdad to begin these negotiations. The first draft presented to the Iraqis by these diplomats revealed the extent of US ambitions in Iraq beyond 2012, asking for the use of 58 military bases, control of Iraq's airspace and immunity from prosecution for American soldiers and private contractors.[2] Baghdad's complete rejection of the draft signified how little the United States understood the transformation of Iraqi politics over the course of 2008.

By the time substantive negotiations on the SOFA were under way, Maliki had already launched the *Charge of the*

Knights, a military operation that took place at the end of March 2007 and saw the Iraqi army wrest control of Basra from the militias that had long dominated Iraq's second city. Although the ultimate success of that operation depended on US logistics and air support, the boost it gave to Maliki's popularity demonstrated to him the expediency of playing the nationalist card to rally popular support. As SOFA negotiations dragged on, Maliki increasingly couched his opposition to some of their more objectionable clauses in terms of Iraqi national sovereignty. This gave him popular approval and encouraged an even tougher negotiating stance.

In addition, electoral timetables in both countries strengthened Maliki's hand.[3] It became increasingly apparent that Bush was eager to conclude a SOFA before he left office, bringing some degree of closure to the most contentious issue of his presidency. Through the summer and autumn of 2008, negotiations ground to a halt. Maliki was happy to use the SOFA to demonstrate his nationalist credentials and independence from Washington, safe in the knowledge that an Obama presidency would give him a similar, if not better, agreement. The American presidential cycle and the growing confidence of the Iraqi prime minister combined to give much greater leverage to the Iraqi side. The final agreement saw the Iraqi government obtain the majority of its demands, and the US was forced into making a series of significant and far-reaching concessions.

The most important of these was extracted from the United States by tough Iraqi negotiating, and demanded an unambiguous timetable for US troop withdrawal. Both then-US Secretary of State Condoleezza Rice and the Chairman of the Joint Chiefs of Staff, Admiral Michael Mullen, made Washington's opposition to specific dates for withdrawal very clear,[4] but the final document left no room for doubt. All US combat forces were withdrawn from Iraqi cities, towns and villages to their bases by 30 June 2009. Thereafter, they had two and a half years to leave the country entirely. Article 24 of the treaty stated that 'all US forces are to withdraw from all Iraqi territory, water and airspace no later than the 31st of December of 2011'.[5] The speed and extent to which the US was forced to cede ground in the negotiation is evident in the fact that the SOFA went much further than Barack Obama's own electoral promises on Iraq. Obama's commitment to pulling two brigades of US combat troops per month out of Iraq would mean that none would remain in the country by the summer of 2010. However, this was balanced by his commitment to leave a 'residual force' of US troops in Iraq. This force of around 30,000 would train the Iraqi military, fight al-Qaeda and deal with the 'potential re-emergence of Shia militias'.[6] Under the SOFA signed by the Bush administration, however, no troops could remain in Iraq after 2011.

The continued decline of US influence accelerated after American troops left the country at the end of 2011. Plans to shape Iraqi politics after troop withdrawal shifted to the State Department and the CIA. Initial plans for the post-withdrawal embassy envisaged a staff of between 15,000–16,000 diplomats and contractors,[7] housed in the largest American embassy in the world and in three consulates in Basra, Irbil and Kirkuk. The CIA laid plans for the continuance of its largest station, which had 700 staff at its peak. However, even these largely civilian plans for influence were undermined by two unforeseen constraints. Firstly, the Iraqi government, after 2011, aimed to steadily reduce America's diplomatic influence in the country. The Prime Minister's Office took direct responsibility for approving every US diplomatic visa, dramatically slowing down the process of bringing American government personnel in and out of the country.[8] Once US troops had departed, Iraqi government officials imposed new constraints on American diplomatic access to Iraqi civil servants and politicians, drastically limiting America's ability to understand and influence the workings of government. Secondly, US government budgetary constraints meant plans to set up consulates in Mosul and Kirkuk were postponed.[9] The CIA likewise announced a decision to cut its staff in Baghdad by 40%.[10] Overall, the departure of US troops in December 2011 was more of a turning point than the American government had anticipated. Iraqi political opinion, the policy of Maliki himself and American budget cuts conspired to reduce US influence across the country, and finally allowed Iraqi politics to function under their own indigenous logic, nine years after regime change.

Iraq and Iran

Baghdad's interactions with Tehran, like its relations with Washington, allow for a great deal more autonomy than is at first apparent. Iranian interests in Iraq are shaped by the trauma of Iraq's 1980 invasion of Iran, and its employment of chemical weapons during the eight-year war. Against this historical background, Iran remains intent on curtailing Iraq's power and limiting the threat it poses. However, the Iraqi challenge for Tehran is not merely military: Najaf remains the seat of Shia learning, with its position in a resurgent Iraq contesting Iran's claim to lead the Shia world. From this perspective, Iranian policy seeks to keep Iraq in a dependent relationship.

For the two years following the invasion, from 2003–2005, Iran sought to achieve this by encouraging the Shia Islamist parties, who had largely been exiled in Iran before returning to Iraq, to push for democratic elections that would bring them to power.[11] However, as civil war engulfed Iraq, Iran exercised its influence through funding one side, the Shia militias, in the bloody conflict. The Quds Forces of Iran's Revolutionary Guard, and its commander, Qassem Suleimani, became the main conduit of this funding. Mowaffak al-Rubaie, former member of the Iraqi Governing Council and Iraq's National Security Adviser from 2004 to 2009, in 2010, went so far as to proclaim Suleimani, 'the most powerful man in Iraq without question. Nothing gets done without him'.[12] It is certainly true that Iran's ability to influence Iraq's state and society was strongest during the civil war. The US military claimed that the Quds Force had 150 members in Iraq at any one time and arrested small numbers of them in 2007 and 2008.[13] There was also sustained evidence to show that Iran supplied advanced weapons and destructive technology to its client militias in the country. These allegations reached a peak when a Lebanese member of Hizbullah, Ali Musa Daqduq, was arrested in Basra in the company of a radical Shia militia leader, Qais al-Khazali.[14]

However, Iran's influence in Iraq extends beyond the financing of militias. Iranian President Mahmoud Ahmadinejad paid a successful state visit to Baghdad in March 2008, and Maliki has since then been a frequent visitor to Tehran. Suleimani retains very close ties to Iraqi President Jalal Talibani, as well as to Moqtada al-Sadr, and used these relations to broker the end of the conflict between Maliki and Sadr after the *Charge of the Knights* in 2008.[15]

In the run-up to the March 2010 national elections, it was clear that Tehran feared Maliki had amassed too much power and enjoyed greater autonomy than they had envisaged; thus, Iran backed his rival for the Shia vote, the Iraqi National Alliance (INA), which contained Sadr's party and the Islamic Supreme Council of Iraq (ISCI). According to US government estimates, in 2009, Iranian support for Iraqi parties with which it sympathised amounted to between US$100 million to US$200m, with an estimated US$70m donated to the ISCI alone.[16] However, the size of the Iraqqiya (Iraqi National

Movement) vote, and its potential to marginalise those parties aligned with Iran, forced Tehran to change its policy and push for Maliki to retain the premiership, in spite of its reservations. This enabled Tehran to act as a major influence on the post-election parliamentary merger of Maliki's State of Law Coalition and the Iraqi National Alliance in May 2012. Sadr's public but very grudging support for Maliki's continued premiership can be traced directly to the pressure applied on him by Iran.

Following the elections, ties between Baghdad and Tehran have grown significantly, with Maliki paying an official visit to Iran in April 2012. Trade between the two countries has also increased, estimated by Iran to have topped US$11 billion a year in 2012.[17] The poor performance of Iraq's own electricity grid has been ameliorated by the import of electricity, gas and oil products from Iran.[18] There have been persistent rumours that Iraq is being used as a covert Iranian conduit for arms and money to support the Assad regime in Syria, and as a vehicle for subverting international sanctions on Iran. However, since becoming prime minister in 2006, Maliki has sought to maximise his autonomy from Iran as a main plank of his strategy for remaining in power. This is, in part, a recognition of a strong Iraqi nationalism that views Iran, at best, with suspicion. This nationalist attitude, and Maliki's own need to retain autonomy, will most likely continue to curb Iran's ability to turn its neighbour into a satellite.

Iraq and Turkey

Of all its neighbours, Iraq's relations with Turkey have declined the furthest and fastest, as a direct consequence of Maliki's consolidation of power in Baghdad. In 2003, the Turkish parliament refused to give the United States permission to use its territory as a launchpad for the invasion. From then until 2011, Turkey focused its interests in the north of Iraq. Turkish businesses became the main economic beneficiaries of the Kurdish Regional Government (KRG) in Iraq, as it continued to pursue an independent oil policy and developed its regional economy. This, however, touched on long-standing concerns in Ankara about its own Kurdish-populated territory. In particular, the Turkish authorities feared that successful Iraqi Kurdish autonomy would encourage Turkey's own Kurdish minority to push for greater autonomy. To that end, Ankara maintained strong links with Baghdad in an attempt to limit the growth of Iraqi Kurdish aspirations. Much to the fury of the KRG president, Masoud Barzani, Turkish military forces frequently carried out raids across the Iraqi border, targeting the camps of their own Kurdish separatist group, the Kurdistan Worker's Party (PKK), who trained in the remote Qandil mountains in northern Iraq. In addition, Turkey projected both its overt and covert influence into Iraq by claiming for itself a right to protect the Turkoman population based in and around the Iraqi city of Kirkuk. Kirkuk holds a strategic position at the gateway to Iraq's northern oil fields, which run from Iraqi government territory into the KRG. By supporting Turkoman claims to the city, Ankara hoped to limit the KRG's expansion and confidence, but by doing so, it blatantly interfered in Iraq's domestic affairs.

Ankara's relationship with Baghdad soured in 2010, when the Turkish government became embroiled in a double game. They supported Maliki's rival for the premiership, Ayad Allawi, in the national elections, while also acting as a conduit for Saudi financial support for Allawi's Iraqiyya. Relations further deteriorated when there were sharp verbal exchanges between Maliki and the Turkish Prime Minister Recep Tayyip Erdoğan, on the issue of Iraq's vice-president, Tareq al-Hashemi. In December 2011, Hashemi fled Iraq to avoid what are thought to be politically motivated murder charges, and eventually found refuge in Turkey. Ankara refused to hand him over, and Hashemi was subsequently sentenced to death in absentia.[19] Erdoğan warned Maliki that the Hashemi issue put Iraq's democracy at risk. Maliki retaliated by accusing Turkey of intervening in Iraq's affairs and 'playing a role that could lead to a catastrophe or civil war in the region'.[20] There followed an unseemly diplomatic row, with Iraq branding its neighbour a 'hostile state'. Turkey escalated tensions when its Foreign Minister, Ahmet Davutoglu, visited Kirkuk without notifying or seeking permission from Baghdad. Further, Turkey's energy minister, Taner Yildiz, shared a platform with the KRG's natural resources minister, Ashti Hawrami, when he announced the KRG's plans to build an independent pipeline to export its oil via Turkey, which clearly undermines Baghdad's ability to control the KRG's oil policy and economy.[21]

Iraq's relations with Turkey are being driven by two sets of dynamics. Firstly, Turkey, like Saudi Arabia, has embarked on a more active regional policy in the wake of the Arab Spring. Ankara seeks to project its power in a region in political turmoil, making up for declining US interest and seeking to counter what it sees as Iran's hegemonic aspirations. Secondly, Turkey is seeking to check Maliki's authoritarian ambitions, and remind him of the destabilising effect his sectarian rhetoric is having on Iraqi politics. Both these dynamics appear to have a degree of longevity, which could ensure that Iraq–Turkey relations remain fraught. However, it behoves Ankara in one respect to exercise restraint because, by using its ties with the KRG to pressure Baghdad, Turkey risks exacerbating its own long-running domestic problems with its Kurdish minority. This should constrain Ankara's regional ambitions, and could bring its relations with Baghdad back into a balance built on their mutual interests in constraining the KRG.

Iraq and the Arab Gulf states

Oddly, given the destabilising role that Iraq has played in the Persian Gulf region, Iraq's relations with its Arab Gulf neighbours are amongst the least problematic of its diplomatic relations. Since Iraqi independence, the country's border with Kuwait has been regarded by many in the country as illegitimate. Iraq's dissatisfaction with its limited access to the Gulf, and the dependence this breeds on its neighbours for the export of its oil, is the closest thing the country has to an enduring national interest.[22] Kuwait's decision in May 2011 to begin development on the uninhabited Bubyan Island, at the mouth of the Shatt al-Arab waterway, triggered renewed political agitation in Iraq concerning the border. Many Iraqis were disturbed that such a large port near its own border would choke shipping, particularly for oil tankers, and also make the planned new port in Iraq at Grand Faw unprofitable.[23] This dispute, however, was mediated through diplomatic negotiations, which indicate that in Iraq–Kuwait relations at least, Maliki is placing more weight on improving his ties with his Arab Gulf neighbours than seeking to mobilise Iraqi popular opinion by reviving long-running border disputes. This pragmatic approach was further in evidence when Iraq settled another of its long-standing disputes in the run up to the March 2012 Arab League Conference in Baghdad. There, as part of its 'regional charm offensive', Iraq agreed to pay its neighbour US$300m in reparations, to settle a US$1.2bn dispute dating back to 1990, when the Ba'athist regime was accused of stealing a number of planes from Kuwait during the invasion.[24] This approach reaped dividends: the Emir of Kuwait was the most senior state representative to attend the Arab League Summit in Baghdad, thus helping to burnish Maliki's regional diplomatic credentials.

In spite of its success with Kuwait, Iraq's relations with Saudi Arabia remain poor. The roots of the tension between Riyadh and Baghdad go back to the 2005–08 civil war. On the Iraqi side, resentment stems from the support senior religious figures within Saudi Arabia gave to the insurgency in its early days[25] and thereafter, by the supply of Saudi money and a sizeable number of irregular fighters to the insurgency.[26] On the Saudi side, there is continued anger and resentment over the number of Sunnis killed during the civil war. Saudi King Abdullah is said to blame Maliki personally for the violence directed against the Sunni population of Baghdad from 2005 to 2008.[27] However, in the wake of the Arab Spring, as the Middle East is increasingly caught in the midst of a competition for influence between Iran, Saudi Arabia, Qatar and Turkey, tension also springs from the Saudis' view that Iraq has, since regime change, become nothing less than an Iranian puppet. In March 2009, Abdullah told a senior US diplomat that he did not trust Maliki and thought he was 'an Iranian agent'.[28] Thus Riyadh funded Maliki's rival, Ayad Allawi, during the 2010 national elections, further damaging relations between the governments. Things looked to be improving in February and March 2012, when Riyadh appointed a non-resident ambassador to Baghdad for the first time since the invasion and signed a security agreement with Iraq. However, a visit to Riyadh by Hashemi, after he had fled murder charges in Iraq, ignited another war of words between Saudi Arabia and Iraq. Given Maliki's use of sectarian rhetoric in Iraqi politics and the rising tensions across the Middle East between Saudi Arabia and Iran, relations between Baghdad and Riyadh are likely to remain strained. With Saudi foreign-policymakers viewing Iraq as little more than a conduit for Iranian influence, the temptation for Riyadh to interfere in Iraqi politics to the detriment of Maliki looks set to remain.

Iraq and Syria

The tensions in Iraq's relations with Saudi Arabia, Iran and Turkey can be summed up in Baghdad's contradictory approach to Syria. Until the revolt against the regime of Bashar al-Assad began in April 2011, Syria was seen, with good reason, by Maliki and the rest of Iraq's ruling elite as the prime source of funding for the insurgency, and a place of sanctuary for senior Ba'athists. Two of the most prominent Iraqi Ba'athists thought to be leading the initial stages of the insurgency, Mohamed Younis and former vice-president, Izzat Ibrahim al-Douri, were in exile in Damascus.[29] In 2007, some 75–80% of the foreign suicide bombers, who proved to be central in driving Iraq into civil war, entered the country from Syria.[30]

However, once the Syrian uprising gathered sufficient moment to threaten the survival of the Assad regime, Iraq's position shifted. First, the government came under extended pressure from Iran to support its allies in Damascus. As a result, Iraq sold oil to the Assad regime, provided its airspace for resupply flights between Iran and Syria, and allowed the regime to use its banking institutions. Baghdad continued this policy despite the extended diplomatic pressure exerted by the United States.[31]

To attribute this support to Iranian pressure alone is too simplistic. The collapse of the Syrian regime would undoubtedly lead to greater instability in Iraq. There are sustained reports of former Iraqi insurgents actively fighting against the Assad regime in Syria. If that fight was successfully concluded, they would be expected to use Syria as a base for mounting attacks on Iraq, with the objective of bringing down the government. Secondly, if the Assad regime did fall, it would likely be replaced by a government with Sunni Islamist radicals in positions of power. This, if anything, would make Syria a greater source of opposition to Maliki than the Ba'ath. Finally, if Iran were to lose Syria as an Arab ally, it would place more demands on Iraq and thereby threaten Maliki's preciously built autonomy. The statement of the Iraqi foreign minister, Hoshiyar Zebari, that Iraq is 'trying to take a independent position, based on our national interests', and that 'things are not black and white', appears to be a masterly example of diplomatic understatement, given the perils and complexities of the situation Baghdad faces.[32]

Conclusion

One of the central aims of regime change in Baghdad was to radically reduce the foreign-policy autonomy that Saddam Hussein had amassed since becoming president in 1979. This autonomy allowed him to invade Iran in 1980 and carry on an eight-year war, invade Kuwait in 1990, and withstand 13 years of the harshest sanctions ever imposed upon a state by the international community. In this aim, the United States has been, if anything, too successful. The state collapse and civil war triggered by the invasion have made Iraq highly vulnerable to the machinations of its neighbours. As a consequence, a muscular or militarily assertive Iraqi foreign policy will not be a major destabilising force in the region for many years to come.

While Iraq will not be an assertive independent player, neither will it be a reliable ally for the United States. Maliki's government is susceptible to external (especially Iranian) influence, but it has amassed enough political autonomy vis-à-vis the United States to rebuff Washington's demands in regard to Iraq's domestic and foreign policies. This was especially evident in the fact that the withdrawal of US forces from Iraq, at the end of 2011, became one of the Obama administration's only unambiguous first-term foreign-policy success stories. Washington needed to believe in Maliki's success, and the stability of Iraq's democracy, more than those in Iraq did. As a result, it was no longer in a position to press Baghdad into supporting US interests in the Middle East.

That said, Iraq's borders, especially with Iran, Turkey and Syria, still remain highly porous; both overt and covert military forces are able to enter the country without Baghdad doing much to stop them. Its ruling elites also remain divided and in conflict with each other. In this battle, they look to regional powers for support, and in return offer promises of allegiance. As the Middle East heads into a regional cold war between Iran and its adversaries in Ankara, Riyadh and Doha, Iraq is likely to become a major site of conflict, as each side seeks allies and proxies to carry on the fight.

Notes

1 See I. William Zartman, 'Posing the Problem of State Collapse', in I. William Zartman, ed., *Collapsed States: The Disintegration and Restoration of Legitimate Authority* (Boulder, CO: Lynne Rienner, 1995).

2 Leila Fadel and Mike Tharp, 'Maliki Raises Possibility That Iraq Might Ask US to Leave', *McClatchy*, 13 June 2008, http://www.mcclatchydc.com/iraq/story/41047.html; Patrick Cockburn, 'Revealed: Secret Plan to Keep Iraq Under US Control; *The Independent*, 5 June 2008, http://www.independent.co.uk/news/world/middle-east/revealed-secret-plan-to-keep-iraq-under-us-control-840512.html.

3 Nancy A. Youssef, 'Why the US Blinked on its Troop Agreement With Iraq', *McClatchy*, 19 November 2008, http://www.mcclatchydc.com/iraq/story/56182.html.

4 Tina Susman and Raheem Salman, 'Iraq Lawmakers Approve Security Pact With US', *Los Angeles Times*, 28 November 2008, http://www.latimes.com/news/nationworld/iraq/complete/la-fg-iraq28-2008nov28,0,4965965.story.

5 Sahar Issa, Jenan Hussein and Hussein Kadhim, 'Unofficial Translation of U.S.-Iraq Troop Agreement from the Arabic Text', *McClatchy*, 18 November 2010, http://www.mcclatchydc.com/iraq/story/56116.html.

6 Barack Obama: Turning the Page in Iraq', http://www.barackobama.com/issues/pdf/IraqFactSheet.pdf.

7 Nathan Hodge, 'In Iraq, US Shifts to a Large, New Footprint', *Wall Street Journal*, 10 December 2011, http://online.wsj.com/article/SB10001424052970204319004577088804024140494.html.

8 Tim Arango, 'US Planning to Slash Iraq Embassy Staff by Up to Half', *New York Times*, 7 February 2012, http://www.nytimes.com/2012/02/08/world/middleeast/united-states-planning-to-slash-iraq-embassy-staff-by-half.html?pagewanted=al.

9 Tim Arango and Michael S. Schmidt, 'US Scales Back Diplomacy in Iraq Amid Fiscal and Security Concerns', *New York Times*, 22 October 2011, http://www.nytimes.com/2011/10/23/world/middleeast/us-scales-back-diplomacy-in-iraq-amid-fiscal-and-security-concerns.html.

10 Siobhan Gorman and Adam Entous, 'CIA Prepares Iraq Pullback; US Presence Has Grown Contentious; Backers Favor Focus on Terror Hot Spots', *Wall Street Journal*, 5 June 2012, http://online.wsj.com/article/SB10001424052702303506404577446703581496154.html.

11 Kenneth Katzman, 'Iran's Activities and Influence in Iraq', Congressional Research Service (CRS), *Reports and Issue Briefs* (October 2007), http://fpc.state.gov/documents/organization/106178.pdf.

12 Martin Chulov, 'Qassem Suleimani: the Iranian General "Secretly Running" Iraq', *The Guardian*, 28 July 2011, http://www.guardian.co.uk/world/2011/jul/28/qassem-suleimani-iran-iraq-influence.

13 Dafna Linzer, 'Troops Authorised to Kill Iranian Operatives in Iraq', *The Washington Post*, January 26 2007, http://www.washingtonpost.com/wp-dyn/content/article/2007/01/25/AR2007012502199.html.

14 John F. Burns and Michael R. Gordon, 'US Says Iran Helped Iraqis Kill Five G.I.'s', *New York Times*, 3 July 2007, http://www.nytimes.com/2007/07/03/world/middleeast/03iraq.html.

15 Hannah Allam, Jonathan S. Landay and Warren P. Strobel, 'Iranian Outmaneuvers US in Iraq', *McClatchy*, 28 April 2008, http://www.mcclatchydc.com/iraq/story/35146.html.

16 See Gordon, 'Meddling Neighbors Undercut Iraq Stability'.

17 See 'Iran–Iraq Trade Transactions Stood at Over $11bn Last Year: Envoy', *Tehran Times*, 24 May 2012, http://www.tehrantimes.com/economy-and-business/98157-iran-iraq-trade-transactions-stood-at-over-11bn-last-year-envoy.

18 Ben Lando, 'Iraq Increases Reliance on Iranian Energy', *Iraq Oil Repor*, 1 July 2011, http://www.iraqoilreport.com/energy/natural-gas/iraq-increases-reliance-on-iranian-energy-5916/.

19 'Tariq al-Hashemi: Turkey "Will Not Hand Over" Iraq VP', BBC News, 11 September 2012, http://www.bbc.co.uk/news/world-middle-east-19554873.

20 See 'Erdogan to Maliki: Take steps to Reduce Tensions in Iraq', *Zaman*, 10 January 2012, http://www.todayszaman.com/news-268246-erdogan-to-maliki-take-steps-to-reduce-tensions-in-iraq.html; and Joe Parkinson, 'Iraq Lashes Out at Turkey as Sunni-Shiite Rift Grows', *Wall Street Journal*, 17 January 2012, http://online.wsj.com/article/SB10001424052970203735304577165140234013650.html.

21 Marwan Ibrahim, 'Turkish Minister's Kirkuk Visit Infuriates Iraq', Agence France-Presse, 2 August 2012, http://www.google.com/hostednews/afp/article/ALeqM5jD_W2IL_AnNHbvg2INSMXvsdrq_Q; and Patrick Osgood, 'Turkey Preparing Major Kurdistan oil', *Iraq Oil Report*, 8 November 2012, http://www.iraqoilreport.com/politics/oil-policy/turkey-preparing-major-kurdistan-oil-entry-9253/.

22 Phebe Marr, 'Iraq: balancing foreign and domestic realities', in L. Carl Brown ed., *Diplomacy in the Middle East. The International Relations of Regional and Outside Powers* (London: I. B. Tauris, 2006), pp. 185–6.

23 See David Roberts, 'Kuwait's War of Words With Iraq', *Foreign Policy*, 20 July 2011, http://mideast.foreignpolicy.com/posts/2011/07/20/kuwatis_war_of_words_with_iraq.

24 Michael Peel and Camilla Hall, 'Iraq Launches Regional Charm Offensive', *Financial Times*, 21 March 2012, http://www.ft.com/cms/s/0/57241272-733b-11e1-9014-00144feab49a.html.

25 Brian Whitaker, 'Saudi Call for Jihad', *The Guardian*, 8 November 2004, http://www.guardian.co.uk/world/2004/nov/08/iraq.saudiarabia.

26 Ned Parker, 'Iraq Insurgency Said to Include Many Saudis', *Los Angeles Times*, 15 July 2007, http://articles.latimes.com/2007/jul/15/world/fg-saudi15; and Joel Wing, 'Wikileak Documents Show Continued Saudi Opposition to Shiite Rule in Iraq', *Musings on Iraq*, 15 December 2010.

27 Toby Harden, 'We'll Arm Sunni Insurgents in Iraq, Say Saudis', The Daily Telegraph, 14 December 2006, http://www.telegraph.co.uk/news/worldnews/1536936/Well-arm-Sunni-insurgents-in-Iraq-say-Saudis.html.

28 Michael R. Gordon, 'Meddling Neighbors Undercut Iraq Stability', *New York Times*, 5 December 2010, http://www.nytimes.com/2010/12/06/world/middleeast/06wikileaks-iraq.html.

29 Peter Beaumont, 'Saddam Aide in Exile Heads List of Most Wanted Insurgents', *The Observer*, October 17 2004, http://www.guardian.co.uk/world/2004/oct/17/iraq; Hugh Naylor, 'Syria Is Said to Be Strengthening Ties to Opponents of Iraq's Government', *New York Times*, 7 October 2007, http://www.nytimes.com/2007/10/07/world/middleeast/07syria.html?pagewanted=all.

30 Daniel Dombey, 'Influx of Suicide Bombers "Entering Iraq from Syria"', Financial Times, 31 January 2007, http://www.ft.com/cms/s/0/7f80109c-bocf-11db-8a62-0000779e2340.html

31 Michale Gordon, Eric Schmitt and Tim Arango, 'Flow of Arms to Syria Through Iraq Persists, to US Dismay', *New York Times*, 1 December 2012, http://www.nytimes.com/2012/12/02/world/middleeast/us-is-stumbling-in-effort-to-cut-syria-arms-flow.html.

32 Patrick Markey and Suadad al-Salhy, 'In Syrian Shadow, Iraq's Maliki juggles Tehran, Washington', Reuters, 1 October 2012, http://www.reuters.com/article/2012/10/01/us-syria-crisis-iraq-idUSBRE89005W20121001.

CONCLUSION

Iraq's post-invasion history has been tumultuous. The ambitious optimism that shaped the US-led invasion and plans for the country's transformation were swept away by a tide of politically motivated violence. What began as a fractured and highly localised revolt against a foreign invasion was soon transformed into a sustained insurgency that operated across the whole of south and central Iraq. By the time of Iraq's first democratic elections in 2005, there was no doubt that the insurgency had evolved into a bloody civil war that was increasingly justified in sectarian terms. The watershed moment for Iraq came two years into that civil war, in 2007. The announcement of a major shift in American policy by Bush in February heralded the start of the surge and the final attempt to pull Iraq out of a war caused by the invasion and the flawed US plans for its aftermath.

The data on contemporary violence are somewhat contradictory and unreliable. The United Nations stopped publishing information on violent deaths in Iraq in the summer of 2012. The figures published by the Iraqi government are inconsistent and have been, on occasion, politically manipulated. This leaves the Iraq Body Count, a non-governmental organisation, as the only independent group using press reports to collate data on the numbers of civilians murdered in Iraq each month. As with all the other sources of data, Iraq Body Count tracked a steady decline in civilian deaths from September 2007 onwards. Yet, since 2009, it estimates that over 4,000 people a year have been murdered.[1] The first thing to note about these figures is that they are almost certainly an under-estimation of overall levels of violence and murder across the country.[2] However, they do indicate a rise in the average numbers of Iraqis murdered on a monthly basis from 2009 onwards. In 2009, an average of 337 people were murdered each month. This rose to 342 in 2010, and then 385 in the first nine months of 2012. In April 2012, Joel Wing examined all the data available and concluded that in the aftermath of the 2007 surge, as violence declined, the deadliness of insurgent attacks increased, with each violent incident killing more people.[3] This situation is such that although the US military and Iraqi government have successfully removed the majority of those deploying violence from Iraqi society, those left are more proficient at killing people.

It is thus pertinent to wonder where Iraq is heading after US troop withdrawal in 2011, and to return to the three questions posed at the outset. Is Iraq in danger of sliding back into civil war? Is the country on a pluralistic political trajectory that gives hope for a stable, democratic future? And does the new Iraq pose a threat to its neighbours?

The drivers of violence and the threat of renewed civil war

Has the application of counter-insurgency doctrine to Iraq in 2007 and the policies of the Iraqi government vanquished the three drivers of insurgency and civil war? It would be possible to have greater confidence in the security situation had all three of the main causes of instability been tackled.

The first driver of the violence, outlined in Chapter One, was socio-cultural: namely, a general legitimation of the use of violence and the flourishing of sectarianism. The weakening of the societal norm against killing is common to societies that have been through extended periods of conflict. This saw the customary prohibitions on killing weaken in the face of war and civil strife. Iraq has been through three decades of conflict; from the start of the Iran–Iraq war in 1980, through the extended aerial bombardment that forced its armies out of Kuwait in 1991, to the socio-economic damage brought by sanctions. On top of this, the mass killings of the civil war made the extended use of violence a common experience for the population of south and central Iraq. This test has not yet been met. It is clear that Iraqi society will need many years to recover from decades of state-sponsored violence, invasion and state collapse.

Sectarian rhetoricism, far from being treated, has become entrenched. As detailed in Chapter Five, Prime Minister Nuri al-Maliki, has from at least 2010 onwards, repeatedly evoked the 'Ba'athist threat' as a key part of his political strategy to unite the Shia electorate behind his continued rule. The idea that the Ba'ath Party, universally discredited after 35 years of brutal and corrupt rule, purged from government in 2003 and persecuted by the security services ever since, could pose any sustained threat to Iraq is simply ludicrous. In evoking the 'hidden hand of Ba'athist conspiracy', Maliki is deploying a coded sectarian message. He is seeking to widen the guilt for the abuses committed in the party's name to the whole of the Sunni section of society, using blame by association, for the myriad ills and abuses of past and present Iraq. With the prime minister so frequently reverting to a sectarian message, it is clear this test has also not been met, and there is little hope in the near future that Iraqi politics will move beyond the communalist rhetoric that justified its civil war.

The second and most important driver of Iraq's civil war was the profound weakness of the state. This created the space in which the protagonists of the civil war operated, deploying politically motivated violence but also seeking to convince the population that sectarian militias were the only defence available against the rising tide of inter-communal conflict. There has clearly been measurable progress in rebuilding the Iraqi state since 2007, but this has been skewed heavily in favour of the internal security apparatus. As detailed in Chapter Four, in 2004, the United States, in the face of a sustained revolt against its presence in Iraq, quickly set about rebuilding and expanding the Iraqi security services. By 2011, over US$24 billion had been spent on recreating the armed forces, employing nearly a million people across the Ministries of Defence and Interior. However, attempts at rebuilding the civilian institutions of the state have been much less successful. Some US$200bn was allocated for reconstruction, but progress was severely hampered by the increasing levels of violence from 2005–07, incoherent management and rampant corruption.

Today, the civilian arm of the state is still very weak; a fleeting presence within Iraqi society and subsequently the focus of popular exasperation and resentment. Since 2003, the United States and the Iraqi government have prioritised raising electricity output as the single most important reconstruction project. This did result in significant increases in output, although the gains fell short of rising demand and the ambitious targets set by government. Independent assessments judge that the average Iraqi household still receives only seven hours of electricity a day, with opinion polls consistently indicating that public opinion assesses electricity delivery to be declining, not improving. Beyond electricity, the availability of fresh water and effective sewerage were never a prime focus of government targets, and have seen little sustained improvement.

The third and final driver of instability was the political settlement established in the wake of invasion. Iraqi politics since 2003 have been structured by an exclusive elite pact, specifically designed to mobilise people along sectarian lines and minimise the role of the Sunni and secular sections of society in government. The politics of exclusion sent increasing numbers of alienated people into the ranks of the insurgency. The 2010 national elections saw an extended attempt both to challenge and defend this exclusive elite pact. The victory of Iraqiyya, who campaigned on an overtly nationalist and secular platform, was greeted by a series of machinations to deny them meaningful power within government, fracture their presence in parliament and force them to integrate into the cabinet on the basis of the existing sectarian formula. The 2.85 million people who voted for Iraqiyya in March 2010 have seen the role of their elected representatives in government systematically reduced. The continuation of this exclusive elite pact cannot help but alienate increasing numbers of Iraq's population from the state, exacerbating the already powerful popular sense that the government is failing to deliver their needs because it is corrupt.

In summary, only one of the three drivers of violence has been tackled, and that one only partially. What, then, are the dangers of Iraq heading back into a high-intensity civil war, in light of evidence that, since 2009, the monthly death toll has crept upwards?

At present, politically motivated violence is both highly localised and focused on the northern and central areas of the country, in the provinces of Baghdad, Salahuddin, Diyala, Anbar and Ninewa. The area controlled by the Kurdish Regional Government (KRG) is the most peaceful in the country. Southern Iraq also has comparatively few security incidents. Of the five most violent provinces, incidents are usually concentrated in specific urban areas; Mosul in Ninewa, Baghdad city, Baquba in Diyala, and Fallujah and Ramadi in Anbar remain the most turbulent.[4]

The fact that violence is largely concentrated in central and northern Iraq indicates that one of the two major non-state actors that drove Iraq into civil war, al-Qaeda in Mesopotamia, remains active. It, along with its umbrella organisation, the Islamic Emirate of Iraq, remains the major perpetrator of violence. Al-Qaeda is responsible for the vast majority of the mass casualty attacks in Iraq as well as smaller car bombs and attacks on the security forces.[5] Its ultimate aim, to drive Iraq back into civil war, has changed little since the height of its activities in 2006. It hopes to achieve this by targeting the Shia population with mass casualty bombings, triggering both militia retaliation and overreaction by security forces. Al-Qaeda has undoubtedly benefitted from the political stalemate in the aftermath of the 2010 national election.

Militancy has been stoked by alienation in central and northern Iraq over the failure of Iraqiyya's strong performance in the 2010 election to translate into more representative and responsive government. Iraqi and US government experts estimate this political situation has allowed al-Qaeda to double the size of its membership from 1,000 in 2011, to anything between 2,500 and 3,000 in October 2012.[6]

Broadly speaking, the militias that claimed to represent the Shia population during the civil war have not reorganised and gone back on the offensive. Moqtada al-Sadr's militia, the Jaish al-Mahdi, declared a ceasefire in August 2007 and announced its cessation of violence in 2008. Unfortunately, in 2004, one of Sadr's former lieutenants, Qais al-Khazali, formed a more radical and violent group, Asaib Ahl al-Haq, or the League of the Righteous. Funded by Iran, Asaib Ahl al-Haq were responsible both for targeting US forces, kidnapping foreign workers and terrorising Sunni populations in and around Baghdad during the civil war. Prime Minister Nuri al-Maliki developed a close relationship with Khazali in an attempt to burnish his own radical nationalist credentials but also to divide the support base of Sadr. In 2012, this relationship led to Asaib Ahl al-Haq declaring a ceasefire and entering into the political process, thus ending the destabilising role of one of the most violent and effective militia in Iraq.[7]

In spite of the sectarian rhetoric that still resonates within Iraqi politics, and the exclusive elite bargain that shapes how governments are formed and who serves in cabinet, Iraq will not return to civil war. The security services, rebuilt since 2004, remain by far the strongest military force within Iraqi society. The aftermath of the 2010 national elections has encouraged an increase in al-Qaeda's membership and there has been a gradual increase in the numbers of people murdered in politically motivated violence. However, a close examination of where that violence is taking place indicates that the Iraqi state is able to limit the range and effect of al-Qaeda's activities, but not stop them altogether. Mass-casualty attacks aimed at civilians and sustained operations against the security forces largely happen in five cities; Mosul, Baghdad, Baquba, Fallujah and Ramadi in north and central Iraq. Baghdad and Mosul are the two largest cities in the country, which means politically motivated violence still shapes the lives of a great deal of Iraq's population. That said, the violence is not a challenge to the status quo or to Maliki's rule. Iraq's security forces are too strong and coherent to let that happen.

The thwarting of democracy and the slide to authoritarianism

Were the security situation not worrying enough, Iraqi politics have gone through another transformation since 2008;

the increasingly authoritarian centralisation of power in the hands of the prime minister and his office. As politically motivated violence declined and Iraq moved away from civil war, Maliki has sought to control the overbearing armed forces that the United States bequeathed to Iraq upon its departure. He has successfully secured his grip over Iraq's army and its intelligence services. He has then used them to intimidate his rivals within the ruling elite and suppress popular movements against his rule. There is now little doubt amongst the rest of Iraq's ruling elite, those outside Maliki's own Dawa Party, that his intention is to move the country back to authoritarian one-party rule.

As detailed in Chapter Five, Maliki has successfully co-opted and marginalised the power of Iraqiyya both in the cabinet and in parliament. He continues to use a pliant judiciary to weaken constraints upon his power and target those who oppose him. The only coherent political force left in Iraq with the power and autonomy to mount a sustained challenge to the prime minister is the dominant party within the KRG, the Kurdistan Democratic Party, and its leader Masoud Barzani.

From 2008 onwards, tensions between the Iraqi government and the KRG mounted. As the military strength of the Iraqi state gathered pace and Maliki consolidated his control over the government, he confronted the power of the KRG. Maliki used similar tactics in his struggle with the KRG to those he had deployed when seizing control of the Iraqi government. In November 2012, he set up a new operational command to coordinate the security services in Kirkuk, Diyala and Salahuddin. As with previous operational commands, he appointed a favoured general, Abdul Amir al-Zaydi, to run it, and flouted the constitution by refusing to ask parliament to approve the appointment. The formation of the Tigris Operational Command was a direct challenge to the KRG, which has long argued that Kirkuk should be part of its jurisdiction, not Baghdad's. Maliki has directly challenged this by increasing Baghdad's military presence in Kirkuk, and by placing those forces under his direct control.[8] It appears that there is little the KRG can do but continue to develop its economic autonomy as quickly possible by offering better deals to international oil companies than Baghdad does, and courting the Turkish government in the hope that it will facilitate much higher volumes of KRG crude-oil exports.

The protests surrounding the 'Iraq Spring' reflect the predicament faced by urban populations in Iraq, particularly the youth, who have become deeply alienated from the new governing elite.[9] The government in Baghdad has failed to reduce unemployment and cannot deliver sufficient electricity to meet the country's needs. The KRG is blamed for widespread corruption and for using non-democratic means to facilitate the KDP's continued dominance of government. Overall, these complaints seem likely to persist for as long as the government fails to deliver either jobs or electricity. But will this popular resentment pose a sustained challenge to the political system as a whole, and to Maliki's domination of the system?

With the armed forces strong enough to keep politically motivated violence contained, his main parliamentary opposition in disarray and the KRG militarily on the back foot and economically constrained, Maliki's position as prime minister looks unassailable. If anything, his dominance of government is set to increase over the next few years. In November 2012, Iraq's oil output hit three million barrels a day for the first time in 30 years. The International Energy Agency (IEA) sees this as the start of a sustained growth in Iraqi oil production, which could see its output double to six million barrels a day by 2020 and over eight million barrels a day by 2035. The vast majority of this increase would come from the super-giant oil fields in the south of the country around Basra, securely under the control of Maliki's security forces. Under this scenario, the IEA estimates that Iraqi government revenue will average US$200bn a year.[10] Such financial gains, even if only partially realised, would give the Iraqi state more than enough money to turn the country into a rentier state, comparable to its Arab Gulf neighbours, and further secure Maliki's rule.

A neutered regional power

One of the major goals of regime change was to drastically restrain the ability of Iraq to destabilise the Gulf region. This has been realised to such an extent that it could possibly destabilise Iraq itself. An unintended consequence of the invasion and the state collapse and civil war that followed was that the Iraqi state lost the ability to control its own borders, which has left Baghdad vulnerable to extended covert and overt interference from its neighbours.

The consolidation of Maliki's rule gave him the ability to drive US troops from the country with greater speed than Washington had expected. It also allowed him to gain a degree of autonomy from Iranian influence. However, Maliki remains vulnerable to direct Iranian pressure that continues to shape his foreign-policy decision-making. In addition, the rapid decline in Baghdad's relations with Ankara has encouraged Turkey to improve its economic and strategic ties with the KRG. In addition, the 2010 election campaign saw Saudi Arabia, another Gulf state, and Turkey all fund Maliki's main rival, Ayad Allawi, in a sustained attempt to unseat him.

In spite of Maliki's consolidation of domestic power, he continues to face an uncertain regional and international environment. In this situation, the main objectives of Iraqi foreign policy are to shape the domestic situation in Iraq in Maliki's favour. For the moment, both the United States and Iran back his continued rule, but the prime minister is keenly aware this may not remain the case. This applies particularly if Tehran loses its principal regional ally, the Assad regime in Syria, and seeks to compensate by bringing Iraq more closely into its orbit. Nor is Iran Maliki's only regional concern; Saudi Arabia and Turkey have shown an extended commitment to remove him from office. His fear must be that external backing for his political rivals could grow and pose a serious challenge to his ability to make and impose policy.

Humanitarian intervention after the invasion of Iraq

The US National Security Strategy, published in September 2002, reveals not only the justification of invasion, the regime's previous use of weapons of mass destruction and the danger they could use them again, but also the source of the reconstruction agenda implemented in Iraq after conventional fighting had stopped. Page One of the Strategy boldly states, 'We will actively work to bring the hope of democracy, development, free markets, and free trade to every corner of the world.'[11] Beyond terrorists and weapons of mass destruction, the United States' main enemies post-9/11 were identified as 'tyrants' and 'totalitarians, holding a creed of power with no place for human dignity'.[12] George W. Bush, speaking before the invasion in February 2003, claimed, 'A liberated Iraq can show the power of freedom to transform that vital region, by bringing hope and progress into the lives of millions.'[13] For President Bush, Iraq's sovereignty was to be abrogated and its territory breached in the name of transforming the lives of its own population. In the aftermath of Saddam Hussein's removal, the fruits of liberation would be guaranteed by the root and branch reform of the Iraqi state, transforming its role in Iraqi society and the economy. Iraq was to become a beacon of liberal capitalism and democracy at the heart of the

Middle East, a post-war case study highlighting the benefits to be gained from the application of muscular intervention and economic transformation.[14]

However, the approach to Iraqi reconstruction adopted by the Bush administration in Iraq did not develop in a vacuum. If the end of the Cold War created the space for a new norm of international interventionism, it was the aftermath of the 1990–91 Gulf War that heralded its arrival. *Operation Provide Comfort*, backed up by the apparently stunning battlefield dominance of the US during its war against Iraq, gained UN Security Council backing for a suspension of Iraq's sovereignty to provide humanitarian relief and protection to the Kurdish population in the north of the country. What followed were a series of UN-sanctioned humanitarian interventions in Somalia (1992–93), Haiti (1994), Bosnia (1993–95), East Timor (1999) and Sierra Leone (2000–01).[15]

Throughout the 1990s, Western powers in the UN Security Council lowered the threshold for intrusive interventions into sovereign states that were riven by conflict or were thought to pose a security threat beyond their borders, under Chapter VII of the United Nations Charter. This muscular and transformative humanitarianism reached its height with a series of lectures given by Kofi Annan and the report of the International Commission on Intervention and State Sovereignty.[16] If the first generation of international interventions had been centred on conflict mediation, and the second generation on conflict resolution, the temporary post-Cold War consensus in the UN Security Council allowed for the birth of a third generation of intervention, based on rebuilding states across the developing world and transforming their relations with society.[17] This new peacebuilding doctrine was given ideational and instrumental coherence by its identification of the main causes driving the increase in humanitarian suffering: the myriad sins of the state. In the aftermath of the Cold War, an increasing number of states were labelled weak, failing or simply despotic.[18] Interventions in the name of humanitarianism were now much more ambitious. Conflicts were not to be mediated, but their root causes identified and banished.[19] These root causes lay in malfunctioning, weak or malign states.

What has this costly doctrine of intervention and state reconstruction achieved in Iraq? By the time US troops left Iraq, 4,487 US military personnel had died.[20] Iraq Body Count conservatively estimates civilian deaths as a result of the invasion and ensuing violence at between 110,110 and 120,293 up to November 2012.[21] By September 2012, US$212bn of US and Iraqi government money had been allocated for post-war reconstruction of the Iraqi state.[22]

Iraq's armed forces were rapidly rebuilt after 2004 as the United States attempted to limit its own casualties and hence reduce the domestic political cost of occupying the country. However, the speed with which this was done and the massive investment channelled into Iraq's security forces leave the country, once again, subservient to a huge military machine. The way that this military is now used by its prime minister makes Iraq comparable not only to the repressive Arab regimes of the pre-spring Middle East, but also to the country's own history, from its independence in 1932 to regime change in 2003.

Economically, there has, if anything, been even less progress. Iraqi state revenue is reliant on the export of oil, which gives the government a massive amount of autonomy from a population from which it does not need to collect taxes. The reconstruction of a rentier economy in Iraq, after 2003, has left the state in control of the majority of economic activity. As early as 2005, the number of people employed by the state had actually risen to 2.3m from 1.2m around the time of the intervention. In 2006, the statistics agency of the Iraqi Ministry of Planning estimated that the state employed 31% of Iraq's labour force and estimated this would rise to 35% by 2008. This would put state employment just 5% lower than the CIA's estimates for pre-invasion Iraq.[23]

The skewed reconstruction of the Iraqi state does not provide a sustainable basis for the consolidation of Iraq's democratic stability in the years ahead. The population, ill-served by government institutions and rightly blaming corruption amongst the political elite, is increasingly alienated from its government and vocal in its criticism. However, the state, empowered by a security service that is now the strongest military force in the country, can, and frequently does, rely on its coercive powers, both overt and covert, to suppress mass protest against its own incompetence. This is obviously problematic, especially when used in conjunction with sectarian rhetoric of Maliki. It leaves the government too reliant on the security services for its survival, because it is unable physically to deliver basic services to its population. Instead of uniting the population behind the state through the use of a unitary and nationalist ideology, Maliki has chosen a divisive rhetoric in an attempt to tie a section of the population, the Shia, to his continued rule. It remains unclear, given poor service delivery and pervasive corruption, whether Maliki can count on the quiescence, let alone the active support, of Iraq's Shias. It leaves Iraq an alienated and fractured society with a ruling elite that is increasingly authoritarian and violent.

Thus, despite the tens of thousands of civilians who have died and the billions of dollars that have been spent, the lives of ordinary Iraqis, in terms of the relationship to their state and to their economy, are comparable to the situation they faced in the country before regime change. The significant positive differences – the composition of the current ruling elite and the democratic national elections – appear to be under sustained threat, and were bought at an unimaginably high cost. In the face of such meagre results and with a comparable lack of success in Afghanistan, the appetite for exogenous attempts at transforming the internal political systems of states targeted for intervention has evidently waned. More fundamentally, the Iraqi experience calls into question whether external powers can actually deliver sustainable economic and political change to the states in which they intervene.

Notes

1 See Iraq Body Count, http://www.iraqbodycount.org.

2 On the statistical problems in assessing violence, see Michael Knights, 'Blind in Baghdad', *Foreign Policy*, 5 July 2012, http://www.foreignpolicy.com/articles/2012/07/05/blind_in_baghdad.

3 See Joel Wing, 'Which Direction is Violence Heading in Iraq?' *Musings on Iraq*, 9 April 2012, http://musingsoniraq.blogspot.co.uk/2012/04/which-direction-is-violence-heading-in.html.

4 Joel Wing, 'The Localized Nature Of Violence In Iraq', *Musings on Iraq*, 17 September 2012, http://musingsoniraq.blogspot.co.uk/2012/04/which-direction-is-violence-heading-in.html.; Joel Wing, 'What is Security Like Today in Iraq? An Interview with Dr. Michael Knights', *Musings on Iraq*, 31 July 2012, http://musingsoniraq.blogspot.co.uk/2012/07/what-is-security-like-today-in-iraq.html.

5 Wing, 'What Is Security Like Today In Iraq? An Interview With Dr. Michael Knights'.

6 'Al Qaida "is Rebuilding in Iraq"', Press Association, 10 October 2012, Khaled Waleed, 'Al-Qaeda in Iraq: Group has New Offices, New Deadly Plans for Dissent', *Niqash*, 6 February 2012, http://www.niqash.org/articles/?id=2990.

7 Khaled Waleed, 'Weapons for Words: Extremists Enter Politics, Threaten Government Power Balance', *Niqash*, 26 January 2012, http://www.niqash.org/articles/?id=2980.

8 Bassem Francis and Mohammad al-Tamimi, 'Kurds Reject Maliki's Demand For Control of Peshmerga Militia', *Al-Hayat*, 10 November 2012, republished in http://www.al-monitor.com/pulse/politics/2012/10/kurds-reject-malikis-demand-to-control-pesherga-militia.html, and 'New Iraq Army HQ Fuels Arab–Kurd Row', Agence France-Presse, 16 November 2012, http://www.france24.com/en/20121116-new-iraq-army-hq-fuels-arab-kurd-row.

9 Raad Alkadiri, 'Rage Comes to Baghdad: Will Iraq's Recent Protests Lead to Revolt?', *Foreign Affairs*, 3 March 2011, http://www.foreignaffairs.com/articles/67557/raad-alkadiri/rage-comes-to-baghdad; Alice Fordham, 'Up in Arms', *Foreign Policy*, 28 February 2011, http://www.foreignpolicy.com/articles/2011/02/28/up_in_arms; Daniel

Serwer, 'Behind Iraq's Protests, a Call for Better Democracy', *Washington Post*, 3 March 2011, http://www.washingtonpost.com/wp-dyn/content/article/2011/03/02/AR2011030204886.html?nav=rss_opinion%2Fcolumns.

10 See International Energy Agency, *Iraq Energy Outlook*, October 2012, http://www.worldenergyoutlook.org/media/weowebsite/2012/iraqenergyoutlook/Fullreport.pdf.

11 See the introduction to The National Security Strategy of the United States of America, September 2002, http://georgewbush-whitehouse.archives.gov/nsc/nss/2002/.

12 *Ibid*.

13 George W. Bush, 'President Discusses the Future of Iraq at the American Enterprise Institute', 26 February 2003, http://georgewbush-whitehouse.archives.gov/news/releases/2003/02/20030226-11.html.

14 See Toby Dodge, 'The Sardinian, the Texan and the Tikriti: Gramsci, the Comparative Autonomy of the Middle Eastern State and Regime Change in Iraq', *International Politics*, Vol. 43, No. 4 (2006), pp. 453–73.

15 See Chris Brown, 'Selective Humanitarianism: in Defence of Inconsistency', in Deen K. Chatterjee and Don E. Scheid (eds), *Ethics and Foreign Intervention* (Cambridge: Cambridge University Press, 2003), p. 32.

16 Ken Menkhaus, 'State Failure and Ungoverned Space', in Mats Berdal and Achim Wennmann (eds), *Ending wars, Consolidating Peace: Economic Perspectives*, (Abingdon: Routledge for the International Institute for Strategic Studies, 2010), p. 172 and Alex Bellamy, 'Responsibility to Protect or Trojan Horse? The Crisis in Darfur and Humanitarian Intervention after Iraq', *Ethics and International Affairs*, vol. 19, no. 2, (2005), p. 34.

17 Oliver P. Richmond, *The Transformation of Peace*, (Basingstoke: Palgrave MacMillan, 2007), p. 86.

18 Menkhaus, 'State Failure and Ungoverned Space'.

19 Richmond, *The Transformation of Peace*, p. 14.

20 Michael E. O'Hanlon and Ian Livingston, *Iraq Index*, 31 January 2012, p. 7. http://www.brookings.edu/~/media/Centers/saban/iraq%20index/index20120131.PDF.

21 Iraq Body Count, http://www.iraqbodycount.org.

22 Special Inspector General for Iraq Reconstruction, *Quarterly Report and Semiannual Report to the United States Congress*, 30 October 2012, p. 3; http://www.sigir.mil/publications/quarterlyreports/October2012.html.

23 Campbell Robertson, 'Iraq Private Sector Falters: Rolls of Government Soar', *New York Times*, 10 August 2008, http://www.nytimes.com/2008/08/11/world/middleeast/11baghdad.html and Central Intelligence Agency, *World Fact Book*, https://www.cia.gov/library/publications/the-world-factbook/geos/iz.html.

APPENDIX

National Elections

January 2005 National Election

Coalition	Number of votes[1]	Number of seats[2]	Percentage of votes[3]
Iraqi National Alliance	4,075,292	140	48.2%
Kurdistan Alliance	2,175,551	75	25.7%
Iraqis List	1,168,943	40	13.8%
Kurdistan Islamic Group	60,592	2	0.7%
Iraqis Party	150,680	5	1.8%
Iraqi Turkmen Front	93,480	3	1.1%
National Independent and Elites	69,938	3	0.8%
People's Union	69,920	2	0.8%
Islamic Action	43,205	2	0.5%
National Democratic Alliance	36,795	1	0.4%
Rafidain National List	36,255	1	0.4%
Liberation and Reconciliation Gathering	30,796	1	0.4%
Ummah (Nation) Party		0	
Other[3]	444,819[4]	0	5.3%
Voter Turnout for this election	58%[5] Turnout by sect/ethnicity:[6] Shi'ite Turnout – 75% Kurdish Turnout 90% Sunni Turnout: less than 10%		

December 2005 National Election

Coalition	Number of votes[7]	Number of seats[8]	Percentage of votes[9]
Iraqi National Alliance	5,021,137	128	41.19%
Kurdistan Alliance	2,642,172	53	21.67%
Iraqis List	977,325	25	8.02%
Iraq Accord Front	1,840,216	44	15.09%
National Iraqi Dialogue Front	499,963	11	4.10%
Kurdistan Islamic Group	157,688	5	1.29%
Iraqi Turkmen Front	87,993	1	0.72%
Rafidain National List	47,263	1	0.39%
Liberation and Reconciliation Gathering	129,847	3	1.07%
Mithal al-Alusi List	32,24522	1	0.26%
Yazidi list	21,908	1	0.18%
Upholders of the Message[23]	145,028	2	1.2%
Progressives[24]	145,028	2	1.19
Islamic Action		0	
National Democratic Alliance		0	
Iraqi National Congress		0	
Voter Turnout for this election	79.6%[12]		

March 2010 National Election[13]

Coalition	Number of votes	Number of seats	Percentage of votes
Iraqi National Alliance	2,092,066	70	18.2%
Iraq Accord Front	298,226	6	2.6%
Kurdistan Islamic Group	152,530	2	1.3%
Iraqi National Movement	2,849,612	91	24.7%
Kurdistan Alliance	1,681,714	43	14.6%
Kurdistan Islamic Union	243,720	4	2.1%
Movement for Change	476,478	8	4.1%
State of Law Coalition	2,792,083	89	24.2%
Unity Alliance of Iraq	306,647	4	2.7%
Minorities	61,153	8	.5%
Others	572,183	0	5.0%
Voter Turnout for this election	62%[14]		

Notes

1 Electoral Knowledge Network, 'Iraq: Provincial Population Estimates and Voter Turnout', at http://aceproject.org/ero-en/topics/ electoral-participation/turnout/updatedelectionresults.pdf.

2 Kenneth Katzman, 'Iraq, Politics, Governance and Human Rights', Congressional Research Service Reports on the Middle East and Arab World, 9 November 2012, p. 48, http://www.fas.org/sgp/crs/mideast/RS21968.pdf.

3 Adam Carr's Election Archive, 'Iraq 2005', at http://psephos.adam-carr.net/countries/i/iraq/iraq2005.txt.

4 *Ibid.*

5 Edward Wong, 'Turnout in the Iraqi Election is Reported at 70 Per Cent', *New York Times*, 22 December 2005, http://www.nytimes.com/2005/12/22/international/middleeast/22iraq.html.

6 Kenneth Katzman, 'Iraq: Elections and New Government', Congressional Research Service Reports on the Middle East and Arab World, 24 June 2005, http://fpc.state.gov/documents/organization/50254.pdf.

7 Shak Bernard Hanish, 'The Post 2003 Iraqi Electoral Laws: A Comparison and An Assessment', International Journal of the Humanities and Social Science, vol.1, no. 17, Special Issue November 2011, at http://www.ijhssnet.com/journals/Vol_1_No_17_Special_Issue_November_2011/13.pdf.

8 Katzman, 'Iraq, Politics, Governance and Human Rights', 2012.

9 Iraq Independent High Electoral Commission, Final Report 2005, at http://www.ihec-iq.com/ftpar/regulation2005/finalreport2005.pdf; Adam Carr's Election Archive, 'Iraq December 2005'; http://psephos.adam-carr.net/countries/i/iraq/iraqdec2005.txt.

10 Hanish, 'The Post 2003 Iraqi Electoral Laws: A Comparison and An Assessment'.

11 Iraq Independent High Electoral Commission, Final Report 2005.

12 Hanish, 'The Post 2003 Iraqi Electoral Laws: A Comparison and An Assessment'.

13 Adam Carris Election Archive, 'Iraq 2010' at http://psephos.adam-car.net/countries/1/iraq/iraq2010.txt

14 'Iraq Election Turnout 62%, Officials Say', BBC, 9 March 2010, http://news.bbc.co.uk/2/hi/8556065.stm; 'Turnout for Iraq Election Solid at 62%', Reuters, 8 March 2010, http://www.reuters.com/article/2010/03/08/us-iraq-election-idUSLDE62505A20100308; Hanish, 'The Post 2003 Iraqi Electoral Laws: A Comparison and An Assessment'.

Adelphi books are published eight times a year by Routledge Journals, an imprint of Taylor & Francis, 4 Park Square, Milton Park, Abingdon, Oxfordshire OX14 4RN, UK.

A subscription to the institution print edition, ISSN 1944-5571, includes free access for any number of concurrent users across a local area network to the online edition, ISSN 1944-558X. Taylor & Francis has a flexible approach to subscriptions enabling us to match individual libraries' requirements. This journal is available via a traditional institutional subscription (either print with free online access, or online-only at a discount) or as part of the Strategic, Defence and Security Studies subject package or Strategic, Defence and Security Studies full text package. For more information on our sales packages please visit www.tandfonline.com/librarians_pricinginfo_journals.

2013 Annual Adelphi Subscription Rates			
Institution	£557	$979 USD	€824
Individual	£199	$338 USD	€270
Online only	£487	$857 USD	€721

Dollar rates apply to subscribers outside Europe. Euro rates apply to all subscribers in Europe except the UK and the Republic of Ireland where the pound sterling price applies. All subscriptions are payable in advance and all rates include postage. Journals are sent by air to the USA, Canada, Mexico, India, Japan and Australasia. Subscriptions are entered on an annual basis, i.e. January to December. Payment may be made by sterling cheque, dollar cheque, international money order, National Giro, or credit card (Amex, Visa, Mastercard).

For a complete and up-to-date guide to Taylor & Francis journals and books publishing programmes, and details of advertising in our journals, visit our website: **http://www.tandfonline.com.**

Ordering information:
USA/Canada: Taylor & Francis Inc., Journals Department, 325 Chestnut Street, 8th Floor, Philadelphia, PA 19106, USA. **UK/Europe/Rest of World:** Routledge Journals, T&F Customer Services, T&F Informa UK Ltd., Sheepen Place, Colchester, Essex, CO3 3LP, UK.

Advertising enquiries to:
USA/Canada: The Advertising Manager, Taylor & Francis Inc., 325 Chestnut Street, 8th Floor, Philadelphia, PA 19106, USA. Tel: +1 (800) 354 1420. Fax: +1 (215) 625 2940. **UK/Europe/Rest of World**: The Advertising Manager, Routledge Journals, Taylor & Francis, 4 Park Square, Milton Park, Abingdon, Oxfordshire OX14 4RN, UK. Tel: +44 (0) 20 7017 6000. Fax: +44 (0) 20 7017 6336.

The print edition of this journal is printed on ANSI conforming acid-free paper by Bell & Bain, Glasgow, UK.